**Studies in the History of Art**
Published by the National Gallery of
Art, Washington

This series includes: Studies in the
History of Art, collected papers on
objects in the Gallery's collections and
other art historical studies (formerly
*Report and Studies in the History of
Art*); Monograph Series I, a catalogue
of stained glass in the United States;
Monograph Series II, on conservation
topics; and Symposium Papers
(formerly Symposium Series), the
proceedings of symposia sponsored by
the Center for Advanced Study in the
Visual Arts at the National Gallery
of Art.

* Forthcoming

# Stained Glass before 1700 in American Collections: Silver-Stained Roundels and Unipartite Panels

VOLUME 39

# Studies in the History of Art

*Monograph Series I*

# Stained Glass before 1700 in American Collections: Silver-Stained Roundels and Unipartite Panels

*(Corpus Vitrearum Checklist IV)*

Timothy B. Husband

Addendum to Checklist III
Madeline H. Caviness and Timothy B. Husband

editorial assistance from Marilyn Beaven

National Gallery of Art, Washington

*Distributed by the University Press of New England*
*Hanover and London*

*Front cover:* **Allegorical Figure: Goatherdess.** South Lowlands, c. 1510–1520. Silver-stained roundel. The Metropolitan Museum of Art, The Cloisters Collection, New York. *See page 147.*

*Frontispiece:* **Susanna and the Elders.** After the Pseudo-Ortkens. South Lowlands, Antwerp ?, c. 1520. Silver-stained roundel. The Metropolitan Museum of Art, The Cloisters Collection, New York. *See page 157.*

*Back cover:* **Apes Assembling a Trestle Table.** Germany ?, c. 1480–1500. Silver-stained roundel. The Metropolitan Museum of Art, The Cloisters Collection, New York. *See page 132.*

This publication was produced by the Editors Office, National Gallery of Art, Washington
Editor-in-chief, Frances P. Smyth

Printed by Wolk Press, Baltimore, Maryland
The type is Trump Medieval, set by ARTECH Graphics, Inc., Baltimore, Maryland

Distributed by the University Press of New England, 17½ Lebanon Street, Hanover, New Hampshire 03755

Abstracted by RILA (International Repertory of the Literature of Art), Williamstown, Massachusetts 01267

ISSN 0091-7338
ISBN 089468-175-3

The Corpus Vitrearum is published under the auspices of the Comité international d'histoire de l'art and the Union académique internationale.

Supported by an Interpretive Research Grant from the National Endowment for the Humanities

# CONTENTS

Fig. 1. **Joab Murdering Abner.** North Lowlands, Amsterdam ?, c. 1510–1520. The Metropolitan Museum of Art, The Cloisters Collection, New York. *See page 144.*

# FOREWORD

In 1952 the International Committee of the History of Art (CIHA) officially authorized a research and publication project called Corpus Vitrearum Medii Aevi; in 1956 this cataloguing project was also granted the patronage of the Union Académique Internationale. According to the original directives, the catalogue was confined to religious stained glass of the Middle Ages. All secular panels—including the silver-stained roundels made for the most part to adorn the windows in the homes of well-to-do burgers or the castles of local nobility—were excluded, even if they had been installed in a church at a later date. Also outside the confines of the Corpus project were all civic glazing programs, including the armorial panels made for the municipal palaces and guild halls of the towns.

At the time the Corpus Vitrearum was conceived in 1949, Europe had only recently survived a war of major proportions. Uppermost in everyone's mind were visions of destroyed buildings and shattered windows. The intent of Swiss art historian Hans R. Hahnloser when he proposed the Corpus Vitrearum Medii Aevi to a small number of colleagues was to preserve a record, at least, of this fragile medium. Two factors favored the idea of such a catalogue. First, most of the important church windows had been dismounted for safety during the war, and in the interim scholars had studied them at close range, many for the first time. Second, most of the monuments commissions of the various countries had taken this opportunity to photograph the glass and, in many cases, to restore the windows. Thus documentation never before available existed for vast numbers of windows throughout Europe. The first volume of the Corpus Vitrearum Medii Aevi appeared in Switzerland in 1956 (see "Status of Publications" at the end of this volume).

Since that time both the content and the scope of the project have changed. Perhaps the most important change was the decision of the French committee in 1971 to initiate a pre-Corpus series of Recensements encompassing broad geographic areas. And in 1975 the international committee elected to extend the date limit beyond the Middle Ages, renaming the project Corpus Vitrearum. Thus the brief notices in the Recensement volumes also include the glass of the Renaissance up to the nineteenth century. The French census idea was adapted in the United States for a Checklist series, of which this is the fourth volume. In many countries, an additional change in Corpus format has been the recent decision to include in their catalogues all of the heraldic emblems as well as the unipartite panels in private collections, museums, and churches; it was agreed at the international colloquium of the Corpus Vitrearum in Amsterdam in 1987 that this material might alternatively be published in specialized supplements.

Fig. 2. **Portrait of General Gustavus Horn.** Northern Germany or Sweden ?, dated 1633. Silver-stained roundel. Private Collection, New York. Photo: T. B. Husband. *See page 186.*

In the case of the Checklists of Stained Glass in American Collections, we chose a date limit of about 1700 in order to divide collector's items of European origin from windows made for buildings in the United States. The large number of colorful Swiss panels of secular origin were included alongside the leaded panels with religious subjects in each collection; these were studied by a team of researchers as a collaborative effort and published in the first three volumes of the Checklist. Also included in volumes 1–3 are a number of heraldic roundels, generally of Dutch or German origin; by agreement between the international group of authors who are concerned with roundels, these do not come under their purview. The wisdom of this decision may be questioned, since it is likely that a donation to a civic hall would include the patron's arms as well as narrative panels, just as in religious programs. The study and cataloguing of figural unipartite panels (those in which no leading was originally needed) has, however, proceeded independently. This specialized area, in which expertise in late Medieval and Renaissance prints and drawings is needed, was assigned to a single author, Timothy B. Husband. He has been solely responsible for the examination of these pieces, whose authenticity is often hard to assess both because expert copies abound and because many original pieces have not borne the ravages of exposure to the elements.

In this volume of the Checklist the entries for silver-stained roundels conform to the system initiated for the Fichier International de Documentation du Rondel, housed in the Institut Royal du Patrimoine Artistique in Belgium. For each roundel a listing of "related material" is included, comprising other known versions of the same composition, whether glass paintings, drawings, or prints. The international archive is an invaluable clearinghouse and has been actively kept up to date by a small group of scholars, who have also held regular meetings to exchange information. One of the pioneers is Dr. William Cole, whose first volume, on the unipartite panels of Great Britain, will soon be published. Publication of the roundels in this country begins with this Checklist and includes all examples of unipartite glass known to date in the United States. It is always possible that there are omissions, and the author will be glad to have information on roundels that he has not examined. One major collection, the James Herbert Rawlings Boone bequest to the Johns Hopkins University, was dispersed through the sale room when this checklist was in preparation; some items from it are catalogued under the Metropolitan Museum of Art, New York, and under a private collection in Hillsborough, California, but the whereabouts of some others is currently unknown. Indices to the silver-stained roundels section will give the reader a coherent analysis of this category by subject, artist, and previous owners.

Appended to this volume is a section that brings the collection of leaded glass in Hillsborough up to date; it is separately indexed. Further supplemental material will await publication, either in the more detailed catalogue entries of the full volumes and fascicules now in preparation, or in a further Checklist Supplement in this journal.

Jane Hayward
*The Cloisters*
President, CORPUS VITREARUM (USA)

Madeline H. Caviness
*Tufts University*
President, International Board, CORPUS VITREARUM

# ACKNOWLEDGMENTS

The compilation of this volume would not have been possible without the full cooperation and generous assistance of the curators and owners who made all the roundels and panels available for examination and publication. While everyone's help was invaluable, I would like to make special mention of several—in addition to the anonymous lenders—who were especially supportive and generous with their time: Laurie Polhemus, Hillsborough, California; Tina Oldknow, formerly with the Los Angeles County Museum of Art; Amy Stewart, J.B. Speed Museum, Louisville, Kentucky; Gregory M. Wittkopp, Cranbrook Academy of Art Museum, Bloomfield Hills, Michigan; Peter Barnet, Detroit Institute of Arts; Dr. Henry G. Hood, Jr., Greensboro, North Carolina; and Cara Denison, Pierpont Morgan Library, New York.

Many colleagues abroad have made the collections in their care available for study, thus broadening our knowledge of roundel production; others have offered invaluable advice and support. In particular, I am grateful to John Rolands, keeper, Department of Prints and Drawings, British Museum; Margret Stuffmann, director, Graphische Sammlung, Städelschen Kunstinstitut, Frankfurt; J. van Tatenhove, Prentenkabinet der Rijksuniversiteit, Leiden; and Jan Piet Filedt Kok, former curator of the Rijksprentenkabinet, Amsterdam, for allowing me to study numerous drawings in their rich collections that relate to silver-stained roundels in American collections.

My many colleagues at the Metropolitan Museum have been tirelessly supportive throughout. William D. Wixom was steadfastly encouraging and understanding even when he might have wished to divert my attention to more immediate museum matters. And, as always, the keen eye and exacting standards of Jane Hayward remain an inspiration to all those who wish to undertake a serious study of stained glass.

Colleagues from the Corpus Vitrearum are likewise owed a debt of gratitude. Jennifer Eskin's administrative assistance was an immense boon for which I am very appreciative. The computerized sales and dealer records compiled by Marilyn Beaven produced a number of otherwise unrecorded provenances, while her skillfully organized index constitutes a significant contribution to the usefulness of this volume. I am also grateful to Madeline H. Caviness for her unflagging support, her valued editorial suggestions, and her continuing understanding in the face of delays occasioned by my other responsibilities.

To Dr. William Cole, Hindhead, Surrey, I owe particular gratitude for giving me access to his photographic archive of silver-stained roundels in English parish churches. This indispensable resource provided a visual record of thousands of relatively inaccessible and virtually unknown roundels and made the partial reconstruction of many roundel series possible. I am grateful to Kees Berserik, The Hague, for continually informing me of the whereabouts of newly rediscovered, related roundels, frequently providing photographs, and ever sustaining this project with his contagious enthusiasm. To my friend Jan Piet Filedt-Kok I owe special thanks for the benefit of his many insightful observations, his formidable interpretive powers, and his generosity in making an array of scholarly resources available to me. His continuing interest has lent much support not only to this project but also to a heightened appreciation of silver-stained roundels in general. I also owe special gratitude to Yvette Vanden Bemden, who has from the beginning supported my work with roundels in any number of ways, be it providing photographs or extending warm hospitality during my several stays in Brussels; she has also made significant contributions to scholarship in this field. And finally, I would like to express particular thanks to Sibyll Kummer-Rothenhäusler, who introduced me, in my callow youth, to silver-stained roundels and who has ever since sought—with some degree of success, it is hoped—to accord interest with knowledge and to temper enthusiasm with discernment. To her I dedicate my efforts in this volume.

The opportunity to study the many collections across this country and the research for this publication have been supported largely by a grant for Interpretive Research from the National Endowment for the Humanities that was extended through June 1990 for this purpose. Assistance had also been provided by the J. Paul Getty Trust, which continues through 1990 to underwrite the preparation of the fuller entries for Corpus Vitrearum fascicules. A grant from the Kress Foundation has paid for new photography, notably by Constancio del Alamo on the West Coast and by Lee Cook in the East and Midwest. The support of these funding agencies is gratefully acknowledged.

Timothy B. Husband

Fig. 3. **Flight into Egypt from a series of the Infancy of Christ.** Master of the Seven Acts of Charity, Pieter Cornelisz. Kunst ?, North Lowlands, Leiden, c. 1515–1525. Silver-stained roundel. Detroit Institute of Arts. *See page 111.*

# INTRODUCTION

By the late Middle Ages, Europe had transformed from a largely agricultural, feudal, and ecclesiastical society to an urban, national, and secular one. The essentially mercantile economic fabric had become dependent on far-flung trade linked with overseas empires. For the first time since the Roman Empire, banking, manufacturing, and commerce established a middle class as the backbone of society. This new plutocracy often modeled itself on the aristocratic class it was supplanting, but in the end it asserted its own developing tastes and prerogatives. By the end of the fifteenth century the urban patriciates had created a demand for new architectural forms that accorded with their sociopolitical and economic needs. The resulting town houses, guild halls, and civic buildings in turn required decorative embellishments that were fashioned to the tastes, pocketbooks, and values of their patrons and were visual testimony to the power and status of a burgeoning sociopolitical order. Stained glass was one art that was greatly innovated as a consequence.

Stained glass had consisted almost exclusively of large-scale pot metal windows destined for ecclesiastical structures. By the end of the Middle Ages, however, immense cathedral building programs characteristic of the High Gothic period had become such a strain on the resources of church and state that they were rarely undertaken. Stained glass, like architecture, became reduced in scale. New urban wealth created a large market for small-scale stained glass destined predominantly for secular buildings. The preponderance of this glass, at least north of the Alps, took the form of silver-stained roundels.

The broad term silver-stained roundel encompasses any single piece of white glass (that is, colorless or non–pot-metal), whether round, square, rectangular, or oval, rarely more than thirty centimeters in any dimension, that is painted with a vitreous paint and enhanced with a silver oxide or sulphide which, when fired, fuses with the glass, imparting translucent tones ranging from pale yellow to deep amber or copper color.[1] Roundels are not to be confused with stained glass, a general term that refers to leaded panels composed of colored and painted pot-metal glass. In the first half of the sixteenth century, additional materials used in roundels included sanguine, sanguine lees, and "Jean Cousin," all of which are hematite-based enamels ranging from flesh tones to deep red, as well as gray and sepia enamels. By mid-century, a wide range of translucent enamels were used; in Bohemia and other regions of Central Europe, opaque enamels identical to those ordinarily used to decorate the walls of glass vessels were also utilized for roundels. In the seventeenth century, particularly in the North Lowlands,[2] roundels frequently were set in large rectangular diamond-pane windows con-

Fig. 4. **Isaac and Rebekah.** North Lowlands, Leiden, c. 1480. Pen and brown ink on paper. Museum Boymans van Beuningen, Rotterdam. Inv. no. N 192.

ceived as a decorative whole. Elaborate ornamental borders surrounded the roundels, while the quarries were decorated with festoons, inscriptions, and a variety of ornament inhabited by flora, fauna, and insects, all executed in varying tones of silver stain and brilliant translucent enamel (figs. 13, 14).

Roundels—often surrounded by a border of ornament, inscription, or plain colored glass—were set in windows composed of small colorless panes or quarries leaded together in diamond-shaped or other patterns (frontispiece, fig. 7).[3] In the Lowlands, these windows were often framed by a fillet of colored glasses, usually a mixture of green, blue, red, yellow, or white. In Germany, although quarry windows were not uncommon, heavy Butzenscheiben—the circular, thick-centered remnant attached to the pontil or blow pipe in the making of crown glass—were widely favored.

The production of roundels thrived primarily in or around the principal artistic centers in the Lowlands, notably Amsterdam, Antwerp, Bruges, Brussels, Ghent, Haarlem, Leiden, Maastricht, and Louvain (figs. 1, 3, 4, 5). Major centers were also located in Germany, particularly in Nuremberg, Augsburg, and Cologne (back cover, figs. 2, 6, 9, 20, 21). French production seems to have been concentrated in or near the Burgundian territories. Although Lowlands influence is frequently evident, French roundels have their own distinctive stylistic identity. Production seems to have flagged by the early sixteenth century, however, at the very moment silver-stained roundels were entering a golden age in the Lowlands. The extent of production in England is less clear, as so much was destroyed during the reign of Henry VIII. Extant examples are frequently of secular subject matter, their presumed domestic settings and inoffensive imagery being largely responsible for their survival (fig. 8). The production, again judging from scanty remains, appears to have flourished largely in the fifteenth century, as in France, and the few Renaissance examples are known mostly from eighteenth- and nineteenth-century drawings (fig. 16).[4] If there was any extensive roundel production in either Italy or Spain, little evidence of it survives.

The silver-stained roundel was ideally suited to new forms of urban domestic and civic architecture as well as to the temperaments of increasingly prosperous and independent-minded patrons. Since both the windows of these buildings and the rooms they illuminated were relatively small, the preponderance of colorless glass in the roundels and surrounds and the sparse use of opaque paint maximized the admission of light. The scale of the roundels also suited the intimate spaces of the rooms, as the detailed painting invited close inspection. Commonly conceived in series, roundels afforded the continuity of a single narrative within a given space. And as roundels were generally intended for private, domestic spaces, their subject matter often provided a far more candid reflection of individual moral, ethical, and spiritual attitudes or preoccupations than large-scale stained glass conceived for public edifices.

The earliest surviving examples that technically satisfy the definition of a roundel date to the late thirteenth or early fourteenth century, when the technique of silver stain was either discovered or first widely used.[5] The original contexts of most examples have been lost, but they were probably set as bosses in band or grisaille windows and were thus components of a larger, ornamental whole. The earliest examples of true roundels, mostly excavated and fragmentary, can by their archaeological context be dated to the second and third quarters of the fourteenth century. Fragments of roundels from this period were excavated, for example, at the site of the Dominican convent known as the "Pand" in Ghent.[6] These fragments represent the symbols of the Evangelists and appear to form part of an independent series.

Few roundels dating earlier than the middle of the fifteenth century survive. With increased production toward the end of the century, roundels had developed from simple iconic or heraldic imagery[7] into complex and sophisticated serial narratives (fig. 6, compare figs. 3, 19, 23, 27). The greatest period of production—both in quantity and quality—spanned the first half of the sixteenth century; indeed, examples are so numerous that a quasi-industrial production may be inferred, located chiefly in the Lowlands but also in Germany and to a lesser degree in France and England.

As no fifteenth-century roundels are documented to have survived in their original secular settings, our knowledge of the format and design of these windows is based on secondary sources, largely depictions in panel paintings (fig. 7).[8] The visual evidence indicates that, at least in the Lowlands, the more common domestic window was rectangular and composed of a fixed transom glazed in leaded diamond panes, usually filling the upper third of the aperture, and an unglazed lower section, often filled with lattice and invariably fitted with hinged shutters.[9] In this type of window, a single roundel was set in the upper fixed transom. Each roundel was customarily surrounded by colored borders, and the window itself had a surround of colored fillets (fig. 7).

One of the few secular glazing programs that can be reconstructed is that made for the bailiff of Rijnland, Adriaen Dircxz. van Crimpen, at 9 Pieterskerkgracht in Leiden dating from the apogée of silver-stained roundel painting.[10] Three double-light, mullioned oak windows were installed in an upstairs hallway and two more elsewhere in the house. A drawing of 1846 records the original installation, which is no longer intact. The window frames, two of which survive,[11] are elaborately carved with caryatids of monsters and female herms; the glazings, designed and executed by Dierick Crabeth and his atelier in 1543, juxtapose scenes from the story of Samuel with others from the life of St. Paul.[12] These rectangular panels are surrounded by architectural ornament with open arcades resting on aedicules, strapwork, festoons, and other classicized and Italianate motifs that, in contrast to the fifteenth-century arrangement, fill the entire aperture.

The instances of roundels being incorporated into the glazing programs of churches are rare.[13] In a highly unusual setting at Anderlecht near Brussels, for example, roundels representing St. John the Baptist Preaching in the Wilderness and the Baptism of Christ are set in gables in the canopies above full-length figures of St. Jerome

Fig. 5. **Isaac and Rebekah.** North Lowlands, Leiden ?, c. 1480. Silver-stained roundel. Rijksmuseum, Amsterdam. Inv. no. NM 12243.

Fig. 6. **Christ as the Man of Sorrows.** Germany, c. 1485–1495. Silver-stained roundel. The British Museum, London. OA 1792.

with a donor and St. Servais.[14] Less rare are secular programs con-
sisting of heraldic badges set in fields of quarries such as those
partially preserved in the fifteenth-century chapels of Canterbury
Cathedral.[15]

Roundels were frequently glazed into the windows of hospitals,
alms houses, or monastic foundations, particularly in contemplative
areas such as cloisters or individual cells. The cloister of Sint-
Pietersgasthuis is today glazed with diamond-panes, but original
borders of foliated running ornament in the flamboyant tracery sur-
rounding the central lights—dated variably 1520 or 1521—suggest
that they might originally have been glazed with a series of roundels,
at least in the upper registers.[16] A window with a similar border in
the church of Saint-Étienne of the large Begijnhof was glazed with
twelve roundels comprising a Passion series in 1525 by Gérard Boels;
another window in the same church was similarly ornamented with
six roundels around the same time by Jean Aep.[17] An instance of
roundels being ordered for private monastic quarters is recorded in
a 1506–1507 document stating that "Cornelis the painter"—most
likely Cornelis Engebrechtsz.—designed silver-stained roundels for

the "Blue Room," which was part of the suite of the abbess of Rijnsburg Abbey.[18]

In the almost total absence of documentation, little is known about the location of roundel workshops, the craftsmen employed by them, or the methods they used. However, a large number of drawings related to the production of silver-stained roundels have survived, and a study of them provides some insights into their function as well as into the relationship of the designers to the roundel painters. The nature and form of these drawings vary,[19] but in addition to rare sketches and studies, in general there appear to be three basic types: original designs, copies of these designs, and highly finished presentation drawings (compare figs. 9, 10, 11, 15, 17).

The designs, frequently executed by highly gifted artists, were drawn to scale and informed both patron and glass painter of all the compositional and stylistic details, providing indications of lead lines where borders were involved, inscriptions, and often technical instructions in the margins (fig. 9). Rendered in ink on paper, these designs were typically highly finished, often enhanced with brush-work, washes, and different colored inks or chalk. Among the many renowned Lowlands artists who produced roundel designs in the first half of the sixteenth century were Cornelis Engebrechtsz., Lucas van Leyden, Dierick Vellert (figs. 11, 15), Pieter Cornelisz. Kunst, Jacob Cornelisz. van Oostsanen, the Pseudo-Ortkens, Jan Gossaert (fig. 17), Pieter Coecke van Aelst, Dierick Crabeth (figs. 24, 25), Jan Swart van Groningen, Maarten van Heemskerck (fig. 22), Lambert van Noort, and Maarten de Vos. At the same time in Germany, designs were being produced by Heinrich Aldegrever, Albrecht Altdorfer, Hans Sebald Beham, Jörg Breu der Älter (fig. 20), Hans Burgkmair, Albrecht Dürer, Hans Baldung Grien, Augustin Hirschvogel, Wolf Huber, Hans Süss von Kulmbach, Georg Pencz (fig. 9), and Hans Leonhard Schäufelein.

Proportionately larger numbers of copies of designs have survived (fig. 15). These copies are the work of lesser hands; although compositionally faithful to the original, the drawing, clearly outlined with minimal shading, is comparatively deliberate and stiff, and the inscriptions, instructions, and the like are typically omitted. Several probable circumstances that required these copies can be postulated. If, for example, the design was commissioned by an individual rather than a roundel workshop, it likely became the property of the patron. A copy would then have to be provided to the glass painting shop as a model for executing the roundel and as a record of the trans-action. In stained glass workshops this copy, called a *vidimus* ("we have seen"), was considered a contractual document, clearly estab-lishing what the painter would produce and what the patron would receive.[20] A full-scale cartoon (*patron*) was then made for the stained glass window. In roundel production, the copy could have served both as a *vidimus* and as a full-scale model.

If the design were commissioned by a workshop, as the evidence shows was more often than not the case, a working copy would be desirable to preserve the original, an item of no small expense. Work-

Fig. 8. **Cancer from a series of the Zodiac.** England, c. 1490. Silver-stained roundel. Church of St. Mary, Shrewsbury. Photo: National Monuments Record.

Fig. 9. **Design for a roundel with the arms of Marco Baro and his ancestors.** Georg Pencz. Germany, Nuremberg c. 1530–1540. Brown ink and wash on paper. The J. Paul Getty Museum, Malibu. 83.GA.193.

Fig. 10. **Design copy for a roundel with the Triumph of Time from a series of the Triumphs of Petrarch.** Workshop of Pieter Coecke van Aelst. South Lowlands, c. 1535–1545. Brown ink, wash, and white highlights on paper. École nationale supérieure des Beaux-Arts, Paris. Inv. no. M625.

ing copies, stored in portfolios, might also have been used to show prospective roundel clients available designs. A working copy could be used as well to update or alter details of the design.[21] A large number of copies have been well preserved, suggesting that multiple working copies were made from the design copy and that these second-generation copies were actually used as models at the bench.[22] In large workshops these multiple copies would allow, as demand required, a given design to be executed by several painters simultaneously. The number of surviving replicas and close versions of popular series is evidence of this practice, as is the existence of design copies pricked for transfer. Whether placed under the glass and traced or pinned up and copied free-hand by the painter, the working copy would eventually be worn out and have to be replaced.

Presentation drawings were meticulously finished autonomous works of art (fig. 17). They were executed on prepared paper, usually green, gray, or brown in tone, in brown, black, or gray ink, often enhanced with one or more washes, and with highlights in white and even gold. Too subtle and delicate to serve as workshop designs, these drawings may have been intended for the general market or as presentation pieces for clients rather than as actual designs for glass. If they were simply intended to exercise the artist's gifts and to delight the eye of the beholder, these drawings establish the high regard sixteenth-century collectors accorded superb sheets, perhaps explaining the relatively numerous extant examples.[23]

While engravings, woodcuts, and book illustration were primary sources for roundel designs in the fifteenth century,[24] by the early sixteenth century they were superseded by drawings. Because this more expensive design alternative was commissioned and therefore unique, it entailed a measure of copyright protection, whereas xylographic sources were essentially in the public domain. This distinction must have become increasingly important as roundel pro-

Fig. 11. **Design for a roundel with the Adoration of the Magi from a series of the Life of the Virgin.** Dierick Vellert. South Lowlands, Antwerp, 1532. Brown ink and wash on paper. Albertina, Vienna. Inv. no. 7802.

Fig. 12. **Adoration of the Magi from a series of the Life of the Virgin.** Dierick Vellert. South Lowlands, Antwerp, probably 1532. Silver-stained roundel. Hessisches Landesmuseum Darmstadt. Inv. no. Kg 31:33.

Figs. 13, 14. **Two Leaded Windows with Ornament and Scenes from a series of the Seven Acts of Charity.** After Maarten van Heemskerck, Netherlands, Haarlem ?, dated 1618. The Metropolitan Museum of Art, New York. *See page 175.*

duction expanded and grew more competitive. A design that was not controlled was soon widely disseminated and reproduced by diverse roundel workshops in disparate styles, rapidly spawning many versions and variants (figs. 26, 27).[25] A design controlled by a workshop was reproduced with relative stylistic homogeneity; variants emerged only with time (figs. 18, 19).[26] Roundels based on graphics, on the other hand, were reproduced in widely separated workshops but with stylistic consistency because they used the identical model.[27]

The 1506–1507 Rijnsburg Abbey accounts concerning the silver-stained roundels designed by Cornelis (Engebrechtsz.?) for the abbess indicate that separate funds were paid to Ewout Vos and his two assistants to execute the roundels and to an ironsmith to make the window fittings.[28] Similarly, a civil dispute in 1514 involved a glass painter named Dieloff Clarsz. and the artist with whom he collaborated, Pieter Cornelisz. Kunst.[29] This scant documentation suggests, then, that the roundel designer was generally not the glass painter. The most notable exception was Dierick Vellert, who in addition to being a gifted designer with a particular interest in roundels was a peerless glass painter, to which the surviving roundels that bear his monogram eloquently attest.[30] Other cases are less clear. Although Lucas van Leyden most probably made designs for

Fig. 15. **Working copy of a design for a roundel with the Marriage of the Virgin from a series of the Life of the Virgin.** After Dierick Vellert. South Lowlands, Antwerp, c. 1532. Ink on paper. The British Museum, London. 1923–4–17–3.

Fig. 16. **Christ in the Wine-Press**, inscribed: IF ANY MAN THIRST COME TO ME AND DRINCK. From Lullington Church, Kent. Charles Winston, October 1844. Watercolor on paper. British Library, ms. add. 35211, vol. II, 200, 262–K64.

Fig. 17. **Finished drawing with the Decapitation of St. John the Baptist.** Jan Gossaert. South Lowlands, Malines ?, c. 1510. Brown ink, wash, and white highlights on gray-brown prepared paper. École nationale supérieure des Beaux-Arts, Paris. Inv. no. Masson 487.

roundels[31] and Karel van Mander describes him as a glass painter and even cites an example of his work,[32] no panel that can be securely attributed to his hand survives.

Silver-stained roundels drew from a broad but relatively conventional choice of subject matter up to about 1520. Iconic images such as patron saints of towns, guilds, confraternities, or individuals formed perhaps the largest (and least innovative) group of single roundel subjects. Also common are devotional images such as the Crucifixion, Man of Sorrows, Pietà, and Trinity (figs. 6, 16). Although these subjects were often influenced by specific movements—*Devotio Moderna* in the Lowlands, for example—pre-Reformation imagery is typically too generic to be localized. Less common are a variety of secular subjects, including genre scenes, vanitas or *memento mori* and other allegorical themes, and vignettes of pure whimsy (back cover). But the majority of roundels belonged to narrative series. Not surprisingly, Infancy, Passion, and Marian cycles were common, as were a larger array of Old Testament subjects. But by the end of the fifteenth century, four biblical subjects—the history of Joseph in Egypt and the stories of Esther, Susanna (frontispiece), and Tobit and Tobias (figs. 18, 19)—appear with great frequency, usually as replicas, versions, or variants of the same series of designs.[33] To judge from the disproportionately large number of surviving examples, the demand for these subjects reached a peak in the 1520s. What special implications these particular subjects held for their Lowlands audience, making them so universally popular, remains to be investigated.[34]

After around 1520 in the Lowlands, the repertoire of subjects for silver-stained roundels dramatically expanded, and the painting became more varied and individualized. While traditional subject matter endured, new forms of imagery, often eclectic, unconventional, and polemical, were introduced. This flourishing of roundel production—and of the arts in general—was possible because the Lowlands were at this time exceptionally rich in artistic talent.[35] It is remarkable that in the 1520s, artists of such diverse abilities as Pieter Coecke van Aelst, Pieter Cornelisz. Kunst, Jacob Cornelisz. van Oostsanen, Cornelis Engebrechtsz., Jan Gossaert, Maarten van Heemskerck, Lucas van Leyden, Barend van Orly, the Pseudo-Ortkens, Jan Swart van Groningen, and Dierick Vellert—all of whom created designs for roundels—were active.

Manifold and complex circumstances created a climate conducive to artistic creativity, not the least of which was the fact the patrons in the Lowlands—as opposed to those in Germany, for example—were overwhelmingly lay and private.[36] The population was, in general, largely traditional in its attitudes and parochial in its outlook.[37] It was not, however, an entirely homogeneous society, and points of view varied according to the conditions and circumstances of the immediate area. Thus, when reformist ideas arrived in the Lowlands, reaction was, at least until the middle of the century, far less strident and polarized than in Germany.[38] It was, in fact, decades before the North Lowlands fully converted to the reformed church.[39]

Reformist thought was, moreover, greatly tempered by the concurrent influence of humanism. Changes in religious views occurred in a climate of relative intellectual receptivity and individual freedom, and thus the reevaluation of church doctrine yielded diverse conclusions[40] that affected attitudes more than dogma and were more apparent in private than in public spheres.[41] Reformist and humanist thought profoundly influenced sixteenth-century imagery, but it did not preclude the commingling of old and new ideas. In this climate, the treatment of biblical subjects took a variety of new forms that more often than not eschewed the purely doctrinal forms.[42]

This eclectic treatment is apparent, for example, in a group of fifteen designs for roundels by Dierick Vellert, all signed and dated 1523, which appear to have formed a typological series in which two, or perhaps three, scenes from Moses are juxtaposed with one scene from the life of Christ. The drawing of Moses Sweetening the Waters at Marah would have been paired with another representing the Marriage Feast at Cana. Two further drawings that may belong to the same series link Moses with Gideon and the Miracle of the Fleece, a subject conventionally associated with a Mariological context.[43] While the rarely depicted Old Testament scenes evidence current humanist interest in biblical texts, the juxtaposition of types and antitypes relies on a purely medieval model.[44]

Similarly, a group of large woodcuts with biblical scenes by Jacob Cornelisz. and Lucas van Leyden have recently been reconstructed in a more conventional typological series analogous to the *Biblia pauperum*.[45] Earlier, between 1511 and 1514, Cornelisz. published a circular passion series that is unusual as it was widely used as designs for silver-stained roundels.[46] In about 1520, the circular woodcuts were incorporated within elaborate Renaissance frames flanked by Old Testament prefigurations, again analogous to those found in the *Biblia pauperum* and the *Speculum humanae salvationis*. It is tempting to think that these typological arrangements were, like the unframed earlier addition, used as designs for windows. In this regard, it is interesting to note that these series of

Fig. 20. **Design for a roundel with Coquinaria from a series of the Septem Artes Mechanicae.** Jörg Breu the Elder. Germany, Augsburg, c. 1530. Brown ink, gray, green, and rose wash, and strengthening in charcoal on paper. Staatliche Graphische Sammlung, Munich. Inv. no. 19 441.

Fig. 21. **Coquinaria from a series of the Septem Artes Mechanicae.** After Jörg Breu the Elder. Germany, Augsburg, c. 1530–1535. Silver-stained roundel. Victoria and Albert Museum, London. 604.72.

outsized woodcuts (when assembled, the Jacob Cornelisz. and Lucas van Leyden typological series was almost three and a half meters long) were intended to be mounted on canvas and hung or attached directly to the wall as a freize.[47] A analogous arrangement of roundels in one or more windows is really only a variation of the same idea. The Leiden windows by Dierick Crabeth, in fact, formed just such an arrangement. In this cycle, an early work painted by Crabeth in 1543, six scenes from the life of Saul are juxtaposed, one over the other, with six from the story of St. Paul (fig. 23). Expounded on are the role of the individual man, his relationship to God, and his responsibilities as a devout Christian.[48] Although the subject matter alludes to the Protestant doctrine of justification by faith, the imagery is too muted to be interpreted as explicitly reformist.

Only after the middle of the century when reformist activity inexorably drifted toward violence do prints as well as silver-stained roundels become overtly polemical.[49] An eclectic example is found in a group of twelve prints comprising twenty-four allegorical scenes that address man's fall, his vain attempt to gain salvation through good works, and his final redemption through the grace of God.[50] These scenes, one of which bears the monogram of the Antwerp engraver Frans Huys, were conflated by Dierick Crabeth in a series of designs for silver-stained roundels. Eight of the drawings and four roundels from the series have survived.[51] Certain iconographic details closely link this series to both Lutheranism and Spiritualism. This admixture is characteristic of reformism in the Lowlands, which frequently blurred distinctions between particular Protestant movements.[52] A set of six woodcuts executed by Cornilsz. Anthonisz., which give an allegorical reading of the parable of the Prodigal Son, contains a similar conflation of reformist theologies.[53]

The Prodigal Son was the ultimate source of another polemic that addressed a more wordly preoccupation. Largely under the influence of the Rederijker, or rhetoricians' chambers, which had become extremely popular in the sixteenth century throughout the Lowlands,[54] the Prodigal was transformed from a parable illustrating God's forgiveness of the repentant to a moralistic allegory of a profligate known as Sorgheloos (Careless), who ends up in abject and unredeemed misery for his wasteful and spendthrift ways. This subject, frequently encountered in silver-stained roundels,[55] gives additional insight into the changing moral values of Lowlands society.[56]

The creative atmosphere that nurtured silver-stained roundel production through the first half of the sixteenth century was soon dissipated—at least in the Lowlands—by the violence of iconoclasm and the rigidity of the Counter-Reformation sentiment. Without the support of artistic and intellectual diversity, the salience of the roundel was lost.

## Brief Guide to Silver-Stained Roundel Literature

Scholarship in the field of silver-stained roundels, compared to that of stained glass, is still in its infancy. As a consequence, the literature is scant and, in the absence of any bibliographical compilation, the material that does exist is not easily found.[57] The following is a brief survey of existing research tools, some of which in turn will direct the reader to further bibliography.

The best general introduction to roundels and other small-scale domestic panels is Hermann Schmitz, *Die Glasgemälde der königlichen Kunstgewerbemuseums in Berlin*. His 1923 volume, *Deutsche Glasmalereien der Gotik und Renaissance: Rund- und Kabinettscheiben*, however, is more valuable for the illustrations than for the text.[58]

Drawings related to the production of silver-stained roundels inform us of individual and local styles, iconographic repertory, and workshop methods, and they often allow the reconstruction of narrative series. Collection catalogues of German and Lowlands drawings are therefore valuable reference tools. Among the more important are those of the Rijksprentenkabinet, Rijksmuseum, Amsterdam; the Kupferstichkabinett, Berlin; the Städelsches Kunstinstitut, Frankfurt; the Department of Prints and Drawings, British Museum, London; the Cabinet des Dessins, Musée du Louvre, Paris; and the Graphische Sammlung Albertina, Vienna.[59]

Surveys and Corpora of national or regional stained glass collections are also useful references in those few instances where roundels are included. Jean Helbig included roundels in his survey of stained glass in Belgium but only those that are glazed in monuments, and the information provided on individual pieces is scant. The Corpus Vitrearum Medii Aevi has tended to exclude roundels from its volumes, again except for those installed in the windows of monuments. The greatest number appear in the Belgian volumes.[60]

The major public collections of silver-stained roundels are those of the Victoria and Albert Museum, London; the Rijksmuseum, Amsterdam; the Musées Royaux d'Art et d'Histoire, Brussels; and the Metropolitan Museum of Art, New York. The collection of the latter is published for the first time in this volume. Regrettably, none of the other collections, all of which are larger, have been published, although Bernard Rackham did treat roundels in his sur-

Fig. 22. **Allegory of the Blood of Christ.** Maarten van Heemskerck. North Lowlands, Haarlem, 1559. Brown ink on paper. Prentenkabinet der Rijksuniversiteit, Leiden. PK 5303.

Fig. 23. **Paul before the Areopagus from a typological series of the stories of Samuel and Paul.** Dierick Crabeth. North Lowlands, Gouda ? Silver-stained roundel. Musée des Arts Décoratifs, Paris. 46518 B.

vey of the collections of stained glass in the Victoria and Albert. Some articles devoted to former private collections are useful in identifying material as it reappears in the market. Another private collection recently installed at the McGill University School of Architecture, Montreal, has been published in its entirety. Several catalogues of museum collections have included informative entries on roundels. And more recently, Hilary Wayment has catalogued the stained glass installed in the side chapel of King's College Chapel, Cambridge, which includes a large number of roundels.[61]

Bernard Rackham long ago recognized that several thousand silver-stained roundels were collected wholesale in the nineteenth century and installed in parish churches throughout Great Britain.[62] Over many years, Dr. William F. Cole has compiled an invaluable photographic and documentary archive of these roundels, aspects of which he has published.[63] By sheer volume alone, this archive has greatly broadened our knowledge of the stylistic and iconographical range of roundel production.

Renewed interest in silver-stained roundels has occasioned their inclusion in several recent exhibitions, the catalogues of which have contributed to the study of this material. Notable examples are *Magie du Verre* at Galerie CGER in Brussels, which included roundels from the fourteenth through the nineteenth centuries; *Kunst voor de Beeldenstorm* at the Rijksmuseum in Amsterdam, which included a number of North Lowlands roundels of the first half of the sixteenth century; and *Northern Renaissance Stained Glass* at the Cantor Art Gallery, College of the Holy Cross, Worcester, Massachusetts.[64]

Periodical literature remains relatively scant. E. A. Popham wrote several useful articles on silver-stained roundels. His attempts to establish authorship were pioneering efforts in this essential aspect

Fig. 24. **Design with Man's struggle between God's wrath and the Devil from an allegorical series of Man's Fall and Redemption.** Dierick Crabeth. North Lowlands, Gouda ? Brown ink and charcoal on paper. Rijksprentenkabinet, Rijksmuseum, Amsterdam. 47:2.

Fig. 25. **Design with the Allegory of Christ as the Redeemer of Man from an allegorical series of Man's Fall and Redemption.** Dierick Crabeth. North Lowlands, Gouda ? Brown ink and charcoal on paper. Rijksprentenkabinet, Rijksmuseum, Amsterdam. 60:175.

Fig. 26. **Drawing of Sorgheloos with Aermoede and Pouer Rejected from a series of the story of Sorgheloos.** Master of the Death of Absalom ? North Lowlands, c. 1500. Black ink and white highlight on gray prepared paper. P. and N. de Boer Stichting. Photo: Rijksmuseum, Amsterdam.

Fig. 27. **Sorgheloos with Aermoede and Pouer Rejected from a series of the story of Sorgheloos.** North Lowlands, c. 1500–1520. Silver-stained roundel. Hessisches Landesmuseum, Darmstadt. Inv. no. Kg 31–35.

of roundel studies; his articles also connected certain designs with executed roundels. Mention must also be made, of course, of Jean Lafond's study of the silver-stained medium itself.[65]

Kurt Steinbart in his study of Jacob Cornelisz. was among the first to consider in depth an individual artist's involvement with roundel production. Among the more important and recent efforts that investigate the work of particular artists or workshops are studies by Linda Evers and Hilary Wayment on the Pseudo-Ortkens, Ellen Konowitz on Dierick Vellert, Paul Maes on sixteenth-century Louvain roundel production and nineteenth-century reproduction, and Zsuzsanna van Ruyven-Zeman on Lambert van Noort. Recent articles that consider iconographical aspects include those by Jeremy Bangs on Heemskerck, Yvette Vanden Bemden on a history of Joseph series, and this author on Sorgheloos.[66]

The Fichier International de Documentation du Rondel, housed in the Institut Royal du Patrimoine Artistique in Brussels, was conceived as a central repository of photographs and documentation of roundels whatever their location; as this archive expands, it will become an increasingly important resource.[67]

The largest single collection of silver-stained roundels in the United States is that of the Metropolitan Museum of Art in New York. The largest portion of the collection is in The Cloisters, one of the few institutions to systematically acquire roundels; other collections have been formed largely by gift or bequest. A number of other institutions have distinguished, if small, collections: the Art Institute of Chicago, the Detroit Institute of Arts, and the J. B. Speed Art Museum in Louisville, to name a few. A group of roundels in the Baltimore Museum of Art is notable not only for its high quality, but also for its distinguished provenance that can be traced to the eighteenth-century collection of Horace Walpole at Strawberry Hill.

Large private collections of roundels have always been a rarity in the United States. The average known collection generally numbers less than eight. Holdings such as those of William Randolph Hearst are exceptional and have long been dispersed. Fortunately, the most important pieces, including the Walpole pieces, are now in various public collections. The more recent sale of the fine collection of

James Herbert Rawlings Boone of Baltimore resulted in the exportation of a number of important pieces, while only three are now in a public collection, The Cloisters, and three are in a California house.

This volume, a compilation of roundels up to 1700 from public and private collections in the United States, does not presume to be complete. If, however, it serves to bring more examples to light, stimulate interest, and, ultimately, advance knowledge of the material, then it will have more than served its purpose.

Timothy B. Husband
*Metropolitan Museum of Art*

NOTES

1.   For the early use of silver-stain, see Jean Lafond, "Un vitrail du Mesnil-Villeman (1313) et les origines du jaune d'argent," *Bulletin de la Société nationale des antiquaires de France* (1954), 93–95, and Meredith P. Lillich, "European Stained Glass around 1300: The Introduction of Silver-Stain," *Europäische Kunst um 1300* (XXV Internationaler Kongress für Kunstgeschichte Wien 6) (Vienna, 1985), 45–60.

2.   The North Lowlands refers to those territories generally incorporated into the modern Netherlands, while the South Lowlands corresponds in general to modern Belgium. Together, the Lowlands are the equivalent of the French term Anciens Pays-Bas. The linguistic division in the fifteenth and sixteenth centuries, however, fell farther south than it does today, with Courtrai, Audenarde, Brussels, Louvain, and Maastricht on the Flemish side and Lille, Tournai, Mons, Namur, Huy, and Liège on the French side. The North Lowlands becomes the Netherlands with the union of the northern counties of Zeeland, Holland, Utrecht, Gelderland, Groningen, Friesland, and Overijssel toward the end of the sixteenth century, even though independence from Spain was not fully achieved until well into the seventeenth century.

3.   Quarries correspond in terms of technique to the definition of roundel, but they were generally components of larger leaded windows rather than entities unto themselves. Because their scale and function are quite different from those of roundels, they are excluded from this study. Other panels that conform to the definition of a roundel but lack silver-stain are, on the other hand, included in this volume.

4.   The watercolor studies of Charles Winston from the 1830s, 1840s, and early 1850s, now in the British Library, include renderings of now-lost English roundels dating to the fifteenth and sixteenth centuries. Examples include a sixteenth-century roundel with the symbol of St. Mark (Ms. add. 33851, no. 99) or a group of four fifteenth-century roundels once in Thaxted Church, Essex (Ms. add. 35211, nos. 55–58) and, in the same manuscript, depictions of roundels once installed in the mayor's chapel, Bristol (no. 512, 121–G60). Similar volumes of drawings and watercolors by A. Buckler, also executed in the nineteenth century, include illustrations of English heraldic silver-stained roundels (Ms. add. 37139, fol. 93). Early topological books can often have illustrations of lost roundels. Hasted's *History of Kent* (23 vols.), with illustrations dating to the 1820s and 1830s, includes, for example, a watercolor of an early sixteenth-century roundel representing a eucharistic Man of Sorrows, once in Luddenham Church, Kent (Ms. add. 32367, fol. 62).

5.   See note 1. For the earliest example in this Checklist, see Illinois, Art Institute of Chicago, accession number 49.209.

6.   See Yvette Vanden Bemden, "Moyen Age," in *Magie de Verre* [exh. cat., Galerie CGER, Brussels] (Brussels, 1986), 39, 43, no. 5d.

7.   Silver-stained roundels with coats of arms survive in considerable numbers. Following the guidelines of the Fichier International de Documentation du Rondel,

roundels whose compositions are restricted to purely heraldic devices are not included in this Checklist but were listed instead among the stained glass in Checklists I–III. If, however, the heraldic shield is supported by a figure set in a landscape, for example, the roundel is included here.

8.  For an analysis of window construction based on depictions in panel painting, see Luc-François Genicot, "Un châssis de fenêtre du XVIe siècle au musée de Louvain-la-Neuve," *Revue des Archéologues et Historiens d'Art de Louvain* 20 (1987), 234–252. See also A. Brouyaux, *Histoire de la clôture des fenêtres dans l'architecture civile, de la fin de l'Antiquité à la fin du Moyen Âge* (Brussels, 1984) and Eva Frodl-Kraft, "Das Bildfenster im Bild, Glasmalerei in den Interieurs der frühen Niederländer," *Bau- und Bildkunst im Spiegel internationaler Forschung* (Berlin, 1989).

9.  The reasons for employing this rather inflexible system instead of glazed moveable casements are unclear, especially in a northern climate. The comfort gained by better control of air flow would seem to more than warrant the expense of hinged windows.

10.  See J. F. Dröge, *De bouw- en bewoningsgeschiedenis van Pieterskerkgracht* 9 (Leiden, 1982).

11.  The three upstairs window frames have disappeared; two others were removed from the house in 1897 and acquired by the Stedelijk Museum De Lakenhal, Leiden, inv. no. 2449.

12.  See *Kunst voor de Beeldenstorm: Noordnederlandse kunst 1525–1580* [exh. cat., Rijksmuseum] (Amsterdam, 1986), 288–289, no. 161.1–2 (window frames); 284–288, no. 160.1–8 (glass).

13.  For an inventory of stained glass, including roundels, in Belgium, see Jean Helbig, *De Glasschilderkunst in België* (Antwerp, 1943).

14.  See Jean Helbig, *Les Vitraux médiévaux conservé en Belgique, 1200–1500* [Corpus Vitrearum Medii Aevi, Belgium, 1] (Brussels, 1961), 177–190, figs. 81–83.

15.  See Madeline Harrison Caviness, *The Windows of Christ Church Cathedral, Canterbury* [Corpus Vitrearum Medii Aevi, Great Britain] (London, 1981), 281–287.

16.  In 1902, a number of roundels were installed in the cloister of Sint-Pietersgasthuis. These had been removed from several local foundations, including the small church of the small Begijnhof, the Alexian Klooster, and other rooms of Sint-Pietersgasthuis. This installation was removed around 1960. See Paul Victor Maes, "De Leuvense Brandglasmedaillons: Technische, Typologische en Stilistische Kenmerken," *Leuvens Brandglas, Arca Lovaniensis* 13 (Louvain, 1987), 79–89.

17.  See Jean Helbig and Yvette Vanden Bemden, *Les Vitraux de la première moitié du XVIe siècle conservés en Belgique: Brabant et Limbourg* [Corpus Vitrearum Medii Aevi, Belgium, 3] (Ghent/Ledeburg, 1974), 275.

18.  Jeremy Bangs, "Rijnsburg Abbey: Additional Documents of Furniture, Artists, Musicians, and Buildings, 1500–1570," in *Bulletin Koninklijke Nederlandse Oudheidkundige Bond* 74 (November 1974), 186 and n. 63, 64, 68; Bangs, *Cornelis Engebrechtsz.'s Leiden* [Studies in Cultural History] (Assen, 1979), 5.

19.  For a general discussion of the use of drawings in the production of stained glass, see William W. Robinson and Martha Wolff, "The Function of Drawings in the Netherlands in the Sixteenth Century," in *The Age of Bruegel: Netherlandish Drawings in the Sixteenth Century* [exh. cat., National Gallery of Art] (Washington, DC, 1986), esp. 33–34.

20.  The term *vidimus* has been much discussed by Hilary G. Wayment in *The Windows of King's College Chapel, Cambridge: A Description and Commentary* [Corpus Vitrearum Medii Aevi, Great Britain, supp. vol. 1] (Oxford and London, 1972), 30; "The Great Windows of King's College Chapel and the Meaning of the Word *Vidimus*," *Proceedings of the Cambridge Antiquarian Society* 69 (1979), 365–376; "Three Vidimuses for the Windows in King's College Chapel, Cambridge," *Master Drawings* 22 (1984), 43–46. For contract drawings in painting, see Robinson and Wolff 1986, 26.

21.  Costumes in designs for particularly popular series, for example, had to be updated to accord with current fashion. Dierick Vellert's Abraham and Pharoah (?) in the British Museum seems to be an instance of the master using a working copy

to make compositional alterations. See *The Age of Bruegel* 1986, 34, 92–93, no. 115. Another design by Vellert for an unidentified Old Testament subject, also in the British Museum, has been similarly reworked.

22. Presumably these intermediate drawings would not be necessary when the designer and the painter were the same.

23. Robinson and Wolff 1986, 25, 34–39.

24. Graphics were frequently indirect sources, that is, a given composition was not simply copied but elements from several sources were appropriated and reassembled to create a scene. The eight roundels in The Cloisters comprising a Passion series (32.24.1–8), for example, drew on Masters E. S. and Schongauer in this fashion. See Charles I. Minott, "A Group of Stained Glass Roundels at The Cloisters," *Art Bulletin* 43, no. 3 (September 1961), 237–239. In Germany prints were also used as direct sources, a practice that continued in the sixteenth century. This practice was rarely used in the Lowlands until the second half of the century.

25. The designs for a series of the popular morality—Sorgheloos, for example—appear to have originated in the Lowlands by the end of the fifteenth century with later versions in drawings, paintings, and roundels being produced in Leiden, Antwerp, and elsewhere. In at least one case, the composition was so varied as to confuse the subject. See Timothy B. Husband, "'Ick Sorgheloose . . .': A Silver-Stained Roundel in The Cloisters," *Metropolitan Museum of Art Journal* 24 (1989), 173–186.

26. The series of the story of Susanna based on the c. 1510–1520 Antwerp designs of the Pseudo-Ortkens, for example, remain stylistically and compositionally quite consistent in spite of the large numbers of replications until degraded variants begin to appear around the middle of the century.

27. The 1559 engraved series of eight Triumphs by Dierick Volkertsz. Coornhert after Maarten van Heemskerck were, for example, widely reproduced in glass. Fragments of roundels based on this series that had been glazed in one or more windows made for Arendt ten Grotenhuis and his wife Maria Willems van Heemskerck in 1611 have been excavated from the basement of a house on Assenstraat in Deventer. The painting follows the printed source so faithfully that without the inscription, the windows could easily be dated to the 1560s or 1570s.

28. Bangs 1974, 186 and n. 68.

29. Bangs 1979, 89. On the previous page Bangs notes that the 1527 record of payment to Pieter Cornelisz. Kunst was not for stained glass but for a series of heraldic banners with the arms of Leiden painted on paper and commissioned by the city annually.

30. Ellen Konowitz in her dissertation in progress ("The Antwerp Artist Dirck Vellert," Institute of Fine Arts, New York University) is studying this aspect of Vellert's work.

31. The argument that Lucas' drawings of Jael and Sisera and of Judith and Holofernes were intended as roundel designs for a series of the Power of Women is strengthened by the existence of a panel representing Samson and Delilah, now in the Hessisches Landesmuseum, Darmstadt. It is also argued that Lucas designed a series of the life of Christ for glass. See W. Th. Kloek and J. Piet Filedt-Kok, " 'De Opstanding van Christus,' getekend door Lucas van Leyden," *Bulletin van het Rijksmuseum* 31, no. 1 (1983), 4–20.

32. Carel van Mander, *Dutch and Flemish Painters* (New York, 1936).

33. In Germany, a series of the parable of the Prodigal Son that seems to have originated in the Lower Rhineland, probably Cologne, enjoyed comparable popularity. Joseph in Egypt occasionally appears in German roundels, but Tobit and Susanna do not.

34. The story of Tobit and Tobias comes from the Apocrypha, and the canonicity of Susanna was questioned as it did not appear in Hebrew bibles. Both may have been rediscovered with the renewed and intense interest in biblical text. Both also involve themes of moral rectitude and the reward of patience and faith, which might have had a special appeal at the time.

35. The 1986 exhibition devoted to the art of the North Lowlands between 1525 and 1580 at the Rijksmuseum and the scholarship that evolved from it greatly enhanced the understanding of art of this period. In addition to the catalogue, *Kunst*

*voor de beeldenstorm* (note 2), see *Bulletin van het Rijksmuseum* 35, no. 3 (1987) for a number of important papers from the colloquium.

36. Craig Harbison in "Response to James Marrow," *Simiolus* 16, no. 2/3 (1986), 171, notes that in the Lowlands lay donors outnumber clerics by two and half times, whereas in Germany the ratio is about even.

37. R. P. Zijp, "De iconographie van de reformatie in de Nederlanden, een begripsbepaling," *Bulletin van het Rijksmuseum* 35, no. 3 (1987), 178–179.

38. Peter W. Parshall, "Kunst en reformatie in de Noordelijke Nederlanden—enkele gezichtspunten," *Bulletin van het Rijksmuseum* 35, no. 3 (1987), 170.

39. Zijp 1987, 179.

40. Zijp 1987, 177. For the variety of response to religious issues, see K. G. Boon, "Divers aspects de l'iconographie de la Pré-Réforme aux Pays-Bas," *Gazette des Beaux-Arts* 104 (1984), 207–216 and 105 (1985), 1–13.

41. Parshall 1987, 172–173.

42. J. Bruyn, "Old and new elements in 16th-century imagery," *Oud Holland* 102, no. 2 (1988), 109–110.

43. See *The Age of Bruegel* 1986, 291, no. 114, and Ellen Konowitz in Virginia C. Raguin et al., *Northern Renaissance Stained Glass: Continuity and Transformations* [exh. cat., College of the Holy Cross, Iris and B. Gerald Cantor Art Gallery] (Worcester, MA, 1987), 26–27.

44. On the other hand, subjects that in medieval texts were typologically linked to scenes in the Life or Passion of Christ became isolated, exemplary images in the sixteenth century, retaining their medieval, emotive character. The scene of Joab Murdering Amasa, for example, traditionally paired with the Betrayal, was used as an isolated, highly charged *exempla* that at once caused the viewer to recoil at the portrayal of Joab's fratricidal treachery and recall how Christ willingly endured Judas' kiss and its consequences so that man, through His sacrifice, would be redeemed.

45. See Jan Piet Filedt-Kok, "Een *Biblia pauperum* met houtsneden van Jacob Cornelisz. en Lucas van Leyden gereconstrueerd," *Bulletin van het Rijksmuseum* 36, no. 2 (1988), 83–116.

46. A complete series of twelve roundels is in the parish church at Bradford-on-Avon, and numerous and isolated scenes are in various museum collections, including that of the Detroit Institute of Arts.

47. Filedt-Kok 1988, 83.

48. See *Kunst voor de Beeldenstorm* 1986, 284–288, no. 160.1–8.

49. Maarten van Heemskerck, at a later date, betrays both reformist and iconoclastic sympathies. His composition of Bel and the Dragon has been seen as both antimonastic and sympathetic to the outbreak of iconoclasm in 1566. See Jeremy Bangs, "Maerten van Heemskerck's 'Bel and the Dragon' and Iconoclasm," *Renaissance Quarterly* 30, no. 1 (Spring 1977), 8–11. These tendencies are apparent in other works by Heemskerck, such as his Old Testament series of the history of Elijah and Ahab, Athaliah, and Joshua, among others, as well as in more explicit compositions such as his Allegory of the Iconoclasts. See Eleanor A. Saunders, "Commentary on iconoclasm in several prints series by Maerten van Heemskerck," *Simiolus* 10, no. 2 (1978–1979), 59–82.

50. Daniel R. Horst, "Een zestiende eeuwse reformatorische prentenreeks van Frans Huys over de Heilsweg van de Mens," *Bulletin van het Rijksmuseum* 38, no. 1 (1990), 3–24. I am grateful to Jan Piet Filedt-Kok for bringing this article to my attention and providing me with a typescript prior to its publication.

51. *Kunst voor de Beeldenstorm* 1986, 359–361, nos. 240–241.

52. Zijp 1987, 177.

53. Barbara Haeger, "Cornelis Anthonisz.'s Representation of the Parable of the Prodigal Son: A Protestant Interpretation of the Biblical Text," *Nederlands Kunsthistorisch Jaarboek* 37 (1986), 144–145.

54. See Walter S. Gibson, "Artists and Rederijkers in the Age of Breughel," *Art Bulletin* 43, no. 3 (1981), 426–446.

55. The subject also appears in a series of woodcuts by Cornelis Anthonisz. See *Kunst voor de Beeldenstorm* 1986, 271–273, no. 151.

56. For a detailed discussion of this theme, see Husband 1989, 173–188.

57. See Yvette Vanden Bemden, "Les Rondels, cousins mal aimés des vitraux," *Vitrea, Revue du Centre International du Vitrail* 1 (1988), 22–23. There is, for example, no separate category for roundels in Madeline H. Caviness, *Stained Glass before 1540: An Annotated Bibliography* (1983). While many of the entries may include material on roundels, there is no way of knowing this without consulting each publication.

58. Schmitz, *Die Glasgemälde der Königlichen Kunstgewerbemuseums in Berlin* (Berlin, 1913). See, in particular, vol. 1, ch. 12, "Niederrheinische Rundscheiben," 64–69; ch. 13, "Flämische Rundscheiben," 69–71; ch. 14, "Holländische Glasmalereien von Rund 1500–1575," 71–77; ch. 15, "Holländische Glasmalereien seit dem letzten Drittel des 16. Jahrhunderts," 77–82; ch. 20, "Oberrheinisch-Schwäbische Rundscheiben der Spätgotik," 101–116; ch. 23, "Augsburg," 129–137; and ch. 25, "Nürnberger Rundscheiben der Spätgotik und Früh-Renaissance," 150–167. The title of the 1923 volume is a misnomer, as a number of very fine-quality Lowlands roundels are illustrated. Many are said to be in "Amerika, Privatbesitz," but these unfortunately failed to surface during the compilation of this Checklist.

59. Karel G. Boon, *Netherlandish Drawings of the Fifteenth and Sixteenth Centuries*, 2 vols. (Amsterdam, 1978); E. Bock, J. Rosenberg, and M. J. Friedländer, *Die Zeichnungen alter Meister im Kupferstichkabinett Berlin: Die Niederländischen Meister* (Berlin, 1930); E. Schilling, ed., *Katalog der deutschen Zeichnungen: Alte Meister*, 2 vols. (Munich, 1973); E. A. Popham, *Catalogue of Drawings by Dutch and Flemish Artists Preserved in the Department of Prints and Drawings in the British Museum*, vol. 5, *Dutch and Flemish Drawings of the XV and XVI Centuries* (London, 1932); L. Demonts, *Inventaire général des Dessins des Écoles du Nord: École Allemande et Suisse*, 2 vols. (Paris, 1937 and 1938); F. Lugt, *Inventaire général des Dessins des Écoles du Nord: Maîtres des Anciens Pays-Bas nés avant 1550* (Paris, 1968); O. Benesch, ed., *Beschreibender Katalog der Handzeichnungen in der Graphischen Sammlung Albertina*, vol. 2, *Die Zeichnungen der Niederlandischen Schulen* (Vienna, 1928); and H. Tietze et al., eds., *Beschreibender Katalog der Handzeichnungen in der Graphischen Sammlung Albertina*, vol. 4, *Die Zeichnungen der deutschen Schulen bis zum Beginn des Klassizismus* (Vienna, 1933).

60. Jean Helbig, *De Glasschilderkunst in België: Repertorium en Documenten* (Antwerp, 1943). The Belgian volumes of the Corpus Vitrearum Medii Aevi published to date are Jean Helbig, *Les vitraux de la première motié du XVIe siècle conservés en Belgique. Anvers et Flandres* [Corpus Vitrearum Medii Aevi 2] (Brussels, 1968); Helbig and Yvette Vanden Bemden, *Les vitraux de la première motié du XVIe siècle conservés en Belgique. Brabant et Limbourg* [Corpus Vitrearum Medii Avei 3] (Ghent/Ledeberg, 1974); and Vanden Bemden, *Les vitraux de la première motié du XVIe siècle conservés en Belgique. Luxemburg et Namur* [Corpus Vitrearum Medii Aevi 4] (Ghent/ Ledeberg, 1981).

61. Bernard Rackham, *Victoria and Albert Museum, Department of Ceramics: A Guide to the Collections of Stained Glass* (London, 1936). For an article about former private collections, see, for example, Rackham, "Stained Glass in the Collection of Mr. F. E. Sidney II. Netherlandish and German Medallions," *Old Furniture* 30 (1931), 13–19. One of these roundels recently surfaced in the Netherlands and was acquired by The Cloisters. Ariane Isler-De Jongh discusses the McGill roundels in "Retour aux traditions—signe de réussite sociale: les rondels de la Collection Hosmer (Université McGill, Montréal)," *Revue d'art canadienne* 16, 1 (1989), 29–42 and 81–98. Museum collection catalogues include, in particular, Suzanne Beeh-Lustenberger, *Glasmalerei um 800–1900 im Hessischen Landesmuseum in Darmstadt*, 2 vols. (Frankfurt, 1967) and Brigitte Lymant, *Die Glasmalereien des Schnütgen-Museums: Bestandskatalog*, (Cologne, 1982). Wayment, *King's College Chapel Cambridge: The Side-Chapel Glass* (Cambridge, n.d. [1988]).

62. Bernard Rackham, "English Importations of Foreign Stained Glass in the Early 19th Century," *Journal of the British Society of Master Glass-Painters* 2 (1927), 86–94.

63. See, for example, Cole, "Netherlandish Glass in St. Mary's Church, Addington," *Records of Buckinghamshire* 22 (1980), 73–91; "A Description of the Netherlandish Glass on the Church of St. Peter, Nowton, Suffolk," in *Crown in Glory: A Celebration of Craftsmanship-Studies in Stained Glass*, ed. Peter Moore (Nor-

wich, n.d.), 40–47; or "The Flemish Roundel in England," *Journal of the British Society of Master Glass-Painters* 15 (1973/1974), 16–27. Other articles have focused on regional collections, for example, S. A. Jeavons, "Medieval Painted Glass in Staffordshire Churches," *Birmingham Archaeological Society Transactions and Proceedings* 68 (1952), 25–73.

*of Master Glass-Painters* 15 (1973/1974), 16–27. Other articles have focused on regional collections, for example, S. A. Jeavons, "Medieval Painted Glass in Staffordshire Churches," *Birmingham Archaeological Society Transactions and Proceedings* 68 (1952), 25–73.

64.  The *Magie de Verre* exhibition catalogue is Vanden Bemden 1986. For the Rijksmuseum exhibition, see the entries by C. J. Berserik in *Kunst voor de Beeldenstorm* 1986. In 1958, the Rijksmuseum organized an exhibition that included roundels and related drawings of the fifteenth century, although the catalogue entries were rather brief; *Middeleeuwse Kunst der Noordelijke Nederlanden* [exh. cat., Rijksmuseum] (Amsterdam, 1958). For the Cantor Art Gallery exhibition, see Raguin et al. 1987.

65.  Popham, "Notes on Flemish Domestic Glass Painting," pts. 1, 2, *Apollo* 7, 9 (January–June 1928, January–June 1929), 175–179, 152–157; and "A Dutch Designer for Glass," *Mélanges Hulin de Loo* (Brussels and Paris, 1931), 272–277. Lafond 1954, 93–95. See also Lillich 1985.

66.  Steinbart, "Nachlese im Werke des Jacob Cornelisz.," *Marburger Jahrbuch für Kunstwissenschaft* 5 (1929), 1–48. Evers has written an unpublished dissertation on this problematic artistic personality to which I have unfortunately not yet had access. Wayment published a somewhat controversial series of articles in which he claimed to solve the Ortkens problem: "A Rediscovered Master: Adrian van den Houte (c. 1459–1521) and the Malines/Brussels School," pt. 1, "A Solution to the 'Ortkens' Problem," *Oud Holland* 82, no. 4 (1967), 172–201; pt. 2, "Adrian van den Houte as a Tapestry Designer," *Oud Holland* 83, no. 2 (1968), 71–94; and pt. 3, "Adrian's Development and His Relation with Bernard van Orley," *Oud Holland* 84, (1969), 71–94. Konowitz, "The Glass Designs of Dierck Vellert," in Raguin et al. 1987, 22–28. Konowitz's dissertation (see n. 30) will also investigate Vellert's activity in roundel production. Maes, "Leuvens Brandglas: de Produktie tijdens de 16de Eeuw en de Nabootsing van oude Brandglasmedaillons in de 19de en 20ste Eeuw," *Arca Lovaniensis* 13 (1987), 21–319. The van Ruyven-Zeman monograph is in preparation.

Bangs, "Maerten van Heemskerck's Bel and the Dragon and Iconoclasm," *Renaissance Quarterly* 30, no. 1 (1977), 8–11. Although this and many other subjects of Heemskerck were used as designs for roundels, this is not the author's concern here. Vanden Bemden, "Peintures sur Verre Representant l'Histoire de Joseph," *Bulletin des Musées Royaux d'Art et d'Histoire* 48 [1976] (1978), 85–100; see also A.-M. Didier-Lamboray, "Les Vitraux de l'Histoire de Joseph à l'Église Saint-Antoine de Liège et leurs Modèles," *Institut Royal du Patrimoine Artistique Bulletin* 8 (1965), 202–221. Husband 1989.

67.  See Yvette Vanden Bemden, "Le Fichier International de Documentation du Rondel," *Revue des Archéologues et Historiens d'Art de Louvain* 12 (1979), 149–166. The fichier was begun in 1976 and already contains more than 2,000 catalogued photographs of roundels.

# NOTE TO THE READER

A glossary of technical terms was included in Checklist I, 217–218, supplemented by three changes as noted in Checklist III, 36. A glossary of terms specific to silver-stained roundels is included at the end of this volume.

Collections are listed by state and then by city; anonymous private collections are placed at the end of the sections. Within each collection works are arranged chronologically, although in the larger collections roundels from the same country are grouped together to facilitate comparisons. All inscriptions have been transcribed literally, with no attempt to expand contractions or to supply missing parts. Three periods within a bracket indicate the omissions. A virgule is used to mark the end of each line; a semicolon separates inscriptions at different locations on the panel. The references for *Illustrated Bartsch* in *Related Material* cite first the volume and then the illustration number and assume the reader has found the appropriate woodcut, engraving, or drawing section for the artist mentioned. A key to abbreviated references and a roundel index are located at the end of this volume.

# CALIFORNIA

# ALTADENA

*BRUCE J. AXT COLLECTION*

## ANNUNCIATE ANGEL

France
1490–1510
*Inscription:* ave mar gratia
Heavy white glass with impurities
and elliptical bubbles; silver stain;
vitreous paint
Diameter: 17.2 (6¾)
Some minor flaking of paint,
particularly along lower edge
*Provenance:* Dealer, Paris
Unpublished
[1]

## ST. LAWRENCE WITH CLERIC DONOR

Lowlands ?
1510–1530
White glass; silver stain; two shades
of vitreous paint
Diameter: 23.5 (9¼)
Two breaks, leaded; paint flaked in
areas along lower edge; paint
somewhat rubbed in areas
*Provenance:* James W. Newton, San
Antonio, TX
Unpublished
[2]

## PENTECOST

Germany or South Lowlands
1520–1540
Fairly heavy, very uneven white glass
with one large and several small
elliptical bubbles and straw marks;
two hues of silver stain; two shades
of paint
Diameter: 23.2 (9⅛)
One break, leaded; paint rubbed in
areas; loss of silver stain at top edge
*Provenance:* James W. Newton, San
Antonio, TX
Unpublished
[5]

## VISITATION FROM A SERIES OF THE LIFE OF THE VIRGIN

Master of the Seven Acts of Charity,
Pieter Cornelisz. Kunst ?
North Lowlands, Leiden
c. 1515–1525
Very smooth, uneven white glass
with innumerable minute bubbles;
silver stain; two shades of vitreous
paint
Diameter: 24.5 (9⅝); with border:
32.5 (12¾)
Numerous breaks, leaded; several
small losses, restored; paint severely
rubbed in areas; some flaking of
paint; considerable surface accretion;
border composed of old and modern
pot metal glass
*Provenance:* James W. Newton, San
Antonio, TX
Unpublished
*Related Material:* Roundel, based on a
design from a version of the same
series [Flight into Egypt], Dr. Henry
Hood collection, Greensboro, NC;
roundel, slightly earlier, reversed
version of the latter, Detroit Institute
of Arts, Detroit, MI (36.97)
[4]

## WARRIOR BISHOP SAINT

*Arms:* Fessy of six or and argent, a
franc quarter vair
South Lowlands, Louvain ?
1520–1530
White glass; two hues of silver stain;
two shades of vitreous paint
Diameter: 22.3 (8¾)
Nine breaks, leaded; paint loss
(restored ?) in small piece at top edge;
paint rubbed in areas; some loss of
paint; modern border
*Provenance:* James W. Newton, San
Antonio, TX
Unpublished
[6]

## PILGRIM SAINT: JAMES THE GREAT ?

South Lowlands
1520–1530
Fairly heavy white glass with two
large elliptical blisters and
innumerable small elliptical bubbles;
two hues of silver stain; two shades
of vitreous paint; sanguine; back-
painting
Diameter: 21.7 (8½)
Five breaks, leaded; some loss of
paint; paint rubbed in areas; chip at
upper edge
*Provenance:* James W. Newton, San
Antonio, TX
Unpublished
[3]

**ST. JOHN THE EVANGELIST**

South Lowlands
1525–1535
Fairly heavy, uneven, very smooth
white glass; silver stain; two shades
of silver stain; border composed of
some old and mostly modern white
and pot metal glass
Diameter: 21 (8¼); with border:
26 (10¼)
Four breaks, leaded; one crack,
unmended; paint rubbed in areas
*Provenance:* James W. Newton, San
Antonio, TX
Unpublished
[7]

**HOLY KINSHIP (ANNASELBDRITT)
WITH A DONATRIX**

South Lowlands ?
c. 1530
Fairly heavy and very smooth, uneven
white glass with one large and many
small elliptical bubbles; two hues of
silver stain; two shades of paint
Diameter: 23.3 (9⅛)
Four breaks, leaded; paint lifted in
areas; surface abraded; surface
scratches
*Provenance:* James W. Newton, San
Antonio, TX
Unpublished
[6]

# GLENDALE

*FOREST LAWN*

**CHRIST BEFORE PILATE FROM A
SERIES OF THE PASSION**

South Lowlands
1510–1530
White glass; two hues of silver stain;
three shades of vitreous paint
20.2 x 18.5 (8⅛ x 7¼)
Five breaks, leaded; losses at center
and lower right corner, stopgaps;
surface accretions along lead lines; set
into the lower register of a 16th-
century window
*Provenance:* William Randolph
Hearst, New York and Los Angeles
Unpublished
[89b]

# HILLSBOROUGH
*PRIVATE COLLECTION*

## DECEMBER: SLAUGHTERING THE PIG FROM A SERIES OF THE LABORS OF THE MONTHS

England
1490–1510
Very heavy white glass with bubbles and some imbedded impurities; silver stain; two shades of vitreous paint
Diameter: 19 (7½); with border: 25.5 (10)
Paint severely rubbed and abraded in areas; border later, possibly 16th century; large chip in a section of the border
*Provenance:* English private collection; Sibyll Kummer-Rothenhäusler, Zurich
Unpublished
400

## BISHOP SAINT

France or South Lowlands
1500–1510 or 19th–20th century
Heavy white glass with some imbedded impurities; silver stain; two shades of vitreous paint; back-painting
Diameter: 20 (7⅞)
Diagonal break, glued; paint rubbed and lost in areas; some repainting; some surface scratches
*Provenance:* Sibyll Kummer-Rothenhäusler, Zurich
Unpublished
989

## ST. JOHN THE BAPTIST

Northern France or South Lowlands
1500–1510 or 19th–20th century
Very heavy white glass with some elliptical bubbles and surface flaws; two hues of silver stain; vitreous paint; back-painting
Diameter: 19.5 (7½)
Some chips along edge; some surface abrasion
*Provenance:* Sibyll Kummer-Rothenhäusler, Zurich
Unpublished
984

## SAINTED DOMINICAN ABBESS AND MONASTIC DONATRIX

*Arms:* Argent a chevron between three crowns or two and one hung by the guige (unidentified)
France ?
1515–1520 or 19th century
Very heavy, even white glass; silver stain; two shades of vitreous paint; back-painting
Diameter: 8.2 (7³⁄₁₆)
Diagonal break, glued; considerable repainting; surface heavily scratched
*Provenance:* Galerie de Chartres, Chartres
*Bibliography: Vitraux-Tapisseries* sale (1989), lot no. ?, 1231–1236.
1036

## ST. LOUIS

France
c. 1530
White glass with large imbedded impurity; silver stain; two shades of vitreous paint
Diameter: 21 (8¼); with border: 37 (14½)
Some loss of paint; paint rubbed in areas, particularly in the face; border probably 19th century
*Provenance:* French private collection; Sibyll Kummer-Rothenhäusler, Zurich
Unpublished
332

## STS. JOHN THE BAPTIST AND AGNES

France
c. 1520
*Inscription:* Ecce agnus dei
Heavy, smooth white glass with numerous elliptical bubbles; silver stain; vitreous paint; back-painting
Diameter: 20.5 (8⅛)
Some surface accretions around edge; minor surface scratches
*Provenance:* Sibyll Kummer-Rothenhäusler, Zurich
Unpublished
959

## GOD THE FATHER JOINING ADAM AND EVE IN MARRIAGE

France
c. 1520–1530
Heavy, slightly bubbled white glass; silver stain; vitreous paint; back-painting
Diameter: 20.3 (8)
Paint flaked and abraded in areas
*Provenance:* Sarah Bernhardt, Paris; Sibyll Kummer-Rothenhäusler, Zurich
Unpublished
420

## ST. CLAUDE

France
c. 1540
*Inscription:* S glau de
Uneven white glass with some
bubbles and imbedded impurities;
silver stain; two shades of vitreous
paint; back-painting
Diameter: 20 (7⅞); with border: 32.2
(12⁹⁄₁₆)
Paint rubbed in areas; border later,
probably 19th or 20th century
*Provenance:* Galerie Fischer, Lucerne;
Sibyll Kummer-Rothenhäusler,
Zurich
Unpublished
404

## STANDING CARDINAL

France ?
16th century
Heavy glass with some imbedded
impurities; silver stain; two shades of
vitreous paint; back-painting
21 x 15.8 (8¼ x 6¼); with border:
27.8 x 21.5 (10¹⁵⁄₁₆ x 8½)
Paint somewhat rubbed; some breaks
in border, leaded; one other break,
unmended; modern border composed
of stopgaps and modern glass
*Provenance:* Sibyll Kummer-
Rothenhäusler, Zurich
685

## TWO PORTRAIT ROUNDELS OF WIVES OF FAMOUS ROMANS

France or South Lowlands
Late 16th century
*Inscription:* A: POMPEIA · Q· POMPEI·
[.]· C· CAES· VXOR·
B: TVLIA· C· CAS[...]· MPEI· VXOR
Uneven white glass with elliptical
bubbles; silver stain; two shades of
vitreous paint; back-painting
A. 25 x 22.5 (9⅞ x 8⅞); B. 24.5 x 22
(9⅝ x 8⅝)
A. Horizontal break, glued; paint,
particularly inscription, very rubbed
B. Diagonal and one other break,
glued; paint severely rubbed; surface
scratches
*Provenance:* Galerie de Chartres,
Chartres
*Bibliography: Vitraux-Tapisseries* sale
(1989), lot no. ? 1249–1257
A. 1058
B. 1060

A

B

## MARTYRDOM OF ST. STEPHEN WITH A HAUSMARK AND ORNAMENT

France
Dated: 1638
*Arms:* A Hausmark (unidentified)
*Inscription:* Estienne fut de p[.]erres tourmenté / Par gens perver[.] pliens de temerite / [.]au lors gardoit les habits, en courage / [.]es faux tyrans, qui faisoient ces outrage / 1638
White glass; two hues of silver stain; two shades of vitreous paint; sanguine; opaque enamels
25.2 x 18.7 (9⅞ x 7⅜); with surrounds: 59 x 46.6 (23⁵⁄₁₆ x 18⁵⁄₁₆)
Losses at upper and upper right edges, restored; seven breaks, leaded; shatter breaks and numerous other breaks in the quarries, leaded; paint flaked in areas of the border; paint rubbed in areas; some surface abrasion
*Provenance:* Mrs. M. Foss
*Bibliography: Nineteenth Century* sale (1987), 77, lot no. 184.
574

## FORTUNA

France
17th century
*Inscription:* NY LA NAVIRE AVEC VNG / ANCRE NY LA VYE AVEC UNE / ESPERANCE N[.] SE DOIBVE: / FVT A RESTER
Uneven white glass with imbedded impurities; silver stain; two shades of vitreous paint; translucent enamel; back-painting
23.7 x 17.7 (9⁵⁄₁₆ x 7)
Seven breaks, leaded; one break, glued
*Provenance:* Sarah Bernhardt, Paris; Sibyll Kummer-Rothenhäusler, Zurich
Unpublished
322

## COAT OF ARMS WITH HELM AND MANTLING

*Arms:* Argent per fess, the upper half indented or (unidentified)
Germany, Nuremberg
c. 1500
Heavy, smooth white glass with some bubbles; silver stain; vitreous paint; back-painting
Diameter: 23 (9¹/₁₆)
Loss at left edge, filled with lead; one break, leaded; paint flaked in areas of the border
*Provenance:* Dr. Erwin Rothenhäusler, Mels; Sibyll Kummer-Rothenhäusler, Zurich
Unpublished
430

## AGONY IN THE GARDEN

After a design by Albrecht Dürer
Germany, Nuremberg ?
1500–1510
Heavy, very uneven white glass with numerous imbedded impurities; silver stain; two shades of vitreous paint; back-painting
Diameter: 17.2 (6¾)
Repainting on back with sanguine; paint rubbed in areas; surface scratched in areas
*Provenance:* Sibyll Kummer-Rothenhäusler, Zurich
*Related Material:* Woodcut, Albrecht Dürer, from the Small Passion series {Illustrated Bartsch 10:26}
Unpublished
983

## CRUCIFIXION

Germany
1510–1530
Very heavy white glass with imbedded frit and other impurities and one elliptical bubble; silver stain; vitreous paint
Diameter: 21 (8¼)
Loss at left and right sides, restored; paint rubbed in areas; some surface scratches
*Provenance*: Sibyll Kummer-Rothenhäusler, Zurich
Unpublished
988

## AMOROUS COUPLE

Germany, Lower Rhineland, Cologne ?
1530–1550
White glass, slightly bubbled; silver stain; vitreous paint
Diameter: 22.5 (8⅞)
Some minor surface abrasion
*Provenance*: Sibyll Kummer-Rothenhäusler, Zurich
Unpublished
426

## TWO SCENES FROM A SERIES OF THE PARABLE OF THE PRODIGAL SON

A. Prodigal receives his share [1014]
B. Prodigal as a swineherd [1015]
Germany, Lower Rhineland
1535–1550
Heavy, uneven white glass; two hues of silver stain; two shades of vitreous paint
Diameter: 23.8 (9⅜) each
A. One break, leaded; some flaking of paint; corroded areas on back
B. One break, leaded; some surface abrasion
*Provenance*: Scheidvimmer, Munich; Claire Mendel, Miami Beach, FL
*Bibliography*: *Old Master Paintings and Drawings, Continental Furniture, Tapestries, Arms and Armour, Sculpture and Works of Art* [sale cat., Christie's East, 8 January] (New York, 1990), n. p., lot no. 6.
*Related Material*: Two roundels, replicas of or two scenes from the same series [Prodigal receives the best coat, Prodigal is banqueted], private collection, Sion, Switzerland; two roundels, earlier versions from a series based on the same designs, each with a Hausmark and inscribed border, dated 1532, The Metropolitan Museum of Art, New York, (41.190.442, 445); six roundels belonging to the same series [Prodigal bids farewell, Prodigal sets out, Prodigal gambles, Prodigal seeks work, Prodigal is given the best coat, Prodigal is banqueted], The Metropolitan Museum of Art, New York, (41.190.446, 444, 441, 443, 440, 439); roundel, replica of or missing scene from the latter series with identical Hausmark and border [Prodigal returns], Schnütgen-Museum, Cologne (M 670); roundel, from a slightly later replica series without Hausmark and border [Prodigal bids farewell], The Metropolitan Museum of Art, The Cloisters collection, New York (32.24.55); roundel, from another slightly later replica series without Hausmark or border [Prodigal as a swineherd], The Metropolitan Museum of Art, The Cloisters collection, New York (32.24.42); roundel, later close version [Prodigal gambles], The J. B. Speed Art Museum, Louisville, KY (44.31 [h])
1014, 1015

A

B

**FRAGMENT WITH THE DESCENT FROM THE CROSS FROM A SERIES OF THE PASSION OF CHRIST**

Northern Germany
1540–1560
White glass with bubbles; silver stain; two shades of vitreous paint; translucent enamel
17.3 x 16 (6¾ x 6⁵/₁₆)
Shatter breaks and numerous other breaks, leaded; several other breaks, unrepaired; enamel flaking in areas
*Provenance*: Sibyll Kummer-Rothenhäusler, Zurich
*Bibliography: European Works of Art, Armor, Furniture, and Tapestries* [sale cat., Sotheby's, 30 May] (New York, 1987), n.p., lot no. 148.
455

**PERSONIFICATION OF HARVEST OR FALL**

Lowlands
1530–1540
Smooth white glass with some imbedded impurities; silver stain; two shades of vitreous paint; back-painting
Diameter: 20.6 (8½); with border: 35 (13¾)
One vertical and one horizontal break, glued; chips along break lines; one large chip at right edge; some surface abrasion; border composed of 19th- and 20th-century glass
*Provenance*: Sibyll Kummer-Rothenhäusler, Zurich
Unpublished
994

**JUDITH HOLDING THE HEAD OF HOLOFERNES**

Germany, Augsburg ?
Dated: 1563
*Inscription*: COGITACIO MORTIS HORROR PECCATIS 1563
Heavy, uneven, whorled white glass; silver stain; vitreous paint; back-painting
Diameter: 17.7 (6¹⁵/₁₆); with border: 23.3 (9⅛)
Paint rubbed; several breaks in modern border, leaded; one piece of border reversed
*Provenance*: Private collection, France; Sibyll Kummer-Rothenhäusler, Zurich
Unpublished
418

**FEMALE ALLEGORICAL FIGURE WITH A BEAR**

*Arms*: A Hausmark (Johannes Zutfeldt the Younger ?)
Northern Germany
Dated: 1668
*Inscription*: Johannes Zutfeldt Junger / Gesell zur Zeit / 1668
White glass with some impurities; silver stain; two shades of vitreous paint; sanguine; back-painting
22.4 x 17.8 (8 x 7)
*Provenance*: Sibyll Kummer-Rothenhäusler, Zurich
Unpublished
350

## FLAGELLATION

After Lucas van Leiden
North Lowlands, Leiden ?
1520–1530
Heavy, even white glass with some
elliptical bubbles and flaws; two hues
of silver stain; two shades of vitreous
paint
Diameter: 22.5 (8⅞)
Surface slightly rubbed in areas;
minor surface accretion
*Provenance*: Sibyll Kummer-
Rothenhäusler, Zurich
Unpublished
*Related Material*: Engraving, Lucas
van Leiden, from the Circular Passion
series {Illustrated Bartsch 12:61}
957

## PRODIGAL EJECTED FROM THE BROTHEL FROM A SERIES OF THE PARABLE OF THE PRODIGAL SON

North Lowlands
1520–1530
Heavy white glass with some
imbedded impurities; silver stain;
vitreous paint
Diameter: 24.1 (9½)
Two breaks, glued; losses to left and
right sides, restored and leaded;
surface scratches
*Provenance*: Sibyll Kummer-
Rothenhäusler, Zurich
Unpublished
422

## PRODIGAL SEEKING WORK AND AS A SWINEHERD FROM A SERIES OF THE PARABLE OF THE PRODIGAL SON

North Lowlands, Utrecht ?
1540–1560
Moderately heavy, uneven white
glass; two hues of silver stain; three
shades of vitreous paint; back-
painting
Diameter: 24.5 (9⅝); with border:
32.5 (12¾)
Shatter break, glued; considerable
19th-century repainting and
strengthening of lines; paint rubbed
throughout; some chips along break
lines; some surface abrasion; 19th-
century border
*Provenance*: Sibyll Kummer-
Rothenhäusler, Zurich
Unpublished
993

## JOSEPH INTERPRETS THE PHARAOH'S DREAM OF THE BAKER AND THE VINTNER FROM A SERIES OF THE HISTORY OF JOSEPH IN EGYPT

North Lowlands or Germany
1530–1560
Fairly heavy white glass with a
prominent surface flaw, some whorls,
and numerous bubbles; two hues of
silver stain; two shades of vitreous
paint
Diameter: 26 (10¼)
Six breaks, repaired with glue and
dutchmen; surface abraded and
scratched in areas
*Provenance*: Sibyll Kummer-
Rothenhäusler, Zurich
Unpublished
450

## TWO MIRACLES FROM A SERIES OF THE LIFE OF CHRIST

A. Miracle of the loaves and fishes (678a)
B. Dinner at Cana (678b)
North Lowlands
c. 1550
White glass with bubbles, two large-sized; two hues of silver stain; vitreous paint
A. 23.2 x 18.8 (9⅛ x 7⅞); with surrounds: 28.8 x 23.8 (11⅜ x 9⅜)
B. 23.4 x 18.9 (9¼ x 7½); with surrounds: 28.7 x 23.7 (11⁵⁄₁₆ x 9⁵⁄₁₆)
A. Break, leaded; surface scratches; paint worn in areas; border probably 19th century
B. Three breaks, leaded; shatter cracks, unmended; some surface abrasion; border probably 19th century
*Provenance*: Private collection, France; Sibyll Kummer-Rothenhäusler, Zurich
Unpublished
678a, b

## FINDING THE CUP IN BENJAMIN'S SACK FROM A SERIES OF THE HISTORY OF JOSEPH IN EGYPT

North Lowlands
1550–1560
White glass with some bubbles; two hues of silver stain; two shades of vitreous paint
Diameter: 25.5 (10)
Six breaks, leaded; surface paint severely rubbed; some surface scratches
*Provenance*: George Wigley, London
Unpublished
561

A

B

## RETURN OF THE PRODIGAL FROM A SERIES OF THE PARABLE OF THE PRODIGAL SON

After Maarten van Heemskerck
North Lowlands, Haarlem ?
1560–1580
White, moderately heavy, slightly reamy and bubbled glass with some flaws; two hues of silver stain; sanguine; vitreous paint
25.6 x 19.3 (10¹/₁₆ x 7⁹/₁₆)
Four breaks, leaded; loss in upper left corner, restored; several chips along break line; paint somewhat rubbed; some surface scratches
*Provenance*: James R. Herbert Boone, Baltimore, MD; Trustees of Johns Hopkins University, Baltimore, MD
*Bibliography*: *European Works of Art* sale (1988), lot no. 64.
*Related Material*: Woodcut, Maarten van Heemskerck, from a series of the Prodigal Son {Hollstein 53}
908

## AGONY IN THE GARDEN

South Lowlands
c. 1500 or 19th–20th century
Heavy, uneven white glass with numerous, minute bubbles; silver stain; two shades of vitreous paint; back-painting
Diameter: 20.5 (8¹/₁₆)
Four breaks, glued; some repainting
*Provenance*: Sibyll Kummer-Rothenhäusler, Zurich
Unpublished
985

## ST. JOHN THE BAPTIST

South Lowlands
1520–1540 or 19th–20th century
Heavy white glass with some imbedded frit and other impurities; silver stain; vitreous paint; back-painting
Diameter: 21 (8¹/₄)
Front surface heavily corroded; paint slightly rubbed; some surface abrasions
*Provenance*: Sibyll Kummer-Rothenhäusler, Zurich
Unpublished
986

## LAZARUS BEFORE THE HOUSE OF DIVES

South Lowlands
1525–1535
Uneven white glass with numerous bubbles; silver stain; vitreous paint
23.5 x 18 (9¹/₄ x 7¹/₈)
Paint flaked and rubbed in areas; some surface scratches; probably cut down from larger format; modern surrounds
*Provenance*: Mrs. M. Foss
*Bibliography*: *Nineteenth Century* sale (1987), 77, lot no. 179.
571

## PARABLE OF THE STEWARD FROM A SERIES OF THE HISTORY OF JOSEPH IN EGYPT

South Lowlands
1530–1540
White glass; silver stain; vitreous paint
22.5 x 18.5 (8⅞ x 7¼)
One break, leaded; other breaks, unmended; paint rubbed and abraded in areas
*Provenance*: Mrs. M. Foss
*Bibliography*: *Nineteenth Century* sale (1987), 77, lot no. 180.
572

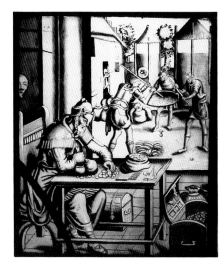

## ANNUNCIATION TO THE VIRGIN

South Lowlands
1530–1550
White, moderately heavy, smooth glass with numerous bubbles; two shades of silver stain; two shades of vitreous paint
18.5 x 18.4 (7¼ x 7¼)
Losses at upper left and lower right corners, restored; one break, leaded; rubbed and abraded; efflorescence on back; deep straw marks; composition probably cut down
*Provenance*: James R. Herbert Boone, Baltimore, MD; Trustees of Johns Hopkins University, Baltimore, MD
*Bibliography*: *European Works of Art* sale (1988), lot no. 64.
909

## PRODIGAL IN THE BROTHEL FROM A SERIES OF THE PARABLE OF THE PRODIGAL SON

South Lowlands
1530–1540
White glass with some bubbles; two hues of silver stain; vitreous paint; back-painting
Diameter: 22.3 (8⅞)
Four breaks, leaded
*Provenance*: Sibyll Kummer-Rothenhäusler, Zurich
Unpublished
448

## SAUL SACRIFICING

South Lowlands
1530–1550
Heavy, even, smooth white glass with whorls, elliptical bubbles, imbedded impurities; two hues of silver stain; two shades of vitreous paint; sanguine
23.5 x 18.8 (9¼ x 7⅜); with border: 29.5 x 24.5 (11⅝ x 9⅝)
One break, leaded; some surface abrasion and scratches; modern border
*Provenance*: Sibyll Kummer-Rothenhäusler, Zurich
Unpublished
980

## TOBIAS RETURNS HOME FROM A SERIES OF THE HISTORY OF TOBIT AND TOBIAS

South Lowlands
1530–1550
Heavy, rippled white glass with straw marks; two hues of silver stain; vitreous paint; back-painting
Diameter: 26 (10¼)
Two breaks, leaded; a small loss, stopgap
*Provenance:* Sibyll Kummer-Rothenhäusler, Zurich
Unpublished
402

## NEBUCHADNEZZAR AS A WILDMAN

South Lowlands
1550–1575
Moderately heavy, even, very smooth white glass; silver stain; two shades of vitreous paint; sanguine
25.5 x 21.5 (10 x 8½); with border: 31 x 27.5 (12³⁄₁₆ x 10⁵⁄₁₆)
One horizontal and shatter break, glued; paint abraded and rubbed in areas; modern border
*Provenance:* Sibyll Kummer-Rothenhäusler, Zurich
Unpublished
968

## ALLEGORICAL ROUNDEL WITH VENUS, AMOR, AND PEGASUS: CUPIDITY FROM A SERIES OF THE SIX TRIUMPHS OF PETRARCH ?

South Lowlands
1530–1550
Heavy white glass with numerous bubbles; two hues of silver stain; vitreous paint; sanguine
Diameter: 22.8 (9)
One break, glued
*Provenance:* Sibyll Kummer-Rothenhäusler, Zurich
Unpublished
394

## ST. CATHERINE OF ALEXANDRIA

South Lowlands
1550–1575
Heavy, uneven white glass; silver stain; two shades of vitreous paint; sanguine; back-painting
Diameter: 18.5 (7¼)
Paint abraded and chipped in places; surface scratches and abrasions
*Provenance:* Sibyll Kummer-Rothenhäusler, Zurich
Unpublished
979

## LOT AND HIS DAUGHTERS

South Lowlands
1550–1575 or 19th–20th century
Heavy, smooth white glass; two hues
of silver stain; vitreous paint
21 x 19.1 (8¼ x 7½)
Two horizontal and one vertical break
and shatter breaks, glued; losses at
top left corner, top edge, and bottom
right corner, stopgaps; chips along
break lines; paint abraded and lost
in areas
*Provenance:* George Wigley, London
Unpublished
562

## DIANA

South Lowlands
1550–1580
Heavy, uneven white glass; silver
stain; two shades of vitreous paint;
sanguine; Jean Cousin; back-painting
20.5 x 17.5 (8⅛ x 6⅞)
Horizontal break, glued; large chip
along break line, another at edge;
format trimmed mostly at top and
bottom; paint somewhat rubbed;
surface scratches and some abrasion
*Provenance:* Galerie de Chartres,
Chartres
*Bibliography: Vitraux-Tapisseries* sale
(1989), 1231–1236, lot no. ?
1061

## IDOLATRY OF SOLOMON

After Philps Galle
South Lowlands, Antwerp ?
After c. 1562
*Inscription:* IRES PER ILLICITVM PATRI
CONTRARIVS AVSV VESANO INSISTIT
SALOMON: INDICIT HONORES DELVBRIS
SACROS CVMVLAT QVE ALTARIA DONIS
SCORTORVM DVM VOTA IMPPLET
FVRIALIA DEMENS
White glass with some bubbles; two
hues of silver stain; two shades of
vitreous paint
Diameter: 24 (9½)
One break, unmended; inscription
rubbed in areas
*Provenance:* Sibyll Kummer-
Rothenhäusler, Zurich
Unpublished
*Related Material:* Engraving, Philps
Galle, from a series of the Power of
Women (Illustrated Bartsch 56:24:5);
five engravings (Illustrated Bartsch
56:1–4, 6) from the same series [Adam
and Eve, Lot and his daughters, Jael
and Sisera, Delilah cuts the hair of
Samson, Judith beheads Holofernes]
454

## RAPHAEL DEPARTING TOBIT AND TOBIAS FROM A SERIES OF THE HISTORY OF TOBIT AND TOBIAS

South Lowlands
1575–1600
White, moderately heavy, smooth glass, flawed and heavily bubbled; silver stain; sanguine; two shades of vitreous paint; translucent enamels
23.5 x 16.5 (9¼ x 6½)
Two breaks, leaded; large areas of flaked enamel; surface badly crizzled in areas of enamel loss; border, perhaps part of the original surrounds, added to bottom edge
*Provenance:* James R. Herbert Boone, Baltimore, MD; Trustees of Johns Hopkins University, Baltimore, MD
*Bibliography: European Works of Art* sale (1988), lot no. 64.
910

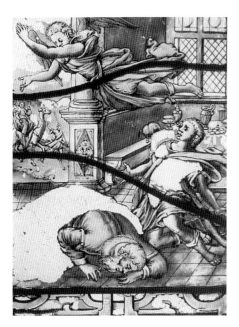

## MONASTIC MEAL PRESIDED OVER BY THREE ABBOTS

South Lowlands
1625–1650
*Inscription:* on scroll: quisquis amat / dictis absentum / rodere vitam / hanc mensam / vetitam noues / it esse sebi
Heavy, very smooth white glass with bubbles; silver stain; four shades of vitreous paint; sanguine; enamel
13.2 x 18 (9⅛ x 7⅛); with border: 29 x 13.2 (11⅜ x 9⅛)
Some surface abrasion and scratches; minor flaking; modern border
*Provenance:* Sibyll Kummer-Rothenhäusler, Zurich
Unpublished
981

## MALE FIGURE

Netherlands
Dated: 1640
*Inscription:* Cornelis Pieter / i 640
Thin white glass; silver stain; vitreous paint; translucent enamels
16.6 x 12.2 (6⅜ x 5¹/₁₆)
Two breaks, leaded; shatter break, glued
*Provenance:* Sibyll Kummer-Rothenhäusler, Zurich
Unpublished
366

## ST. PETER AND A COCK

Netherlands
17th century
*Inscription:* S PETRVS
White glass with bubbles and
impurities; vitreous paint; sanguine
25.3 x 19.6 (9⅞ x 7¾)
Five breaks, leaded; paint somewhat
rubbed in areas
*Provenance:* French private
collection; Sibyll Kummer-
Rothenhäusler, Zurich
Unpublished
323

### ST. JOHN THE EVANGELIST

Netherlands
17th century
*Inscription:* s iohan[. .]s
White glass with some bubbles and
straw marks; silver stain; vitreous
paint
23.9 x 18.3 (9⅜ x 7¼)
Five breaks, leaded; star shatter,
glued; other breaks, glued
*Provenance:* Sibyll Kummer-
Rothenhäusler, Zurich
Unpublished
326

### BATTLE SCENE

Netherlands
Late 17th century
*Inscription:* Excellentsie
Thin white glass; silver stain;
vitreous paint; sanguine; translucent
enamels
19.3 x 22 (7⅝ x 8⅝)
One break, glued
*Provenance:* Sibyll Kummer-
Rothenhäusler, Zurich
Unpublished
376

# LOS ANGELES
*LOS ANGELES COUNTY MUSEUM OF ART*

## ADORATION OF THE SHEPHERDS

Southern Germany
1525–1550
Reamy white glass; two hues of silver
stain; two shades of vitreous paint;
translucent enamel; back-painting
Diameter: 15.9 (5⅞)
Five breaks, leaded; surface rubbed in
areas and abraded; photographed from
the back
*Provenance:* Comtesse de St.-Michel,
Paris; Mr. and Mrs. Vance Thompson,
Los Angeles
Unpublished
A.880.18.1a Gift of Mr. and Mrs.
Vance Thompson

## PORTRAIT OF ULRICH VON WÜRTTEMBERG

*Arms:* Quarterly: 1 or three antlers
fesswise sable; 2 lozengy bendy sable
and argent; 3 argent imperial standard
with imperial eagle displayed sable; 4
gules two fish addorsed proper or
(Ulrich von Württemberg)
Southern Germany
Dated: 1550
*Inscription:* · Ulrich der · 3 · Herzog
Zu Württemberg · u · Sarb Seelig ·
Anno · 1550
White glass; silver stain; two shades
of vitreous paint; sanguine; back-
painting in translucent enamels
Diameter: 13 (5⅛)
Shatter crack, glued; minor chip and
some flaking along edge
*Provenance:* Comtesse de St.-Michel,
Paris; Mr. and Mrs. Vance Thompson,
Los Angeles
*Bibliography: Bulletin of the Museum
of History, Science and Art,
Department of Fine and Applied Arts*
I, no. 4 (July 1920), 31, ill.
A.880.18.2a Gift of Mr. and Mrs.
Vance Thompson

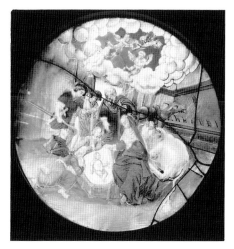

## TWO SCENES FROM A SERIES OF THE STORY OF SUSANNA

A. Judgment of Susanna (45.21.10)
B. Daniel Judges the Elders (45.21.11)
North Lowlands, Leiden or Haarlem ?
1515–1525
*Inscription:* A. Suzana besproghen ioleert hebben ghae[...]isert bleef onge[.]echters van den die haer
B. Daniels geest la[..]n comen haerver [.]nscult Suzana tot vernomen heest verwerkkst uit hebbede (on hem of onlooker) [...]NORVA
White glass with numerous large, elliptical bubbles; two hues of silver stain; vitreous paint
Diameter: 23.2 (9⅛); with border: 29.8 (11¼) each
A. Two breaks, leaded; some surface scratches; circumference trimmed to fit border; 16th-century border added
B. Four breaks and shatter crack, leaded; paint abraded in areas; circumference trimmed to fit border; 16th-century border added
*Provenance:* James A. Garland, Boston, to 1924; William Randolph Hearst, New York and Los Angeles, to 1943
*Bibliography:* Hearst ms. (1943), no. 234 (A), 235 (B); *Rare and Beautiful Works of Art Inherited and Collected by the Late James A. Garland* [sale cat., American Art Galleries, 17–19 January] (New York, 1924), lot no. 327, ill. (A), lot no. 328, ill. (B); *LACMA Quarterly* (1945), 5, ill., 6.
*Related Material:* Roundel, replica without border, Christ Church, Llanwarne, Hereford and Worcester (sI 3b)
45.21.10, 11 William Randolph Hearst Collection

A            B

## STS. HIPPOLYTUS AND MARGARET

South Lowlands
1490–1510
*Inscription:* . S . Ipolite sancte margerite
Heavy white glass; two hues of silver stain; two shades of paint; back-painting
Diameter: 20.3 (8)
Two breaks, leaded; some slight surface abrasion
*Provenance:* Musée van Stolk, Haarlem; A. Seligmann Rey & Co., New York, to 121929; William Randolph Hearst, New York and Los Angeles
*Bibliography:* Hearst ms. (1943), no. 232; *Musée van Stolk* catalogue (1912), 101, no. 442.
45.21.8 William Randolph Hearst Collection

## JESTER WITH A HERALDIC SHIELD AND CANON OF LIÈGE AS A DONOR

*Arms:* Or damascened three piles argent (unidentified)
South Lowlands, Liège ?
Dated: 1557
*Inscription:* D . IASPERVRS HELVE ECCLESIE COL^TE SCTE CRVCÎS LEODIENSIS CANONIC^S . A° : 1557
flanking jester: Digito copes = ce labella
Thin, slightly reamy white glass; two hues of silver stain; vitreous paint
Diameter: 30.5 (12)
Paint rubbed and abraded; some abrasion on back surface; traces of damascene on shield
*Provenance:* Musée van Stolk, Haarlem; A. Seligmann, Rey & Co., New York; William Randolph Hearst, New York and Los Angeles
*Bibliography: Musée van Stolk* catalogue (1912), 101, no. 336; *LACMA Quarterly* (1945), 5, ill.
45.21.9 William Randolph Hearst Collection

## APOLLO AND THE CHARIOT OF THE SUN

South Lowlands
1560–1580 or 19th century
Smooth white glass; two hues of silver stain; two shades of vitreous paint; sanguine trace lines; back-painting
19 x 26 (7½ x 10⅝); with border: 21 x 28.3 (8¼ x 11⅛)
Several breaks and a shatter crack, glued; one large and several minor chips along break lines; overfired paint
*Provenance:* Comtesse de St.-Michel, Paris; Mr. and Mrs. Vance Thompson, Los Angeles
Unpublished
A.880.18.4b Gift of Mr. and Mrs. Vance Thompson

## TWO EMBLEMATIC SCENES WITH CUPID

A. Cupid: a thousand pains for one pleasure (A.880.18.4a)
B. Cupid: absence kills (A.880.18.4c)
After Otto van Veen
Lowlands, Antwerp or Brussels
1625–1650
*Inscription:* A. Pour vn plaisir mille douleurs
B. l'Absence tue
White glass with bubbles; silver stain; vitreous paint; translucent enamels
9.8 x 9.5 (3⅞ x 3¾) each
A. Two breaks, unmended; some surface abrasion
B. Some surface abrasion
*Provenance:* Comtesse de St.-Michel, Paris; Mr. and Mrs. Vance Thompson, Los Angeles
Unpublished
*Related Material:* Two engravings, Otto van Veen, from the *Amorum Emblemata* [Antwerp, 1608]
A.880.18.4a, c Gift of Mr. and Mrs. Vance Thompson

A

B

## TWO LEADED WINDOWS WITH SCENES FROM THE STORY OF ESTHER

A. Ahasuerus giving his ring to Haman (45.21.53)
B. Esther accusing Haman at her banquet (45.21.52)
*Arms:* A. A lozenge argent displaying a leafless tree growing from a mount vert; a lozenge or displaying a Hausmark sable (unidentified)
B. A lozenge argent displaying a lion's head sable; a lozenge or displaying a bird close sable (unidentified)
After Maarten van Heemskerck
Netherlands, Haarlem ?
Dated: 1620
*Inscription:* A. Haman die hooch van Asweero was verheeūen / Sijnde een geswooren Vij[.]ant vande Jooden / Hij Creech sconinckx rinc[.] / Heest haest geschreēuen / In Alle westen Om Haer te Dooden / .1.6.2.0. / Abraham Lieu[.]nsz walop en / Weijntgen Pietersz zijn Huijsvr̄
B. As[..]erus liet Hester Coomen voor sijnen troon / En Creech haer lief Booūen [.]ndere vrouwen Naede / Sij Wert gecroont met Een Conincklijcke Croon / Ende Dat in Vastij Haere Voorsaels steede / .1.6.2.0. / Pieter Corneli[..] Mūll en / Ariaentgen Jans sij huijsvroūw

White glass, leaded; silver stain; two shades of vitreous paint; sanguine; translucent enamels
27.7 x 28.8 (10⅞ x 11⁵/₁₆) each roundel; with surrounds: 96.5 x 61 (38 x 24) each window
A. Ten panes with breaks, leaded; one pane with shatter crack, glued; horizontal break through central medallion, leaded; fragment of one pane lost, restored
B. Ten panes with breaks, leaded; vertical break through central medallion, leaded
*Provenance:* Hamberger Frères, Paris, to 4/24/1913; William Randolph Hearst, San Simeon, CA, to 1943
*Bibliography:* Hearst ms. (1943), nos. 277 (A), 278 (B); James Normile, "The William Randolph Hearst Collection of Medieval and Renaissance Stained and Painted Glass," *Stained Glass* 61, no. 11 (Summer 1946), 42, ill. (B).
*Related Material:* Two engravings, Philip Galle after Maarten van Heemskerck, from a series of the story of Esther, 1563, compositions reversed (Hollstein 250, 255); roundel set in surrounds, from the same series [Records of his reign read to Ahasuerus], Victoria and Albert Museum, London (1257–1855)
45.21.52, 53 William Randolph Hearst Collection

*Enlarged illustrations page 204*

# SAN FRANCISCO
*THE FINE ARTS MUSEUMS OF SAN FRANCISCO*

**CRUCIFIXION WITH THE VIRGIN AND ST. JOHN THE EVANGELIST**

Germany, Lower Rhineland, Cologne?
1500–1520
Heavy, uneven white glass with imbedded impurities and some bubbles; two hues of silver stain, two shades of vitreous paint
37.2 x 18.5 (14⅝ x 7¼); with border: 40 x 21 (15⅞ x 8¼)
Numerous breaks, leaded; losses at lower left and upper right corners, restored; one break, unmended; chipping along break lines; considerable surface abrasion and corrosion; modern border
*Provenance:* Julius Landauer, Anavista, CA; Julius and Selma Kay, Anavista, CA
Unpublished
61.43.29

# SANTA BARBARA

*SANTA BARBARA MUSEUM OF ART*

**EAGLE: SYMBOL OF ST. JOHN THE EVANGELIST ?**

England
1480–1500
Heavy, reamy white glass with imbedded frit and other impurities; silver stain; vitreous paint
Diameter: 17.8 (7)
Three breaks, leaded; vignetted; loss at outer part of eagle's right wing, restored; roundel filled out with modern glass; modern pot metal border
*Provenance:* Arthur Sachs, Santa Barbara, CA
Unpublished
44.11.3

**ST. JOHN THE EVANGELIST**

South Lowlands
1490–1500
Heavy, slightly reamy white glass with imbedded frit; two hues of silver stain; three shades of vitreous paint; back-painting; iridescence on back
Diameter: 22 (8¾); with border: 34.9 (13½)
Four breaks, leaded; one break, unmended; border composed of stopgaps and modern white and pot metal glass
*Provenance:* Arthur Sachs, Santa Barbara, CA
Unpublished
44.11.6

**MARRIAGE OF ESTHER AND AHASUERUS FROM A SERIES OF THE STORY OF ESTHER**

South Lowlands
1540–1560
Even, slightly whorled white glass with elliptical bubbles and imbedded impurities; two hues of silver stain; vitreous paint
Diameter: 35.5 (14)
Break, leaded; border composed of stopgaps and modern white and pot metal glass; photographed from the back
*Provenance:* Arthur Sachs, Santa Barbara, CA
Unpublished
44.11.7

# STANFORD

*STANFORD UNIVERSITY MUSEUM OF ART*

**ALLEGORICAL SCENE: MONKEY PLAYING A SHAWM**

South Lowlands ?
1520–1530
Smooth, moderately heavy white glass with large elliptical bubbles; two hues of silver stain; three shades of vitreous paint
Diameter: 22.5 (8⅞)
Loss in lower portion, restored; original in seven fragments, unrestored; three breaks, leaded; two further breaks, unmended; paint rubbed in areas
*Provenance:* Mrs. Theodore Lilienthal, San Mateo, CA
Unpublished
74.272.1

**Flight into Egypt.** *See page 64.*

# CONNECTICUT

# GREENWICH
*GEORGE A. DOUGLASS COLLECTION*

**TWO MARTYRS IN A CAULDRON:
STS. CYPRIAN AND JUSTINA ?**

1475–1500
Northern France ?
White glass; silver stain; vitreous
paint
Diameter: 15.2 (6)
Three breaks, glued and leaded
*Provenance:* Lion, Paris; Bashford
Dean, Riverdale, NY; Mrs. Bashford
Dean, Riverdale, NY, to 1947
*Bibliography:* Douglass (1972), no.
LG-17; unpublished.
LG-17

**FLIGHT INTO EGYPT FROM A
SERIES OF THE INFANCY OF
CHRIST**

South Lowlands, Ghent or Bruges
1480–1500
White glass; silver stain; vitreous
paint
16.1 x 9.3 (6⁵⁄₁₅ x 3⅝)
Fragment, cut down from larger
format; three breaks, leaded; small
stopgap; modern surrounds composed
of old glass
*Provenance:* Unknown
*Bibliography:* Douglass (1972), no.
LG-10; unpublished.
LG-10

**CRUCIFIXION WITH THE VIRGIN
AND ST. JOHN THE EVANGELIST**

South Lowlands
1500–1510
White glass; silver stain; vitreous
paint
Diameter: 19.2 (7⁹⁄₁₆); with border:
21.7 (8½)
One break, unmended; modern border
*Provenance:* Lion, Paris; Bashford
Dean, Riverdale, NY; Mrs. Bashford
Dean, Riverdale, NY, to 1947
*Bibliography:* Douglass (1972), no.
LG-2; unpublished.
LG-2

*Enlarged illustration page 62*

# NEW HAVEN

*YALE UNIVERSITY, BERKELEY COLLEGE*

**WOMAN SUPPORTING A LOZENGE WITH ARMS**

*Arms:* Or three bugle horns stringed (unidentified)
North Lowlands
Dated: 1593
*Inscription:* Wie Leefter [. .] Beloegen 1593
White glass; silver stain; three shades of vitreous paint; sanguine; opaque enamel
19 x 24 (7½ x 9⁷⁄₁₆)
Five breaks, leaded; shatter crack; another crack; loss at bottom and another at right edge, restored
*Provenance:* Robert W. Forest ?
Unpublished
[1]

# NEW LONDON

*LYMAN ALLYN ART MUSEUM*

### SEVEN-HEADED BEAST OF THE APOCALYPSE AND THE DAMNED

South Lowlands
1550–1600
White glass; silver stain; vitreous paint
34.9 x 26.5 (13¼ x 10½) with border
Two breaks, leaded; modern border; surrounds composed of stopgaps and modern glass
*Provenance:* Pallier, Paris
*Bibliography:* Caviness et al. (1978), 99.
53.31

### WOMAN HOLDING A LOZENGE WITH A HAUSMARK

*Arms:* Azure a Hausmark or
Netherlands
Dated: 1614
*Inscription:* anneke pietersz sijn huisvrou 1614
White glass; silver stain; translucent enamels
27 x 20 (10⅝ x 7⅞) without surrounds
Center horizontal lead; one break, leaded; enamel flaked in areas, repainted; modern surrounds
*Provenance:* Grosvenor Thomas, London; Roy Grosvenor Thomas, New York; George May, Essex, CT; Oliver May, Essex, CT
*Bibliography:* Grosvenor Thomas Stock Book I, 272, item no. 1561; Caviness et al. (1978), 99; Checklist I, 33.
1972.507

### COUPLE WITH TWO SONS AND A DAUGHTER

Netherlands
1625–1675
White glass; silver stain; vitreous paint; sanguine; translucent enamels; back-painting
24.5 x 18.5 (9⅞ x 7¼)
Loss at upper left corner, stopgap; two breaks, leaded; modern surrounds; marked 1096
*Provenance:* Grosvenor Thomas, London; Roy Grosvenor Thomas, New York; George May, Essex, CT; Oliver May, Essex, CT
*Bibliography:* Grosvenor Thomas Stock Book I, 178, item no. 1096; Caviness et al. (1978), 99.
1972.506

# DISTRICT OF COLUMBIA

# WASHINGTON, D. C.

*NATIONAL MUSEUM OF AMERICAN ART*

*Smithsonian Institution*

### SEATED VIRGIN AND CHILD

Germany, Middle Rhineland
1480–1500
Heavy, even flashed blue pot metal
glass, cut and engraved; silver stain;
vitreous paint
Diameter: 24.1 (9½)
Break, unrepaired; minor chipping
along break line; paint slightly
rubbed; surface abrasion
*Provenance:* Maurice Drake, Exeter
(Devonshire) ?; Grosvenor Thomas,
London; Roy Grosvenor Thomas,
New York, to 1928; John Gellately,
New York
*Bibliography:* Grosvenor Thomas
Stock Book I, 80, item no. 956;
unpublished.
1929.8.364

# FLORIDA

# MIAMI BEACH
*CLAIRE MENDEL COLLECTION*

**STS. CORNELIUS AND CATHERINE
OF ALEXANDRIA**

Germany
1550–1575
White glass; two hues of silver stain;
two shades of vitreous paint; sanguine
23.5 x 18.4 (9¼ x 7¼)
One break, leaded
*Provenance*: Grosvenor Thomas,
London; William Randolph Hearst,
New York and Los Angeles
*Bibliography*: Maurice Drake, *The
Grosvenor Thomas Collection of
Ancient Stained Glass*, pt. 1 [exh.
cat., Charles Gallery] (New York,
1913), 24, no. 71.
[1]

# PALM BEACH

*BETHESDA-BY-THE-SEA EPISCOPAL CHURCH*

## ST. PHILIP AND A KNEELING DOMINICAN

Germany
1540–1550
White glass with numerous bubbles; two hues of silver stain; two shades of vitreous paint
Diameter: 21 (8¼); with border: 24.5 (9⅝)
Two breaks, leaded; loss at left edge, restored; small loss at bottom edge; considerable flaking of paint; modern border; set into composed window
*Provenance:* Grosvenor Thomas, London; Mrs. Henry Morgan Tilford, Tuxedo Park, NY; Annette Tilford Haskell, Palm Beach
*Bibliography:* Drake (1913), pt. 1, 23, no. 64; *American, English, French and Italian Furniture . . . Property of the Estate of the Late Mrs. Henry Morgan Tilford, Tuxedo Park, N.Y.* [sale cat., Parke-Bernet Galleries, 24–26 September] (New York, 1942), 15, lot no. 83; Kathryn E. Hall, *Chronicles of Bethesda 1809–1964* (Palm Beach, 1964), 110, 129; Hall, *The Pictorial History of the Episcopal Church of Bethesda-by-the-Sea* (Palm Beach, 1970–1971), 8.
Lady Chapel, Ia

## FOURTH DAY OF CREATION: GOD CREATES THE FISHES AND BIRDS

South Lowlands
1540–1550
White glass with bubbles; two hues of silver stain; two shades of vitreous paint
Diameter: 21 (8¼); with border: 24.5 (9⅝)
Four breaks, leaded; loss at bottom edge, restored; paint rubbed and abraded in areas; modern border; set into composed window
*Provenance:* Grosvenor Thomas, London; Mrs. Henry Morgan Tilford, Tuxedo Park, NY; Annette Tilford Haskell, Palm Beach, FL
*Bibliography:* Drake (1913), pt. 1, 23, no. 63; *American, English, French and Italian Furniture . . . Property of the Estate of the Late Mrs. Henry Morgan Tilford, Tuxedo Park, N.Y.* [sale cat., Parke-Bernet Galleries, 24–26 September] (New York, 1942), 15, lot no. 83; Kathryn E. Hall, *Chronicles of Bethesda 1809–1964* (Palm Beach, 1964), 110, 129; Hall, *The Pictorial History of the Episcopal Church of Bethesda-by-the-Sea* (Palm Beach, 1970–1971), 8.
Lady Chapel, Ib

# WINTER PARK

*THE CHARLES HOSMER MORSE MUSEUM OF AMERICAN ART*

## PORTRAIT PANEL OF MAXIMILIAN I

*Arms:* a shield or with an imperial eagle displayed sable (Holy Roman Empire); in escutcheon, a shield gules fess argent (Austria); crest: an imperial crown or
After Albrecht Dürer
Germany, Nuremberg ?
After 1518–1519, 1520–1530 ?
*Inscription:* IMPERATOR CAESAR DIVVS MAXIMILIANVS PIVS / FELIX AUGVSTVS
Heavy white glass with impurities and minute bubbles throughout; three hues of silver stain; four shades of vitreous paint
19.7 x 17.7 (7¾ x 6¹⁵⁄₁₆)
Some surface corrosion; minor surface scratches
*Provenance:* Berliner
Unpublished
*Related Material:* Woodcut, Albrecht Dürer (Illustrated Bartsch 10:154)
63–2

## TWO SCENES FROM A SERIES OF THE LIFE OF CHRIST

A. Anne and Joachim at the golden gate (62.32)
B. Ascension (62.31)
After Albrecht Dürer
Germany, Nuremberg ?
1530–1540
Heavy white glass with some small elliptical bubbles; silver stain; vitreous paint; sanguine; back-painting
Diameter: A: 10.1 (4); B: 10.4 (4⅛)
A. Some surface scratches
B. Paint slightly rubbed in areas
*Provenance:* Julius Böhler, Munich
Unpublished
*Related Material:* A: woodcut, Albrecht Dürer, from the Life of the Virgin series (Illustrated Bartsch 10:79), variant composition, reversed; B: woodcut, Albrecht Dürer, from the Small Passion series (Illustrated Bartsch 10:50), composition reversed
62–31, 32

## STANDING COUPLE WITH A SHIELD

*Arms:* Or a pair of shears argent (Kiennl)
Southern Germany
Dated: 1598
*Inscription:* ·1·5·9·8· Autmarz Kiennlin · von Allmendingen
White glass; silver stain; three shades of vitreous paint; opaque enamel
Diameter: 10 (3¹⁵⁄₁₆)
Loss at bottom edge; surface rubbed in areas
*Provenance:* Sibyll Kummer-Rothenhäusler, Zurich
Unpublished
GL 41–85

A

B

**Agony in the Garden.** *See page 78.*

# ILLINOIS

# CHICAGO
*THE ART INSTITUTE OF CHICAGO*

**KING DAVID**

France, Nantes ?
Late 13th century
Very heavy, uneven white glass with numerous impurities and surface irregularities; vitreous paint
Diameter: 14.6 (5¾)
Many large chips around edge; numerous scratches through paint; surface accretions along lower right edge; some pitting on back
*Provenance:* L.-J. Demotte, Paris and New York; Joseph Brummer, New York
*Bibliography: Stained Glass from the XIIth to XVIIIth Centuries* [exh. cat., Demotte, Inc.] (New York, 1929), no. 9, ill.; Meyric R. Rogers and Oswald Goetz, *Handbook to the Lucy Maud Buckingham Medieval Collection, The Art Institute of Chicago* (Chicago, 1945), 68, no. 42, ill.; "New Life to the Middle Ages," *Art News* 44, no. 1 (15–28 February 1945), 21–22, ill.
49.209

## BIRTH, CIRCUMCISION, AND NAMING OF JOHN THE BAPTIST

North Lowlands, Leiden
1510–1520
*Inscription:* JOH
Heavy, fairly uneven white glass with whorls, some small bubbles, and one large elliptical bubble; three hues of silver stain; two shades of vitreous paint; marked 50
28.5 x 20.2 (11¼ x 8)
*Provenance:* Grosvenor Thomas, London; Mr. and Mrs. Martin A. Ryerson, Chicago
*Bibliography:* Drake (1913), pt. 2, 13, no. 50.
*Related Material:* Roundel, rectangular format, replica, formerly Kunstgewerbe Museum, Berlin; roundel, circular format, close version, Baltimore Museum of Art, Baltimore (1941.399.2b); roundel, rectangular format, close version, Lampe collection, The Hague
37.864

## MORDECAI OVERHEARS THE CONSPIRATORS BIGTHAN AND TERESH FROM A SERIES OF THE HISTORY OF ESTHER

North Lowlands
1515–1525
Heavy, smooth, uneven white glass with a few elliptical bubbles, surface irregularities, and some imbedded impurities; silver stain; two shades of vitreous paint
28.2 x 20 (11⅛ x 7⅞)
Minor surface abrasion; some iridescence on back surface; marked 51
*Provenance:* Grosvenor Thomas, London; Mr. and Mrs. Martin A. Ryerson, Chicago
*Bibliography:* Drake (1913), pt. 1, 13, no. 51.
37.863

## ALLEGORICAL SCENE: A MAN SERVING A WOMAN

North Lowlands
1520–1530
*Inscription:* WAEBT ONBENIIT THIS / SONDER ARCH
Very heavy, uneven white glass with pronounced whorls and some large bubbles and numerous imbedded impurities; three hues of silver stain; two shades of vitreous paint
Diameter: 23.2 (9⅛)
Break, leaded; a few chips along break line; some minor surface scratches; marked 59
*Provenance:* Grosvenor Thomas, London; Mr. and Mrs. Martin A. Ryerson, Chicago
*Bibliography:* Drake (1913), pt. 2, 15, no. 59.
37.862

**AGONY IN THE GARDEN**

North Lowlands, Amsterdam ?
1500–1510
Fairly heavy, uneven, smooth white
glass with numerous small bubbles
and imbedded impurities; two hues of
silver stain; three shades of vitreous
paint; back-painting
Diameter: 23.5 (9¼)
Horizontal break, leaded; surface
accretions along leadline; some
surface scratches on back surface;
some iridescence on back-paint
*Provenance:* Sibyll Kummer-
Rothenhäusler, Zurich; Timothy
Husband, New York; Blumka Gallery,
New York
*Bibliography: Stained Glass of the
Middle Ages and the Renaissance*
[exh. checklist, The Metropolitan
Museum of Art, The Cloisters] (New
York, 1971–1972), no. 43; Donald F.
Rowe, S.J., *The First Ten Years:
Notable Acquisitions of Medieval,
Renaissance, and Baroque Art, The
Martin D'Arcy Gallery of Art, The
Loyola University Museum of
Medieval and Renaissance Art*
(Chicago, 1979), no. 47, pl. 47.
8.76

*Enlarged illustration page 74*

**THE SON OF ZALEUCUS ACCUSED
OF ADULTERY FROM A SERIES OF
THE HISTORY OF ZALEUCUS OF
LOCRIA**

North Lowlands, Leiden
c. 1530
Fairly heavy, uneven, smooth white
glass with some small and many
minute bubbles and some imbedded
impurities; three hues of silver stain;
three shades of vitreous paint; back-
painting
22 x 19 (8⅝ x 7½)
Cut down from larger, probably
rectangular, format; even breaks,
glued; minor chips along break lines;
considerable abrasion in areas on back
surface; some residual glue on back
surface
*Provenance:* Sibyll Kummer-
Rothenhäusler, Zurich; Hilary G.
Wayment, Cambridge,
Cambridgeshire
Unpublished
Unaccessioned

# IOWA

# DES MOINES

*SALISBURY HOUSE*
*IOWA STATE EDUCATIONAL ASSOCIATION*

## CARRYING THE CROSS FROM A SERIES OF THE PASSION OF CHRIST

Lowlands ?
16th century or 19th–20th century
Heavy white glass with numerous bubbles; silver stain; vitreous paint
24.2 x 18.8 (9½ x 7⅜)
Loss in center; shattered in storm (20 May 1967), unrestored; paint bubbled in areas
*Provenance:* Christopher Weeks, Salisbury, Wiltshire
Unpublished
46.606 [Great Hall, west window d 3]

## HERCULES

Switzerland
16th century
*Inscriptions:* at top: HERCULES; on table, left: VOLUPTA / S; on grotto, below: VIA VITA; on book: BIBLIA
on scroll, left: VIRTVS
below scene: Hercules [.]er verrümbte held, / Als er sich [.]n den scheid weg steldt. / Sein gfall [..]s solt er wellet han / Der Thug[.]ndt ald der laster ban / Als er betr[.]cht ihr beider End / Hatt sich zu[.] weg der Thugend gwendt
White glass; silver stain; vitreous paint; translucent enamels
Diameter: 15.5 (6⅛)
One break, leaded; somewhat rubbed in areas
*Provenance:* Christopher Weeks, Salisbury, Wiltshire
Unpublished
46.2449 [Common Room, west bay window d 2]

## ALLIANCE PANEL WITH A SCENE OF ONE OF THE MILAN BATTLES

*Arms:* (LEFT) Or two crossed banners sable; crest: on a barred helm sinister a flag on a flagstaff between two bull horns of the colors; mantling: of the colors (Willer ?); (RIGHT) Or a canton in sinister azure (charges effaced); crest: on a barred helm dexter a torso or with a moor's head; mantling of the colors (Zolikof ?)
Switzerland, St. Gallen
Dated: 16(49 ?)
*Inscriptions:* above: Sieh an wie Manlich leib und blutt / Dem vor deren magten dir zu gutt / Damitt das sy dich machtend frey / Vor fromden gwalt vnd Thyranen / Bedracht was für gutthatt / sey
below: Herman Von Willer / Bürger / in St. Gallen Fr. Anna / Maria Zolikofferin / sein Ehegmahel / 1649
White glass; silver stain; vitreous paint; opaque enamels
Diameter: 22.5 (8⅞)
Some paint loss in lower portion
*Provenance:* Christopher Weeks, Salisbury, Wiltshire
Unpublished
46.2449 [Common Room, west bay window g 2]

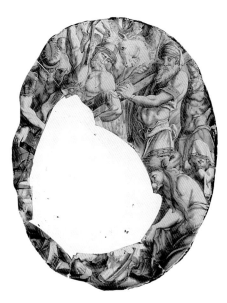

# KENTUCKY

# LOUISVILLE

*THE J. B. SPEED ART MUSEUM*

## ST. MARTIN AND THE BEGGAR

Germany, Rhineland ?
1500–1510
Heavy white glass; silver stain;
vitreous paint
Diameter: 17.8 (7); with border: 35.4
(13¹⁵/₁₆)
Circumference partially cut down;
modern border
*Provenance:* Delannoy collection,
Belgium; A. Seligmann, Rey & Co.,
Paris and New York, to 1933; P. W.
French & Co., New York, to 1944;
Dr. Preston Pope Satterwhite, Great
Neck, NY
*Bibliography:* P. W. French & Co.
Stock Sheets no. 39086–D;
unpublished.
44.31 [a] Preston Pope Satterwhite
Collection

## PRODIGAL GAMBLING FROM A SERIES OF THE PARABLE OF THE PRODIGAL SON

Germany, Cologne ?
1535–1545
Reamy white glass; two hues of silver
stain; three shades of vitreous paint
Diameter: 23.6 (9½); with border:
33.2 (13¹/₁₆)
Some surface scratches; border
composed of 16th-century glass
*Provenance:* Delannoy collection,
Belgium; A. Seligmann, Rey & Co.,
Paris and New York, to 1933; P. W.
French & Co., New York, to 1944;
Dr. Preston Pope Satterwhite, Great
Neck, NY
*Bibliography:* P. W. French & Co.
Stock Sheets no. 39086–E;
unpublished.
*Related Material:* Roundel, earlier
version with Hausmark and border,
dated 1532, The Metropolitan
Museum of Art, New York
(41.190.441); seven roundels belonging
to the same series [Prodigal receives
his share, Prodigal bids farewell,
Prodigal departs, Prodigal seeks work,
Prodigal as a swineherd, Prodigal is
given the best coat, Prodigal is
banqueted], The Metropolitan
Museum of Art, New York
(41.190.442, 446, 444, 443, 445, 440,
439); roundel, replica of or missing
scene from the latter series with
identical Hausmark and border
[Prodigal returns], Schnütgen-
Museum, Cologne (M 670); roundel,
from a slightly later replica series
without Hausmark or border [Prodigal
departs], The Metropolitan Museum
of Art, The Cloisters Collection, New
York (32.24.55); roundel, from a
slightly later replica series without
Hausmark or border [Prodigal as a
swineherd], The Metropolitan
Museum of Art, The Cloisters
Collection, New York (32.24.42); two
roundels, later versions without
Hausmark and borders [Prodigal
receives the best coat, Prodigal is
banqueted], private collection, Sion,
Switzerland; two roundels from the
latter or a replica series [Prodigal
receives his share, Prodigal as a
swineherd], private collection,
Hillsborough, CA (1014, 1015)
44.31 [h] Preston Pope Satterwhite
Collection

## ST. CYPRIAN

Southern Germany
1650–1670
*Inscription:* S. Ciprian . Epis:
Thin white glass; silver stain;
vitreous paint
24.3 x 19.4 (9³⁄₁₆ x 11⁹⁄₁₆)
Three breaks, leaded; modern
surrounds
*Provenance:* Grosvenor Thomas,
London; Mrs. Whitelaw Reid,
Purchase, NY, to 1935; P. W. French
& Co., New York, to 1944; Dr.
Preston Pope Satterwhite, Great
Neck, NY
*Bibliography:* P. W. French & Co.
Stock Sheets no. 39852; Drake (1913),
pt. 1, 24, no. 37; *Whitelaw Reid* sale
(1935), 349, lot no. 1441.
44.31 [k] Preston Pope Satterwhite
Collection

## ST. GUDULA ?

Southern Germany
1650–1670
Thin white glass; silver stain;
vitreous paint; translucent enamels
23.7 x 17 (9⁵⁄₁₆ x 6¹¹⁄₁₆)
Horizontal break, leaded
*Provenance:* Grosvenor Thomas,
London; Mrs. Whitelaw Reid,
Purchase, NY, to 1935; P. W. French
& Co., New York, to 1944; Dr.
Preston Pope Satterwhite, Great
Neck, NY
*Bibliography:* P. W. French & Co.
Stock Sheets no. 39852; Drake (1913),
pt. 1, 25, no. 79; *Whitelaw Reid* sale
(1935), 349, lot no. 1441.
44.31 [l] Preston Pope Satterwhite
Collection

## ECCE HOMO FROM A SERIES OF THE PASSION OF CHRIST

North Lowlands
1520–1530
White glass; two hues of silver stain;
two shades of vitreous paint; back-
painting
Diameter: 22 (8⁵⁄₈)
Four breaks, leaded; paint flaking and
abraded in areas; back-painting
corroded
*Provenance:* P. W. French & Co.,
New York; Dr. Preston Pope
Satterwhite, Great Neck, NY
Unpublished
44.31 [e] Preston Pope Satterwhite
Collection

## ECCE HOMO FROM A SERIES OF THE PASSION OF CHRIST

North Lowlands
1520–1530
White glass; two hues of silver stain; two shades of vitreous paint; back-painting
Diameter: 22.5 (8⅞)
Six breaks, leaded; surface rubbed in areas
*Provenance:* P. W. French & Co., New York; Dr. Preston Pope Satterwhite, Great Neck, NY
Unpublished
44.31 [f] Preston Pope Satterwhite Collection

## PRODIGAL IN THE BROTHEL FROM A SERIES OF THE PARABLE OF THE PRODIGAL SON

North Lowlands
1530–1550
Reamy white glass; two hues of silver stain; vitreous paint
Diameter: 21 (8¼); with border: 33.6 (13³⁄₁₆)
Paint slightly rubbed in areas; border composed of stopgaps and modern white and pot metal glass
*Provenance:* P. W. French & Co., New York; Dr. Preston Pope Satterwhite, Great Neck, NY
*Related Material:* Roundel, a later replica, Longleat House, Wiltshire, panel 9
Unpublished
44.31 [g] Preston Pope Satterwhite Collection

## ST. JOHN THE EVANGELIST

South Lowlands
1510–1515
White glass; two hues of silver stain; vitreous paint
Diameter: 20 (7⅞); with border: 35.6 (14)
Four breaks, leaded; modern border
*Provenance:* E. S. Bayer, New York, to 1931; P. W. French & Co., New York, to 1942; Dr. Preston Pope Satterwhite, Great Neck, NY
*Bibliography:* P. W. French & Co. Stock Sheets no. 16579; unpublished.
44.31 [b] Preston Pope Satterwhite Collection

## ST. MARY MAGDALENE

South Lowlands
1520–1525
White glass; silver stain; vitreous paint
Diameter: 18.2 (7⁵/₁₆); with border: 34.2 (13⁷/₁₆)
Circumference slightly cut down; modern border
*Provenance:* Delannoy collection, Belgium; A. Seligmann, Rey & Co., Paris and New York, to 1933; P. W. French & Co., New York, to 1942; Dr. Preston Pope Satterwhite, Great Neck, NY
*Bibliography:* P. W. French & Co. Stock Sheets no. 39086–C; unpublished.
44.31 [c] Preston Pope Satterwhite Collection

## REPRESENTATIONS OF WORLDLY LOVE

South Lowlands
1520–1530
White glass; two hues of silver stain; two shades of vitreous paint
Diameter: 26.8 (10½); with border: 34.6 (13⁵/₈)
Two breaks, leaded; one background couple (in bed) abraded away; two other couples in part abraded; border composed of stopgaps and modern white and pot metal glass
*Provenance:* Delannoy collection, Belgium; A. Seligmann, Rey & Co., Paris and New York, to 1933; P. W. French & Co., New York, to 1944; Dr. Preston Pope Satterwhite, Great Neck, NY
*Bibliography:* P. W. French & Co. Stock Sheets no. 39086–F; unpublished.
44.31 [d] Preston Pope Satterwhite Collection

## EMBLEMATIC SCENE: GRAPEVINE GROWING AROUND A TREE

South Lowlands
1580–1600
*Inscription:* MORS · FIRMAT AMOREN[.]
Reamy white glass; silver stain; two shades of vitreous paint
28.6 x 25.7 (10³/₁₆ x 10¹/₁₆); with border: 40.2 x 36.3 (16½ x 14⅛)
Paint slightly flaked in areas; modern border
*Provenance:* Galeries Heilbronner, Paris, to 1913; P. W. French & Co., New York, to 1944; Dr. Preston Pope Satterwhite, Great Neck, NY
*Bibliography:* P. W. French & Co. Stock Sheets no. 5561; unpublished.
44.31 [j] Preston Pope Satterwhite Collection

## PERSONIFICATION OF SIGHT (VISUS) FROM A SERIES OF THE FOUR SENSES

After Martin de Vos
South Lowlands, Antwerp ?
1580–1600
Thin white glass; silver stain; two shades of vitreous paint
23.3 x 19.4 (9³/₁₆ x 7⁵/₈)
Loss along bottom edge
*Provenance:* Grosvenor Thomas, London; Mrs. Whitelaw Reid, Purchase, NY, to 1935; P. W. French & Co., New York, to 1944; Dr. Preston Pope Satterwhite, Great Neck, NY
*Bibliography:* P. W. French & Co. Stock Sheets no. 39852; Drake (1913), pt. 1, 23, no. 57; *Whitelaw Reid* sale (1935), 349, lot no. 1441.
*Related Material:* Engraving, Adriaen Collaert after Martin de Vos, from a series of the personifications of the Four Senses (Hollstein 43)
44.31 [i] Preston Pope Satterwhite Collection

## ST. MARTIN AND THE BEGGAR

South Lowlands, Antwerp ?
1680–1700
Thin white glass; two hues of silver stain; vitreous paint
24.1 x 19 (9½ x 7½)
Paint rubbed in areas
*Provenance:* Grosvenor Thomas, London; Mrs. Whitelaw Reid, Purchase, NY, to 1913; P. W. French & Co., New York, to 1944; Dr. Preston Pope Satterwhite, Great Neck, NY
*Bibliography:* P. W. French & Co. Stock Sheets no. 39852; Drake (1913), pt. 1, 26, no. 96; *Whitelaw Reid* sale (1935), 349, lot no. 1441.
44.31 [m] Preston Pope Satterwhite Collection

# MARYLAND

# BALTIMORE
## *THE BALTIMORE MUSEUM OF ART*

**TORMENT OF ST. ANTHONY**

Manner of Martin Schongauer
Germany, Upper Rhineland
1480–1490
White glass; two hues of silver stain;
vitreous paint
Diameter: 22.8 (9)
Five breaks, plated with glass; set in
panel with another roundel (1942.60)
*Provenance:* A. Seligmann, Rey &
Co., Paris and New York; William
Randolph Hearst, New York and Los
Angeles, to 1941; Saidie A. May,
Baltimore, MD
*Bibliography:* C. W. Post Catalogue
(1939), vol. III, lot no. 99, art. 29;
*Hearst* sale (1941), 330, lot no. 99–29.
1942.62 Gift of Saidie A. May

## BIRTH, CIRCUMCISION, AND NAMING OF JOHN THE BAPTIST

North Lowlands, Leiden
1510–1520
*Inscriptions:* on paper in Zechariah's hand: JOH
White glass; two hues of silver stain; two shades of vitreous paint
Diameter: 22.8 (9)
Two breaks, leaded; extensive shatter crack and many other breaks, plated with glass; set with another roundel (1941.399.3c) in panel composed of fragments, stopgaps, and modern glass
*Provenance:* Horace Walpole, Strawberry Hill, Middlesex, to 1842; Sneyd, Keele Hall, Staffordshire, to 1924; Harding, London; Joseph Brummer, New York, to 1927; William Randolph Hearst, New York and Los Angeles, to 1941; Saidie A. May, Baltimore, MD
*Bibliography:* C. W. Post Catalogue (1939), vol. III, lot no. 138, art. 23; Berserik (1982), pt. I, no. 11, fig. 20; *Strawberry Hill* sale (1842), 240–241, lot no. 30, 31, or 32; *Sneyd* sale (1924), lot no. 63; *Hearst* sale (1941), lot no. 138–23, ill. 145.
*Related Material:* Roundel, rectangular format, close version, The Art Institute of Chicago, Chicago (37.864); roundel, rectangular format, close version, formerly Kunstgewerbe Museum, Berlin; roundel, rectangular format, close version of Chicago roundel, Lampe collection, The Hague
1941.399.2b Gift of Saidie A. May

## CRUCIFIXION WITH LONGINUS PIERCING CHRIST'S SIDE FROM A PASSION SERIES

North Lowlands, Leiden ?
c. 1520
White reamy glass; silver stain; two shades of vitreous paint
Diameter: 22.7 (8⅞)
One vertical and four other breaks, plated with glass; some chipping along breaks; set in panel composed of fragments, stopgaps, and modern glass
*Provenance:* Horace Walpole, Strawberry Hill, Middlesex, 1842; Sneyd, Keele Hall, Staffordshire, to 1924; Harding, London; Joseph Brummer, New York, to 1927; William Randolph Hearst, New York and Los Angeles, to 1941; Saidie A. May, Baltimore, MD
*Bibliography:* C. W. Post Catalogue (1939), vol. III, lot no. 138, art. 23; Berserik (1982), pt. I, no. 13, fig. 2; *Strawberry Hill* sale (1842), 239–241, lot no. 20, 30, or 34 ?; *Sneyd* sale (1924), lot no. 64; *Hearst* sale (1941), lot no. 138–23.
*Related Material:* Roundel, variant, from a related Passion series [Carrying of the cross], The Metropolitan Museum of Art, The Cloisters Collection (32.24.50)
1941.399.1a Gift of Saidie A. May

## ST. BARBARA BEFORE A CITYSCAPE

South Lowlands
1515–1525
White, reamy glass with some minute bubbles; deeply impressed straw marks; silver stain; vitreous paint
Diameter: 22.3 (8¾)
Some surface abrasion; set in panel composed of fragments, stopgaps, and modern glass
*Provenance:* Horace Walpole, Strawberry Hill, Middlesex, to 1842; Sneyd, Keele Hall, Staffordshire, to 1924; Harding, London; Joseph Brummer, New York, to 1927; William Randolph Hearst, New York and Los Angeles, to 1941; Saidie A. May, Baltimore, MD
*Bibliography:* C. W. Post Catalogue (1939), vol. III, lot no. 138, art. 23; *Strawberry Hill* sale (1842), 239–241, lot no. 20, 29, 31, or 34 ?; *Sneyd* sale (1924), lot no. 64; *Hearst* sale (1941), lot no. 138–23, ill. 145.
1941.399.2a Gift of Saidie A. May

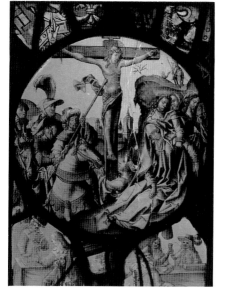

## SUSANNA AND THE ELDERS FROM A SERIES OF THE STORY OF SUSANNA

After a design of the Pseudo-Ortkens
South Lowlands, Antwerp ?
1520–1525
White glass; two hues of silver stain;
two shades of vitreous paint
Diameter: 22 (8⅝)
Extensive shatter crack and three
other breaks, plated with glass; some
chipping and losses along break lines;
set with another roundel
(1941.399.2b) in panel composed of
fragments, stopgaps, and modern glass
*Provenance:* Horace Walpole,
Strawberry Hill, Middlesex, to 1842;
Sneyd, Keele Hall, Staffordshire, to
1924; Harding, London; Joseph
Brummer, New York, to 1927;
William Randolph Hearst, New York
and Los Angeles, to 1941; Saidie A.
May, Baltimore, MD
*Bibliography:* C. W. Post Catalogue
(1939), vol. III, lot no. 138, art. 23;
*Strawberry Hill sale* (1842), 241, lot
no. 33 ?; *Sneyd sale* (1924), lot no. 63;
*Hearst sale* (1941), lot no. 138–23, ill.
145.
*Related Material:* Roundel, close
somewhat earlier version,
Rijksmuseum, Amsterdam (NM
12290); roundel, from a slightly
earlier series based on the same
designs [Stoning of the elders],
Rijksmuseum, Amsterdam (NM
12562); roundel, slightly later and
weaker version, Institut néerlandais,
Fondation Custodia, Paris (546a);
roundel, later and weaker version of
the latter, The Metropolitan Museum
of Art (41.170.73); roundel, later
variant with inscribed border,
Rijksmuseum, Amsterdam (NM
16833); roundel, reversed variant with
inscribed border, formerly Galerie für
Glasmalerei, Zurich; roundel, earlier
and stronger version of the latter
without border, Dr. William Cole
collection, Hindhead, Surrey (148);
drawing, contemporary or slightly
earlier version, Institut néerlandais,
Fondation Custodia, Paris (6612);
drawing, slightly later version of the
latter, formerly Thomas Cremer
collection, now on loan from Vermeer
Associates to the Fogg Art Museum,
Harvard University, Cambridge, MA
{Raguin et al., 1987, 59–60, no. 23A};

two further drawings, from the same
series [Judgment of Susanna, Stoning
of the elders], formerly Thomas
Cremer collection, now on loan from
Vermeer Associates to the Fogg Art
Museum, Harvard University,
Cambridge, MA {Raguin et al., 1987,
59–60, nos. 23B, C}; roundel, version
based on the former Cremer drawing
[Susanna led to judgment], Musées
royaux des Beaux-Arts, Musée de l'Art
ancien, Brussels; drawing, variant of
the former Cremer drawing, J.
Pierpont Morgan Library, New York;
roundel, based on the Paris drawing,
Victoria and Albert Museum, London
(5636–1859); two roundels, versions
from a series based on closely related
designs [Susanna led to judgment,
Daniel judging the elders], formerly
the Eugen Felix collection ? {Schmitz
1923, pls. 66, 67}; two roundels,
versions from a series based on the
same designs [Susanna and the elders,
Daniel condemns the elders], church
of St. Peter, Nowton, Suffolk;

roundel, version from a series based
on the same designs [Susanna led to
judgment], Victoria and Albert
Museum, London (5637–1859);
roundel, variant from a related series
[Susanna and the elders],
Rijksmuseum, Amsterdam (NM
10493); roundel, version from a
related series [Susanna in judgment],
Institut néerlandais, Paris (9114);
roundel, version [Susanna and the
elders], church of St. Mary, Ickworth,
Suffolk; roundel, later and weaker
version based on the Paris drawing,
Musée des Antiquités de la Seine
Maritime; two roundels, versions
from a series based on the same
designs [Daniel judging the elders,
Stoning of the elders], Castle chapel,
Cholmondeley, Cheshire; roundel,
from a series closely related to the
latter [Stoning of the elders], church
of St. Oswald, Malpas, Cheshire;
roundel, another version of the latter,
Long Stratton, Norfolk
1941.399.2c Gift of Saidie A. May

## TWO SCENES FROM A SERIES OF THE HISTORY OF ZALEUCUS OF LOCRIA

A. The son of Zaleucus accused of adultery (1941.399.1c)
B. Zaleucus blinded in one eye to save an eye of his son (1941.399.1b)
After Dierick Vellert ?
South Lowlands, Antwerp
c. 1530
*Inscription:* on woman's cuff: JOA [. . .]
White glass; two hues of silver stain; two shades of vitreous paint
Diameters: A. 21.9 (8⅝)
B. 22.3 (8⁹⁄₁₆)
A. Extensive vertical shatter crack and four other breaks, plated with glass; some chipping along break lines; small loss at center, restored
B. Extensive vertical shatter crack, plated with glass; chipping along several break lines
A and B. Both set in panel composed of fragments, stopgaps, and modern glass
*Provenance:* Horace Walpole, Strawberry Hill, Middlesex, to 1842; Sneyd, Keele Hall, Staffordshire, to 1924; Harding, London; Joseph Brummer, New York, to 1927; William Randolph Hearst, New York and Los Angeles, to 1941; Saidie A. May, Baltimore, MD
*Bibliography:* C. W. Post Catalogue (1939), vol. III, lot no. 138, art. 23; Berserik (1982), pt. 1, no. 12, fig. 21 (A); *Strawberry Hill* sale (1842), 239–241, lot no. 20, 29, 30, 33, or 34 ?; *Sneyd* sale (1924), lot no. 64; *Hearst* sale (1941), lot no. 138–23.
*Related Material:* Roundel, slightly earlier version [Blinding of Zaleucus], chapel R, King's College Chapel, Cambridge (window 51); roundel, later and weaker version [Blinding of Zaleucus], Chapelle castrale, Enghien, Belgium {Helbig 1951, 2:pl. 27, fig. 84}; roundel, later variant [Blinding of Zaleucus], Mentmore, Buckinghamshire
1941.399.1b,c Gift of Saidie A. May

A

B

## ST. GEORGE AND THE DRAGON

*Arms:* Argent a chevron sable (?), three spearheads gules (unidentified)
South Lowlands
1560–1580
White, reamy glass; two hues of silver stain; vitreous paint
Diameter: 22 (8⅝)
Break, leaded; marked 150 ?
*Provenance:* Saidie A. May, Baltimore, MD
Unpublished
1942.60 Gift of Saidie A. May

## LAMENTATION GROUP

Germany
late 15th century ?
White glass; silver stain; vitreous
paint
11.5 x 15.7 (4½ x 6³⁄₁₆)
Fragmentary; three breaks, leaded;
one break, unmended; loss in upper
right corner, restored
*Provenance:* Henry C. Lawrence, New
York; A. Seligmann, Rey & Co., New
York; Laura F. Delano, Baltimore, MD
*Bibliography: The Noteworthy
Gathering of Gothic and other
Ancient Art collected by the Well-
Known Connoisseur Mr. Henry C.
Lawrence* [sale cat., American Art
Association, 28 January] (New York,
1921), n. p., lot no. 341, ill.
46.86

## ABRAHAM AND THE SACRIFICE OF ISAAC

Germany ?
17th century or 19th–20th century
White glass; silver stain; vitreous
paint; translucent enamels
26.5 x 20.7 (10³⁄₈ x 8³⁄₁₆)
Loss at left, restored; numerous
breaks, leaded; numerous breaks,
unleaded; paint and enamel flaked
and rubbed
*Provenance:* Unknown
Unpublished
46.36

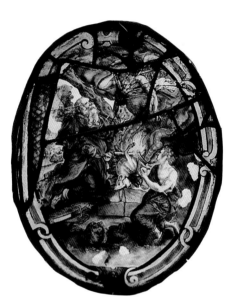

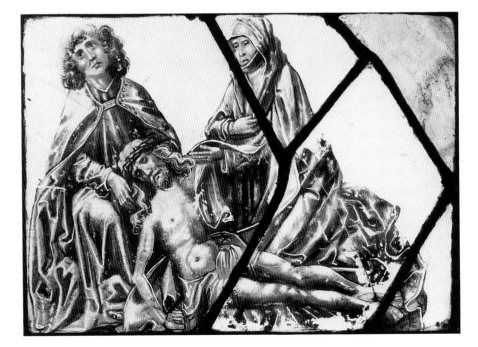

**ADORATION OF THE SHEPHERDS**

Germany ?
17th century or 19th–20th century
White glass; silver stain; vitreous
paint; translucent enamels
26.5 x 21.5 (10⅜ x 8½)
Losses at top, left, right, lower left,
and bottom, restored; eight breaks,
leaded; paint flaked and rubbed
*Provenance:* Unknown
Unpublished
46.35

**FIGURE SEATED AT A TABLE AND
IN A LANDSCAPE WITH RUSTIC
SCENES**

Germany ?
17th century ?
White glass; silver stain; vitreous
paint; translucent enamels
19 x 24.5 (7⁷⁄₁₆ x 9⅝)
Two breaks, leaded; other breaks,
unmended; paint flaked and rubbed in
areas
*Provenance:* Unknown
Unpublished
46.37

## ST. RENAULT

France
1515–1525
*Inscription:* S RENAVLT
White glass with minute bubbles
throughout; two hues of silver stain;
vitreous paint; back-painting
Diameter: 19.4 (7⅝)
Glue on back upper left surface; some
paint possibly strengthened; set in
modern wooden frame
*Provenance:* M. Bach, Paris ?, to 1909;
Albert Lehman, Paris; A. Seligmann,
Rey & Co., New York, to 1926;
William Randolph Hearst, New York
and Los Angeles, to 1941; Mr. and
Mrs. Fred J. Van Slyke, Baltimore, MD
*Bibliography:* C. W. Post Catalogue
(1939), vol. 111, lot no. 106, art. 13;
*Catalogue des Objets d'Art et de
Haute Curiosité . . . Composant la
Collection de M. X . . .* [sale cat.,
Hotel Drouot, 9–12 February] (Paris,
1909), 14, lot no. 54d; *Hearst* sale
(1941), 130, lot no. 106–13a, ill.
46.78

## ST. GEORGE AND THE DRAGON

North Lowlands, Leiden ?
1520–1530
White glass with silver stain; vitreous
paint; back-painting
Diameter: 22.7 (8¹⁵⁄₁₆)
Some minor surface abrasion;
efflorescence on back; photographed
from back; set in modern wood frame
*Provenance:* M. Bach, Paris ?, to 1909;
Albert Lehman, Paris; A. Seligmann,
Rey & Co., Paris, to 1926; William
Randolph Hearst, New York and Los
Angeles, to 1941; Mr. and Mrs. Fred J.
Van Slyke, Baltimore, MD
*Bibliography:* C. W. Post Catalogue
(1939), vol. 111, lot no. 106, art. 13;
*Catalogue des Objets d'Art et de
Haute Curiosité . . . Composant la
Collection de M. X . . .* [sale cat.,
Hotel Drouot, 9–12 February] (Paris,
1909), 14, lot no. 54b; *Hearst* sale
(1941), lot no. 106–13b, ill. 130.
46.79

**TWO PRISONERS BEING LED TO THEIR EXECUTION**

South Lowlands, Antwerp ?
1530–1540
White glass; two hues of silver stain;
two shades of vitreous paint
Diameter: 20.2 (8)
Paint slightly rubbed
*Provenance:* Dealer, Wales
Unpublished
*Related Material:* Close version,
rectangular format, Longleat House,
Wiltshire (18b)
[1]

**CHRIST BEFORE CAIAPHAS FROM A SERIES OF THE PASSION OF CHRIST**

South Lowlands, Antwerp ?
1540–1560
White glass; two hues of silver stain;
two shades of vitreous paint; sanguine
Diameter: 20.2 (8)
Paint slightly rubbed; some chips
along lower edge
*Provenance:* Dealer, Wales
Unpublished
[2]

## PRIVATE COLLECTION

### FIGURE SITTING BENEATH A SHRINE

Lowlands
1510–1520
White glass; silver stain; vitreous paint
Diameter: 21 (8½)
Paint somewhat rubbed in a few areas
*Provenance:* Unknown
Unpublished
[2]

### MOTHER INTERCEDES ON BEHALF OF THE SOLDIER WHO KILLED HER CHILD

North Lowlands, Leiden ?
1510–1520
White glass; silver stain; vitreous paint
Diameter: 24.8 (9¾)
Minor flaking of paint near edge
*Provenance:* Unknown
Unpublished
[1]

### TWO SCENES FROM A SERIES OF THE PARABLE OF THE PRODIGAL SON

A. Prodigal in the brothel (3a)
B. Prodigal driven from the brothel (3b)
North Lowlands
1525–1535
White glass; silver stain; vitreous paint
Diameter: 20 (7⅞) each
*Provenance:* Unknown
Unpublished
*Related Material:* Roundel, later version from a series probably based on the same designs [Prodigal seeks work], formerly Obreen collection [sale cat., F. Müller, 26–29 November] (Amsterdam, 1912), lot no. 1394, C, D [3 a, b]

A

B

# MASSACHUSETTS

# BOSTON
*ISABELLA STEWART GARDNER MUSEUM*

## SELF-MORTIFICATION OF ST. BENEDICT WITH A DONATRIX AND AN ANGEL HOLDING A HERALDIC SHIELD FROM A SERIES OF THE LIFE OF ST. BENEDICT

*Arms:* a shield damascened sable, two prongs crossed (unidentified)
After Albrecht Dürer
Germany, Nuremberg ?
1490–1510
White glass; silver stain; vitreous paint; back-painting
22.5 x 16.3 (8⅞ x 6⅜)
Shatter crack, unmended; loss at lower right edge, unmended; chipping along break lines; some surface scratches and abrasion
*Provenance:* A. Pickaert, Nuremberg
*Bibliography:* Mary-Beth Lacey, "A Saint Benedict Cycle for the Monastery of Saint Egidius in Nuremberg," master's thesis, Tufts University, 1980; Friedrich Winkler, *Die Zeichnungen Albrecht Dürers* (Berlin, 1936–1939), I, 144, no. 207; Winkler, *Albrecht Dürer, Leben und Werk* (Berlin, 1957), 119; Karl Adolf Knappe, *Albrecht Dürer und das Bamberger Fenster in St. Sebald in Nürnberg,* Erlanger Beiträge zur Sprach- und Kunstwissenschaft, IX (Nuremberg, 1961), 60, n. 245, 66; Caviness et al. (1978), 99.
*Related Material:* Drawing, after Albrecht Dürer, Hessisches Landesmuseum, Darmstadt {Winkler 1936, I, no. 207}; eleven drawings from the same series [Benedict in the grotto of Subiaco, Benedict's miracle of the scythe, Maurus talks to

Placidus with the help of Benedict, Benedict as a guest in his sister's house, Benedict as a student, Florentius tries to poison Benedict, Benedict revives a dead child, Benedict in solitude, Benedict and the devil, Totilas is converted by Benedict, Romanus surrenders the monk's habit], {Winkler 1936, I, nos. 198–206, 208–209}; roundel, rectangular format, based on a design from the same series [Benedict dons monk's habit], Schlossmuseum, Gotha; roundel, rectangular format, based on a design from the same series [Benedict and the devil], Germanisches Nationalmuseum, Nuremberg
C6e13

## MOSES AND THE BRAZEN SERPENT

Germany ?
c. 1530
White glass; silver stain; vitreous paint
21.5 x 14.5 (8½ x 5¼)
*Provenance:* A. Pickaert, Nuremberg
*Bibliography:* Caviness et al. (1978), 99.
C6e5

## ST. ANTHONY ABBOT WITH A CLERIC DONOR

North Lowlands, Amsterdam or Utrecht ?
c. 1520
White glass; silver stain; vitreous paint
29.2 x 36.8 (11½ x 14½)
Vertical joining lead, two small breaks, leaded; some paint loss; surface rubbed in areas; marked 1093
*Provenance:* Grosvenor Thomas, London; Roy Grosvenor Thomas, New York, to 1927; Mrs. Charles Hofer, Cincinnati, OH; Philip Hofer, Cambridge, MA
*Bibliography:* Grosvenor Thomas Stock Book I, 178, item no. 1093; Mary-Beth Lacey, in Caviness et al. (1978), 83–84, no. 41; Checklist I, 46; Hilary G. Wayment, *King's College Chapel, Cambridge: The Side-Chapel Glass* (Cambridge, 1988), 62, 66, n. 24.
56.44

## DEATH OF LUCRETIA

After Marcantonio Raimondi
North Lowlands
1520–1530
*Inscription:* LVCRES
White glass; silver stain; vitreous paint; sanguine
Diameter: 22.5 (8⅞)
*Provenance:* Unknown
*Bibliography:* D.C.S., "A Roundel of Vitreous Painted Glass," *Bulletin of the Boston Museum of Fine Arts* 22 (1922), 40; Wendy Stedanan Sheard, *Antiquity in the Renaissance* [exh. cat., Smith College Museum of Art] (Northampton, MA, 1978), no. 102.
*Related Material:* Engraving, Marcantonio Raimondi after a lost drawing of Raphael [figure of Lucretia] (Illustrated Bartsch 26:192); engraving, Lucas van Leiden, Susanna and the Elders [right-hand portion of the background landscape] (Illustrated Bartsch 26:193)
21.10886

**NATIVITY**

South Lowlands
1520–1530
White glass; vitreous paint; silver
stain
Diameter: 23 (9½)
Vertical break, glued
*Provenance:* Unknown
Unpublished
Unaccessioned

**ST. BENEDICT**

South Lowlands
1540–1560
White glass; vitreous paint
25 x 19 (9⅞ x 7½)
Breaks, leaded; section lost at lower
left; another loss at lower right
*Provenance:* Unknown
Unpublished
26.95

# CAMBRIDGE

*HARVARD UNIVERSITY, BUSCH-REISINGER MUSEUM*

**CREATION OF EVE FROM A
SERIES OF SCENES OF GENESIS**

Germany, Nuremberg ?
1520–1530
White glass; silver stain; vitreous
paint
Diameter: 9.5 (3¾); with border:
15 (5⅞)
Some flaking of paint; modern border
composed of fragments and stopgaps
*Provenance:* Private chapel,
Heidenheim, near Nuremberg; Louise
Habemeyer; Mrs. Margaret
Habemeyer, Woodstock, NH
*Bibliography:* Mary-Beth Lacey, in
Caviness et al. (1978), 65, no. 29.
1976.5

**SEATED MADONNA AND CHILD**

After Hans Burgkmair
Germany, Augsburg ?
Dated: 1526
*Inscription:* HB / 1526
White glass; silver stain; vitreous paint
22 x 17.5 (9⅞ x 6⅞)
Shatter crack and other breaks, glued
*Provenance:* Mrs. Naumburg, New York
*Bibliography:* Caviness et al. (1978), 99, no. 29.
*Related Material:* Woodcut, Hans Burgkmair, date added (Illustrated Bartsch 11:9)
Unaccessioned [Naumburg Room]

# HARVARD LAMPOON

**A CAVALIER**

Netherlands
Dated: 1611
*Inscription:* Pietr[.] [.]ertenz Peck /
Captijn [.] de Bor: / gerij Ma[..]ier /
1611
White glass; silver stain; vitreous
paint; sanguine; translucent enamels
19.5 x 14.5 (7¾ x 5¾)
*Provenance:* Gift of E. A. Ahlborn,
1902
Unpublished
Great Hall nIV b2

# CHARLESTOWN

*PRIVATE COLLECTION*

**TWO ROUNDELS FROM A SERIES OF THE LABORS OF THE MONTHS**

A. July
B. October
England, West Country
1450–1500
*Inscription:* A. Iulius; B. Octobr'
White glass; silver stain; vitreous paint
Diameter: A and B: 18.5 (7¼)
A. Considerable surface corrosion; rubbed; some repainting
B. Horizontal crack, unmended; considerable surface corrosion; rubbed; some repainting
*Provenance:* Lt. Col. H. Sidney; dealer, Cheltenham (Gloucestershire)
*Bibliography:* A and B: Herbert Read, "The Labors of the Months: A Series of Stained Glass Roundels," *Burlington Magazine* 43 (1923), 167–168, n. 2; Efrat Porat, in Caviness et al. (1978), 59–61, nos. 26, 27.
*Related Material:* Roundel, based on the same or similar design [October], parish church, Ebrington, Gloucestershire (Sydney A. Pitcher, "Ancient Stained Glass in Gloucestershire Churches," *Bristol and Gloucester Archaeological Society* 47 (1925), 25, fig. 48}
[1,2]

A

B

## ST. LAWRENCE

France, Normandy ?
c. 1490–1510
White glass; silver stain; vitreous
paint
23 x 17 (9 1/16 x 6 11/16)
Losses in upper corners, stopgaps;
some surface abrasion and loss of
paint
*Provenance:* Jean Lafond, Paris
*Bibliography:* Allyson E. Scheckler, in
Caviness et al. (1978), 62–63, no. 28.
[3]

## ST. MATTHEW AND THE ANGEL

After Agostino Veneziano
Lowlands
1550–1600
Reamy white glass with imbedded
impurities; silver stain; two shades of
vitreous paint; sanguine; back-
painting
24.5 x 18.8 (9 5/8 x 7 3/5)
Some loss of back-painting; paint
somewhat rubbed in areas
*Provenance:* Dealer, Cheltenham,
Gloucestershire
*Bibliography:* Charles Lemiszki, in
Caviness et al. (1978), 62–63, no. 28.
*Related Material:* Engraving, Agostino
Veneziano after Giulio Romano, 1518,
from the series of the four evangelists
(Illustrated Bartsch 26:95); roundel,
reversed composition, church of
Saint-Julien, Pruillé-L'Éguillé, Maine
{Grodecki et al. in *Recensement des
vitraux anciens de la France 2*,
CVMA (Paris, 1981), 264}; roundel,
circular format, from a version of the
same series [St. John and the Eagle],
The Cincinnati Art Museum,
Cincinnati, OH (1934.291)
[4]

**Last Supper.** *See page 112.*

# MICHIGAN

# BLOOMFIELD HILLS
*CRANBROOK EDUCATIONAL COMMUNITY, CRANBROOK HOUSE*

**MARCUS CURTIUS RIDING INTO
THE FIERY HOLE**

After Dierick Vellert ?
South Lowlands, Antwerp ?
1520–1530
Thin, very uneven white glass with a
few imbedded impurities; two hues of
silver stain; three shades of vitreous
paint
Diameter: 28.5 (11¼)
Small shatter crack and two breaks,
leaded; some minor flaking of paint;
some abrasion on back surface
*Provenance:* Grosvenor Thomas,
London; Roy Grosvenor Thomas,
New York, to 1923; George G. Booth,
Bloomfield Hills, MI
*Bibliography:* Grosvenor Thomas
Stock Book I, 44, item no. 589;
Bloomfield Hills, MI, Cranbrook
Educational Community, George G.
Booth diary, 161923; unpublished.
CEC-702

## SORGHELOOS WITH LICHTE FORTUNE FROM A SERIES OF THE ALLEGORY OF SORGHELOOS

South Lowlands, Antwerp ?
c. 1530–1540
Smooth, fairly even white glass with some small bubbles, imbedded impurities, and straw marks; two hues of silver stain; three shades of vitreous paint
Diameter: 22.8 (9); with border: 35.5 (14)
Some minor surface scratches; paint slightly rubbed in spots; loss in border at bottom, restored; three breaks in border, leaded; another break, unmended; chip along latter break line
*Provenance:* Delannoy collection, Belgium; A. Seligmann, Rey & Co., New York, to 1933; P. W. French & Co., New York, to 1939; George G. Booth, Bloomfield Hills, MI
*Bibliography:* P. W. French & Co. Stock Sheet no. 39086A; Husband (1989), 173.
*Related Material:* Tondo, distemper on canvas, replica based on same design, Öffentliche Kunstsammlung, Basel (360); three tondi from same series [Sorgheloos attacked by Aermoede and Pouer, Sorgheloos carrying Aermoede, Sorgheloos in poverty], Öffentliche Kunstsammlung, Basel (359, 1579, 1578); roundel, earlier variant based on the same series of designs [Sorgheloos attacked by Aermoede and Pouer], formerly James Herbert Boone and the Trustees of the Johns Hopkins University, Baltimore, MD; roundel, slightly later variant of the latter, K. G. Boon collection, Aerdenhout; roundel, earlier version, based on a design from the same series, Toledo Museum of Art, Toledo, OH (57.49); fragment of roundel, close version, Royal Museum and Free Library, Canterbury, Kent {W. Pugin Thornton, Canterbury, 1899, pl. ill. window on staircase}; roundel, earlier reversed variant, The Metropolitan Museum of Art, The Cloisters Collection, New York (1976.47); drawing for a roundel, earlier variant, Kestner Museum, Hannover (Z 81); tondi, oil on panel, later, debased version, formerly Albert Figdor collection, Vienna {Giroux catalogue, lot no. 58}; roundel,

probably based on a lost composition from the same series [Sorgheloos dancing with Weelde], Stedelijk Museum "De Lakenhal," Leiden (7684); roundel, based on a design from the same series [Sorgheloos carrying Aermoede], Hessisches Landesmuseum, Darmstadt (31:35); roundel, replica, Christ Church, Llanwarne, Hereford and Worcester (sI c2); another replica, Christ Church, Hereford and Worcester (sI a2); roundel, slightly later replica, Österreiches Museum für angewandte Kunst, Vienna (Gl 2798); another slightly later replica with an inscribed border, Victoria and Albert Museum, London (66–1929); roundel, somewhat later version, private collection, Melksham Court, Wiltshire; roundel, earlier version based on a design from the same series [Sorgheloos in poverty], private collection, Sussex; roundel, replica, Christ Church, Llanwarne, Hereford and Worcester (sI c3); roundel, slightly later replica with an inscribed border, Victoria and

Albert Museum, London (65–1929); drawing for a roundel, variant, Nationalmuseum, Stockholm (collection Anckarsvärd 432)
CAAM 1939.57

## NATIVITY FROM A SERIES OF THE INFANCY OF CHRIST

Southern Germany
1625–1650
*Inscription:* Luce am II. cap . / Dan
euch ist heut der Heiland geboren /
Welcher ist Christus der Herr inn der
/ Stadt David etz.
Very uneven, rippled white glass with
some minute bubbles and a few
imbedded impurities; silver stain;
four shades of vitreous paint; back-
painting in translucent enamels
Diameter: 13.2 (5¼)
Break, leaded; considerable flaking of
flesh tones; paint much rubbed in
areas
*Provenance:* Lord Sudeley,
Toddington Castle, Gloucestershire;
Theodor Fischer, Lucerne; George G.
Booth, Bloomfield Hills, MI
*Bibliography:* Bloomfield Hills,
Cranbrook Educational Community,
George G. Booth diary, 3/20/1922;
*Kunstgewerbe* [sale cat., Galerie
Fischer, 18 March] (Lucerne, 1922).
CAAM 1922.7

# DETROIT
*DETROIT INSTITUTE OF ARTS*

## ST. BENEDICT

Master of the St. Alexius Roundels
Germany, Cologne
1530–1540
*Inscription:* S bñdict'
Smooth, uneven white glass with
ridged whorls and several large
elliptical bubbles; three hues of silver
stain; four shades of vitreous paint;
back-painting
Diameter: 22.8 (9); with border:
32.3 (12¹¹/₁₆)
Minor surface abrasion; a few surface
scratches; large flaw in right section
of border; upper three sections of
border restored
*Provenance:* Earl of Essex, Cassiobury
Park, Hertfordshire; Grosvenor
Thomas, London; Roy Grosvenor
Thomas, New York, to 1923; Julius
Haass, Grosse Pointe, MI; Lillian
Henckel Haass and Mrs. Trent
McNath, Detroit
*Bibliography:* Grosvenor Thomas
Stock Book I, 120, item no. C-52;
unpublished.
40.126 Gift of Lillian Henckel Haass
and Mrs. Trent McNath

*Enlarged illustration page 114*

## FLIGHT INTO EGYPT FROM A SERIES OF THE INFANCY OF CHRIST

Master of the Seven Acts of Charity,
Pieter Cornelisz. Kunst ?
North Lowlands, Leiden
1515–1525
Heavy, very uneven white glass with
some imbedded impurities, whorls,
and straw marks; silver stain; five
shades of vitreous paint
Diameter: 23.2 (9)
Break, leaded; some surface scratches,
minor flaking of paint; marked 2041
*Provenance:* Grosvenor Thomas,
London; Thomas and Drake, New
York
*Bibliography:* Grosvenor Thomas
Stock Book II, 80, item no. 2041;
unpublished.
*Related Material:* Roundel, slightly
later reversed replica, Dr. Henry Hood
collection, Greensboro, NC; roundel,
based on a design from a version of
the same series [Visitation], Bruce J.
Axt collection, Altadena, CA
36.97 Founders Society Purchase,
Octavia W. Bates Fund

*Color illustration page 14*

## LAST SUPPER FROM A SERIES OF THE PASSION

After Jacob Cornelisz. van Oostsanen
North Lowlands, Amsterdam ?
1517–1525
Thin, uneven white glass with some large elliptical bubbles and an imbedded impurity; two hues of silver stain; sanguine; two shades of vitreous paint; back-painting
Diameter: 22.2 (8¾)
Break, leaded; paint rubbed in areas; a few minor surface scratches; marked 2002
*Provenance:* Grosvenor Thomas, London; Thomas and Drake, New York
*Bibliography:* Grosvenor Thomas Stock Book II, 74, item no. 2002; unpublished.
*Related Material:* Woodcut, Jacob Cornelisz. van Oostsanen, from the large circular Passion series, monogrammed and dated 1517 (Steinbart, no. 20; Illustrated Bartsch 13:1); eleven woodcuts from the same series, some monogrammed and dated 1511–1517 [Agony in the garden, Betrayal, Taking of Christ, Mocking of Christ, Flagellation, Crown of thorns, Ecce homo, Carrying of the cross, Crucifixion, Mourning of Christ, Resurrection] (Steinbart, nos. 21–31; Illustrated Bartsch 13:2–12); roundel, replica, Christ College, Cambridge, Cambridgeshire (41d2); roundel, close version, chapel, Longleat House, Wiltshire; roundel, version from a series based on the same designs, church of St. Andrew, Watford, Hertfordshire; roundel, another version, Packwood House, Warwickshire; roundel, another version, Stedelijk Museum van der Kelen-Mertens, Louvain (B/III/25); roundel, version from a series based on the same designs, Dr. William Cole collection, Hindhead, Surrey (109); roundel, later version in rectangular format, Rijksmuseum, Amsterdam (F 961–8); roundel, version from a series based on the same designs, Holy Trinity Church, Bradford-on-Avon, Wiltshire; nine roundels, from the same series as the latter [Agony in the garden, Betrayal, Taking of Christ, Mocking of Christ, Flagellation, Ecce homo, Carrying of the cross, Crucifixion, Mourning of

Christ], Holy Trinity Church, Bradford-on-Avon, Wiltshire; roundel, version from a replica series [Betrayal], Rijksmuseum, Amsterdam (RBK 1966–59); roundel, version of the same subject from a series based on the same designs, St. Mary's church, Addington, Buckinghamshire; roundel, another version of the same subject from a series based on the same designs, church of St. Mary Magdalene, Norwich, Norfolk; roundel, from a slightly earlier replica series, monogrammed [Crown of thorns], Rijksmuseum, Amsterdam (NM 12563); roundel, version from a series based on the same designs [Ecce homo], church of St. Peter, Nowton, Suffolk; roundel, fragment, version of the same subject from a series based on the same designs, excavated at Monster near Delft, W. Duyvestyn collection, Delft; roundel, from a replica series of Rijksmuseum RBK 1966–59 [Resurrection], Rijksmuseum, Amsterdam (NM 126080); fragment, close version of the latter, formerly Kunstgewerbemuseum, Berlin {Schmitz 1913, 1:75, fig. 129}; roundel, version of the same subject, Strawberry Hill, Middlesex; roundel, another version of the same subject, Musée des Arts Decoratifs, Paris (20768)
36.96 Founders Society Purchase, Octavia W. Bates Fund

*Enlarged illustration page 106*

## HUNTSMEN AND A DICE THROWER

After Dierick Pietersz. Crabeth ?
North Lowlands, Gouda ?
1549–1560
Heavy, uneven white glass with numerous small bubbles, impurities, whorls, and straw marks; two hues of silver stain; sanguine; three shades of vitreous paint
23.4 x 21.3 (9³⁄₁₆ x 8⅜)
Six breaks, leaded; one break, unmended; five losses in upper left and right corners, restored
*Provenance:* Grosvenor Thomas, London; Thomas and Drake, New York
*Bibliography:* Grosvenor Thomas Stock Book II, 72, item no. 1999; unpublished.
36.99 Founders Society Purchase, Octavia W. Bates Fund

# GROSSE POINTE SHORES

*EDSEL & ELEANOR FORD HOUSE*

**ENTHRONED VIRGIN AND CHILD**

South Lowlands
1520–1530; dated on border: 1542
*Inscription:* on border: 1542
White glass; two hues of silver stain;
two shades of vitreous paint;
border composed of stopgaps and
modern glass
Diameter: 12.1 (4¾); with border:
19.5 (7¹¹⁄₁₆)
Three breaks, leaded; paint severely
rubbed; modern border composed of
16th- and 20th-century glass
*Provenance:* Unknown
Unpublished
[1]

**St. Benedict.** *See page 111.*

# MINNESOTA

# WINONA
*WATKINS HOUSE*

**ALLEGORICAL PANEL**

South Lowlands ?
16th century
*Inscription:* on banderoles: IVSTITIA /
DAVID / SALOMON
White glass; silver stain; vitreous
paint
39.3 x 19 (15½ x 7½)
Paint flaked throughout; surface
scratches and abrasion
*Provenance:* Paul Watkins, Winona,
MN
Unpublished
[1] [Great Hall]

# MISSOURI

# ST. LOUIS
*THE SAINT LOUIS ART MUSEUM*

## FEMALE NUDE SUPPORTING TWO HERALDIC SHIELDS

*Arms:* (LEFT) Gules damasked and bordured a face in profile on a crescent or; (RIGHT) Argent damasked and bordured a griffin rampant azure
After Hans Springinklee ?
Germany, Nuremberg
1520–1530
White glass and flashed and abraded pot metal glass; silver stain; vitreous paint
15.7 x 10.1 (6³⁄₁₆ x 4); with border: 19.3 x 13.6 (7⅝ x 5⅜)
Heraldic shields are later insets; breaks in right shield, unmended
*Provenance:* Minutoli collection ? ; Eugen Felix, Leipzig; private collection, United States; A. Seligmann, Rey & Co., New York
*Bibliography:* Von Eye and Bürner, *Die Kunstsammlung von Eugen Felix in Leipzig* (Leipzig, 1880), 151, not numbered; Schmitz (1913), 1:165, fig. 275; Schmitz (1923), 10, pl. 36; "Recent Accessions, Stained Glass Panels," *The St. Louis City Art Museum Bulletin* 13 (July 1928), 3; *Stained Glass: A Quarterly Devoted to the Craft of Stained and Vitreous Painted Glass* 29, nos. 1–2 (Spring-Summer 1934), 16.
*Related Material:* Roundel, circular format, closely related composition [Woman holding the arms of Welser and Schlüsselfelder], Schloss Hohenschwangau {Fischer 1914, 169, fig. 38}; drawing, closely related composition [Woman holding unidentified arms], Kupferstichkabinett, Berlin
9:1928

# NEW JERSEY

# PRINCETON

*PRINCETON UNIVERSITY, THE ART MUSEUM*

## ECCE HOMO

North Lowlands
1515–1525
*Inscription:* on the hems of the
foreground figures: [. . .]EVA[. . .] / [. . .]
HO[.]AVSOE[. . .] / [. . .]OLSVN[. . .] /
[. . .]OVAEH[. . .]
White glass; silver stain; vitreous
paint
Diameter: 20 (7⅞)
Break, leaded; several cracks,
unmended; photographed from the
back
*Provenance:* Stanley Mortimer, New
York
*Bibliography: Gothic and*
*Renaissance Art, Property from the*
*Estate of Stanley Mortimer, New*
*York* [sale cat., Parke-Bernet Galleries,
2 December] (New York, 1944), 12,
no. 35; *Record of the Art Museum,*
*Princeton University* 22:1 (1963), 19.
62.100 Gift of Stanley Mortimer

## HAMAN BEFORE AHASUERUS
## FROM A SERIES OF THE HISTORY
## OF ESTHER

South Lowlands, Antwerp or Brussels
1525–1535
White glass; silver stain; vitreous
paint
Diameter: 28 (11)
Break, leaded
*Provenance:* Stanley Mortimer, New
York
*Bibliography: Gothic and*
*Renaissance Art, Property from the*
*Estate of Stanley Mortimer, New*
*York* [sale cat., Parke-Bernet Galleries,
2 December] (New York, 1944), 12,
no. 35; *Record of the Art Museum,*
*Princeton University* 22:1 (1963), 19.
62.99 Gift of Stanley Mortimer

# NEW YORK

# CORNING

*THE CORNING MUSEUM OF GLASS*

## FRAGMENT WITH LANDSCAPE

France or Lowlands ?
c. 1650
White glass; two hues of vitreous
paint; two shades of back-painting
15 x 11 (5⁷⁄₈ x 4⁵⁄₈)
Star crack and seven other breaks,
leaded; small loss in upper right
corner, restored
*Provenance:* Bashford Dean,
Riverdale, NY
*Bibliography: Arms and Armor,*
*Gothic and Renaissance Furniture*
*from the Collection Formed by the*
*Late Bashford Dean* [sale cat., Parke-
Bernet Galleries, 26 October] (New
York, 1950), 33, lot no. 160.
50.3.90

## JACOB BLESSING HIS SONS

Manner of Adriaen Pietersz. or
Dierick Pietersz. Crabeth
North Lowlands, Gouda ?
c. 1550; ornament dated: 1529
*Inscription:* in ornament: Heer tomas
van / zwanenburch / T Z
Uneven white glass; three hues of
silver stain; sanguine; three shades of
vitreous paint
Diameter: 25.7 (10¹³⁄₁₆); with border:
30 (11¹³⁄₁₆); with surrounds: 56.7 x
46.2 (22¼ x 18³⁄₁₆)
Two breaks in roundel, leaded;
border, modern; roundel set in panel
of earlier ornament; four losses in
ornament, stopgaps; four additional
losses at joining of border, restored;
further minor loss; one break, leaded;
six further breaks, taped; marked 161
*Provenance:* Marquis, to 1890;
Grosvenor Thomas, London; Roy
Grosvenor Thomas, New York, to
1927; Philip Hofer, Cambridge, MA
*Bibliography:* Grosvenor Thomas
Stock Book I, 16, item no. 161 and 68,
item no. 841; *Catalogue des Objets*
*d'Art. . .composant l'important*
*collection de Feu M. Marquis* [sale
cat., Hôtel Drouot, 10–18 February]
(Paris, 1890), 39, lot no. 280.
*Related Material:* Roundel, replica,
Blumka collection, New York;
roundel, based on a design from the
same series [Isaac begs for the hand of
Rebekah], dated 1550, Blumka
collection, New York; roundel,
slightly later replica [Isaac begs for
the hand of Rebekah], formerly James
A. Newton collection, San Antonio,
TX; ornamental panel of identical
design, inscribed T. Zwanenburch /

Anno 1529, Galilee Chapel, Durham
Cathedral, Durham, Durham
(wIV 2a); ornamental panel of
identical design, inscribed TZ Heer
thomas van Zwanenburch 1529,
Galilee Chapel, Durham Cathedral,
Durham, Durham (wIV 2c)
Unaccessioned

## EXPULSION FROM EDEN FROM A SERIES OF THE HISTORY OF ADAM AND EVE

Netherlands
Johannes Saenredam after Abraham Bloemaert
c. 1650
White glass; silver stain; vitreous paint; sanguine; translucent enamels
21 x 16 (8⅛ x 6¼)
Cut down from larger format; loss at lower right, restored; one break, leaded; one break, unmended; some loss of paint; surface scratches and abrasion
*Provenance:* Unknown
Unpublished
*Related Material:* Roundel, rectangular format with ornamental surrounds, replica, Schweizerisches Landesmuseum, Zurich (LM 21198); roundels, rectangular format, from the same series [Adam naming the animals; Adam and Eve with the Tree of Knowledge; Adam and Eve mourn Abel], Schweizerisches Landesmuseum [LM 21196, LM 21197, LM 21199]; roundel, rectangular format, replica, Rijksmuseum, Amsterdam; roundel, rectangular format, from the same series [Adam naming the animals], Rijksmuseum, Amsterdam (NM 10182); engraving, Johannes Saenredam, from a series of the History of Adam and Eve [*Illustrated Bartsch* 4:16, rest of series 4:13–15, 17–18]
51.3.230

## ST. MICHAEL AND THE DEVIL

South Lowlands or Germany, Lower Rhineland
c. 1530
Heavy, slightly uneven white glass with bubbles and a few imbedded impurities; two hues of silver stain; two shades of vitreous paint
Diameter: 22.5 (8⅞)
Some scratches on front and back surfaces; minor losses of paint
*Provenance:* Sibyll Kummer-Rothenhäusler, Zurich
*Bibliography: Corning Museum of Glass Annual Report 1984* (Corning, NY, 1984), 6, ill. cover; "Recent Important Acquisitions Made by Public and Private Collections in the United States and Abroad," *Journal of Glass Studies* 27 (1985), 99, no. 10, ill.
*Related Material:* Roundel, slightly later replica, Maagenhuismuseum, Antwerp (92/4)
84.3.236

## FORTUNA IN A LANDSCAPE

Switzerland, Lucerne
1600–1625
*Inscription:* Quand fortuna / me Tor mente / Espera[. . .] me conten / te
Slightly uneven white glass with bubbles; two shades of vitreous paint
11.4 x 20.6 (4½ x 8½)
Break, glued; small loss at top of break, restored
*Provenance:* Sibyll Kummer-Rothenhäusler, Zurich
Unpublished
83.3.237

# EAST HAMPTON
*ST. LUKE'S EPISCOPAL CHURCH*

**VIRGIN OF THE IMMACULATE CONCEPTION**

Germany or Switzerland
Dated: 1640
*Inscription:* AGRICOLA FABRY /
BARTOLOME BOVERI
White glass, silver stain; vitreous
paint; sanguine
18.5 x 16 (7¼ x 6¼)
Shatter breaks, leaded; other breaks,
unmended; chipping along some
break lines; paint rubbed in areas
*Provenance:* Unknown
Unpublished
North aisle window

# NEW YORK

## THE BROOKLYN MUSEUM

**INVESTITURE OF A BISHOP**

Northern France or South Lowlands
1510–1520
White glass, two hues of silver stain,
two shades of vitreous paint
Diameter: 20.2 (8)
Some surface scratches; paint slightly
rubbed
*Provenance:* Grosvenor Thomas,
London
*Bibliography:* Drake (1913), pt. 1, 24,
no. 75.
.506

**Note:** In 1932, The Cloisters acquired a significant number of roundels from Roy Grosvenor Thomas with the help of John D. Rockefeller, Jr. At the time, Thomas prepared a presentation scrapbook containing a photograph of each piece accompanied by a brief description. In these old photographs a Thomas number can be seen on most roundels, identifying the roundel with the matching entry in the stock book. The numbers have since been removed. In this checklist, the Thomas inventory numbers, if known, are noted under *Bibliography*.

## WINGED OX: SYMBOL OF ST. LUKE THE EVANGELIST

England
c. 1475–1485 or 19th-20th century
*Inscription:* lucas
Heavy, even white glass with several very large impurities, one large, and several smaller blisters on back surface; two hues of silver stain; two shades of thin vitreous paint
Diameter: 17.5 (6⅞); with border: 20.9 (8³⁄₁₆)
Pitted front surface; some loss of paint around edge; modern border
*Provenance:* Grosvenor Thomas, London; Roy Grosvenor Thomas, New York
*Bibliography:* Grosvenor Thomas Stock Book I, 42, item no. 511; unpublished.
32.24.17 [The Cloisters]

## EAGLE: SYMBOL OF ST. JOHN THE EVANGELIST

England, Norwich ?
1475–1500
*Inscription:* In principio erat v̄bū
Heavy, uneven white glass; two hues of silver stain; four shades of vitreous paint
Diameter: 19.7 (7⅞)
Break, leaded; paint flaked and considerably rubbed; back surface rubbed; modern border
*Provenance:* George William Jerningham, 8th Baron Stafford, Costessey Hall, Norfolk; Durlacher Brothers, New York
*Bibliography:* C.O.C., "Rearrangement of Stained Glass including some Recent Acquisitions," *Bulletin of the Metropolitan Museum of Art* 16 (November 1921), 233–234, ill.
*Related Material:* Roundel, based on a similar design, Weybread, Church of St. Andrew, Suffolk
21.87.19 [Medieval]

**WINGED OX: SYMBOL OF ST. LUKE THE EVANGELIST**

England
1475–1500 or 19th–20th century
*Inscription:* Scts L[. .]as
Very heavy white glass with impurities; silver stain; vitreous paint; iridescence on back
Diameter: 17.7 (7)
Five breaks, leaded; several large chips along edge
*Provenance:* Grosvenor Thomas, London; Roy Grosvenor Thomas, New York
*Bibliography:* Grosvenor Thomas Stock Book II, 30, item no. 1765; unpublished.
32.24.16 [The Cloisters]

**PASTORAL SCENE: DEER UNDER A TREE**

England ?
1475–1500
Fairly smooth white glass; silver stain; two shades of vitreous paint; back-painting
Diameter: 21.6 (8½)
Star fracture at top and two vertical breaks, unmended; chip in star fracture; front surface corroded; modern border
*Provenance:* Grosvenor Thomas, London; Roy Grosvenor Thomas, New York
*Bibliography:* Grosvenor Thomas Stock Book I, 42, item no. 512; unpublished.
32.24.20 [The Cloisters]

**CRUCIFIXION WITH THE VIRGIN AND ST. JOHN**

England ?
1480–1500
*Inscription:* on titulus: inrs
Fairly smooth, slightly reamy white glass with some imbedded impurities; two hues of silver stain; two shades of vitreous paint; back-painting
Diameter: 19.2 (7⁹⁄₁₆)
Some surface abrasion
*Provenance:* William M. Dodson, Tilbury, Essex; Wallis Cash, Wincanton, Somerset; Wilfred Drake, London; Grosvenor Thomas, London; Roy Grosvenor Thomas, New York
*Bibliography:* Grosvenor Thomas Stock Book I, 214, item no. 1275; unpublished.
32.24.19 [The Cloisters]

## ST. CATHERINE OF ALEXANDRIA

England
1480–1500 or 19th–20th century
Smooth, fairly uneven white glass
with one large impurity on back
surface and several other imbedded
impurities; silver stain; two shades of
vitreous paint
Diameter: 18.9 (7⅞)
Six breaks, leaded; loss in center,
restored; spots of glass
decomposition; paint rubbed; surface
scratches
*Provenance:* Grosvenor Thomas,
London; Roy Grosvenor Thomas,
New York
*Bibliography:* Grosvenor Thomas
Stock Book I, 32, item no. 344;
unpublished.
32.24.18 [The Cloisters]

## INSTRUMENTS OF THE PASSION

England
1490–1510 or 19th–20th century
Heavy, uneven white glass with
several large imbedded impurities;
silver stain; vitreous paint
Diameter: 20.3 (8¼)
Eight breaks, leaded; paint flaking and
rubbed in areas
*Provenance:* Grosvenor Thomas,
London; Roy Grosvenor Thomas,
New York
*Bibliography:* Grosvenor Thomas
Stock Book II, 30, item no. 1766;
unpublished.
32.24.25 [The Cloisters]

## HEAD OF A LION WITH FOLIATE ORNAMENT

France
1475–1500
Heavy, uneven white glass with two hues of silver stain and two shades of vitreous paint
Diameter: 14.6 (5¾)
Losses along edge; several large chips along left edge; paint considerably rubbed; surface scratches; back surface corroded
*Provenance:* Bashford Dean, Riverdale, NY; George D. Pratt, Glen Cove, NY
Unpublished
30.73.4 [Medieval]

## ST. GEORGE AND THE DRAGON

France
1490–1510 or 19th–20th century
Heavy, even white glass; silver stain; vitreous paint
Diameter: 21.3 (8⅜); with border: 29.8 (11¼)
Five breaks, leaded; surface heavily corroded; minor pitting on back surface; some abrasion; modern border
*Provenance:* Grosvenor Thomas, London ?; A. Lion, Paris; Edward S. Harkness, New York
*Bibliography:* Drake (1913), pt. 2, 13, no. 53.
29.156.62 [Arms and Armor]

## ST. MICHAEL

France
c. 1500
Heavy, even white glass; silver stain; two shades of vitreous paint; back-painting
Diameter: 20 (7⅞); with border: 23.8 (10⅜)
Paint rubbed at lower left; some surface scratches; spots of white iridescence on back surface; modern border
*Provenance:* Amoureauc, Paris; Edward S. Harkness, New York
Unpublished
29.156.58 [Arms and Armor]

## PLAYING AT QUINTAIN

France, Paris ?
c. 1500
Fairly heavy, smooth white glass; silver stain; two shades of vitreous paint; back-painting
Diameter: 20.3 (8)
Horizontal break through lower portion, glued; shatter break near lower right edge, glued and back plated; loss at lower right edge, restored with polymer
*Provenance:* Bresset Frères, Paris
*Bibliography:* Metropolitan Museum annual report (1980–1981), 42; Hayward (1981), 29–30, ill.; *The Metropolitan Museum of Art, The Renaissance in the North* (New York, 1987), 41, ill.
1980.223.6 [The Cloisters]

## ST. GEORGE AND THE DRAGON

France
1500–1510 or 19th–20th century
White glass; silver stain; vitreous paint
62.9 x 27.3 (24¾ x 10¾)
Lower part restored; break in upper part of central panel, leaded; numerous breaks in ornamental surrounds, leaded
*Provenance:* Edward S. Harkness, New York
Unpublished
29.156.57 [Arms and Armor]

## TWO SOLDIERS IN COMBAT

Germany ?
1475–1500 or 19th–20th century
White glass; silver stain; vitreous paint
46.3 x 39.3 (18¼ x 15½)
Seven breaks, leaded; surface scratched and abraded; border composed of stopgaps and modern glass
*Provenance:* Chassunot, Paris; Edward S. Harkness, New York
Unpublished
29.156.59 [Arms and Armor]

## EIGHT SCENES FROM A SERIES OF THE LIFE OF CHRIST

A. Adoration (32.24.1)
B. Flight into Egypt (32.24.2)
C. Circumcision (32.24.3)
D. Baptism of Christ (32.24.4)
E. Betrayal (32.24.5)
F. Flagellation (32.24.6)
G. Crown of Thorns (32.24.7)
H. Resurrection (32.24.8)
Germany, Upper Rhineland
1480–1490
*Inscriptions:* C. nunc dimittis servm tuu dne
D. du es filius meus dilcs in te michi mo lui
E. Ave rabi
G. Ave rex judeor
A-H. Fairly heavy, uneven white glass with numerous minute bubbles and imbedded frit; two hues of silver stain; three shades of vitreous paint; back-painting
A and B. Straw marks
B. Numerous large elliptical bubbles
C. One large elliptical bubble
Diameters: A, E, F, G: 20 (7⅞); B, C, H: 19.7 (7¾); D: 19.8 (7¹³⁄₁₆)
A-H. Numerous white spots of glass decomposition; minor surface abrasion
C. Horizontal break just above center, glued

A

*Provenance:* William M. Dodson, Tilbury, Essex; Wilfred Drake, London; Grosvenor Thomas, London; Roy Grosvenor Thomas, New York
*Bibliography:* Grosvenor Thomas Stock Book, I, 208, item nos. 1248–1255 (A-H); Charles I. Minott, "A Group of Stained Glass Roundels at The Cloisters," *Art Bulletin* 43:3 (September 1961), 237–239, figs. 1, 3, 5, 6, 8–11 (A-H); Bonnie Young, *A Walk through The Cloisters* (New York, 1979), 90, ill. (A, C); *The Cloisters: The Building and the Collection of Medieval Art in Fort Tryon Park* (New York, 1963), 116–117, ill. (A, F); Hayward (1971–1972), 143, ill., and frontispiece (D, E); *The Metropolitan Museum of Art, Europe in the Middle Ages* (New York, 1987), 154, ill.
*Related Material:* A: engraving, freely adapted from, Master E. S. {Lehrs 27}; C: engraving, figures adapted from, reversed Israel van Mechenen after Master E. S. [Marriage of the Virgin], {Geisberg, 1974, pl. 233}; D: drawing, based on, Master E. S., Cabinet des Dessins, Musée de Louvre, Paris (inv. no. 18.838); engraving, based on latter drawing, Master E. S. {Lehrs 29}; G: engraving, standing figure wielding a club adapted from, Master E. S. [Martyrdom of St. Margaret], {Lehrs 163}
32.24.1–8 [The Cloisters]

B

C

D

E

F

G

H

## ANNUNCIATION TO THE VIRGIN

Southern Germany
c. 1480–1500
Heavy, uneven white glass with
numerous bubbles; two hues of silver
stain; vitreous paint; pot metal glass
border; vitreous paint; pot metal glass
border with black vitreous paint
Diameter: 16.8 (6⅝); with border:
23.2 (9⅛)
Paint considerably rubbed and lost in
areas; one section of border replaced
*Provenance:* Mel Greenland, New
York
*Bibliography: The Metropolitan
Museum of Art, Annual Report for
the Year 1985–1986* (New York,
1986), 33.
*Related Material:* Roundel, somewhat
later version, Seckau (Steiermark)
{Kieslinger, 97, fig. 27}; roundel, later
version, Schloss Hohenschwangau
{Fischer, 1937, 15, fig. 5}
1985.244 [The Cloisters]

## ST. BARBARA OR ST. CATHERINE THROWN INTO PRISON

Germany
1480–1500
Thin, fairly smooth white glass; silver
stain; two shades of vitreous paint;
back-painting
Diameter: 20.8 (8³⁄₁₆)
Ten breaks, leaded; paint rubbed
*Provenance:* Grosvenor Thomas,
London; Roy Grosvenor Thomas,
New York
*Bibliography:* Grosvenor Thomas
Stock Book I, 64, item no. 800;
unpublished.
32.24.9 [The Cloisters]

## THREE APES ASSEMBLING A TRESTLE TABLE

Germany ?
1480–1500
Heavy, fairly smooth white glass;
silver stain; two shades of vitreous
paint
26 x 22.5 (10¼ x 8⅞)
Several minor chips in the paint;
slight abrasion in areas; surface
accretions along edges
*Provenance:* Galerie de Chartres,
Chartres; Sibyll Kummer-
Rothenhäusler, Zurich
*Bibliography: Vitraux-Tapisseries* sale
(1989), lot no. 1231–1236 ?;
Metropolitan Museum annual report
(1989–1990), 29.
1990.119.3 [The Cloisters]

*Color illustration on back cover*

## ST. AGNES

Germany, Swabia
c. 1490
Heavy, uneven white glass with numerous bubbles; silver stain; two shades of vitreous paint; back-painting
Diameter: 17.3 (6¾)
Numerous breaks, glued; shatter break at top, glued; small loss at top, restored with polymer; some flaking of paint
*Provenance:* Walter von Pannwitz, Munich; Julius Böhler, Munich; Ruth Blumka, New York
*Bibliography:* Otto von Falke, ed., *Die Kunst sammlung von Panniwitz, II Skulpturen und Kunstgewerbe* (Munich, 1925), 10, no. 97; Metropolitan Museum annual report (1983–1984), 40.
1983.237 [The Cloisters]

## MARTYRDOM OF ST. LEGER

Germany, Upper Rhineland
c. 1490
Fairly heavy, smooth white glass; silver stain; two shades of vitreous paint
Diameter: 21.6 (8½)
Surface slightly abraded in areas
*Provenance:* Bresset Frères, Paris
*Bibliography:* Metropolitan Museum annual report (1980–1981), 42.
1980.223.4 [The Cloisters]

## ST. MARTIN

Germany, Middle Rhineland
1490–1500
Fairly heavy, smooth, uneven white glass; silver stain; two shades of vitreous paint; pot metal glass border
Diameter: 9.7 (7¾); with border: 23.9 (9⅜)
One break through center, leaded; glass chipped along break; paint somewhat abraded; surface scratches; some abrasion on back surface; modern border
*Provenance:* Sibyll Kummer-Rothenhäusler, Zurich
*Bibliography: The Metropolitan Museum of Art, Annual Report for the Year 1971–1972* (New York, 1972), 45; *The Metropolitan Museum of Art, Notable Acquisitions (1965–1975)* (New York, 1975), 162, ill.; *The Metropolitan Museum of Art, Europe in the Middle Ages* (New York, 1987), 154, ill.
1971.278 [The Cloisters]

## ENTRY INTO JERUSALEM FROM A SERIES OF THE LIFE OF CHRIST

Germany, Middle or Upper Rhineland
1490–1500
Diameter: 21.5 (8½)
Heavy, fairly smooth white glass with several impurities, one adhering to the surface; silver stain; vitreous paint; back-painting
Eight breaks, leaded; a few scratches on back surface
*Provenance:* Fine Arts Society, London
*Bibliography:* D. F[riedley]., "Stained Glass Panels," *Metropolitan Museum of Art Bulletin* 7 (November 1912), 213.
12.137.5 [The Cloisters]

## TWO FIGURAL PANELS FROM A SERIES OF THE NINE HEROES

A. King Arthur (25.135.168)
B. Charlemagne (25.135.169)
*Arms:* A. Azure three crowns or in pale (King Arthur)
B. Or an imperial eagle displayed sable (Holy Roman Empire)
Germany c. 1490–1500
*Inscription:* B. on banner: VCF ?
A. Heavy, smooth uneven white glass with numerous minute bubbles and a large imbedded impurity; silver stain; two shades of vitreous paint
B. Heavy, uneven white glass with many small bubbles; three hues of silver stain; two shades of vitreous paint
32.5 x 11.2 (12¾ x 4⅜) each
A. Two breaks, leaded; loss at upper left, restored; paint slightly rubbed; chip along right edge; minor surface scratches
B. Minor surface abrasion; chip along right edge; minor scratches on back surface
*Provenance:* William H. Riggs, Paris
*Bibliography:* Hayward (1971–1972), 142, ill. (A); unpublished (B).
25.135.168, 169 [Arms and Armor]

A                                      B

## FRAGMENT: HEAD OF A KNIGHT WEARING AN *ARMET-À-RONDELLE*

South Lowlands
1475–1500
Heavy, even white glass with some bubbles; silver stain; two shades of vitreous paint
14.6 x 12.2 (5¾ x 4¾)
Losses along upper and right edges, restored; break, leaded; paint slightly rubbed in areas; corroded on back surface
*Provenance:* Chassunot, Paris; Edward S. Harkness, New York
*Bibliography:* Checklist I, 132, ill.
29.156.61 [Arms and Armor]

## FRAGMENT: HEAD OF AN ANGEL

South Lowlands, Guelders
c. 1480
White glass; silver stain; vitreous paint
14.6 x 14.9 (5¾ x 5⅞)
Extensive pitted corrosion
*Provenance:* George D. Pratt, Glen Cove, NY
Unpublished
28.46.2 [Medieval]

## HOLY KINSHIP (ANNASELBDRITT): ST. ANNE ENTHRONED WITH VIRGIN AND CHILD

South Lowlands
1480–1500
Thin, smooth, even and slightly reamy white glass; silver stain; two shades of vitreous paint
Diameter: 19 (7½)
Five breaks, leaded; some loss of paint at lower edges; surface scratches
*Provenance:* Grosvenor Thomas, London; Roy Grosvenor Thomas, New York
*Bibliography:* Grosvenor Thomas Stock Book I, 8, item no. 51; unpublished.
32.24.15 [The Cloisters]

## VIRGIN WITH SACRED HEART AND CHILD SEATED ON A CRESCENT MOON

South Lowlands or Germany
1490–1500 or 19th–20th century
Thin, even, slightly reamy white glass; silver stain; two shades of vitreous paint; back-painting
Diameter: 17.8 (7)
Paint somewhat rubbed; chip at lower edge; pitted corrosion on back
*Provenance:* Maurice Drake, Exeter; Grosvenor Thomas, London; Roy Grosvenor Thomas, New York
*Bibliography:* Grosvenor Thomas Stock Book I, 80, item no. 958; unpublished.
32.24.13 [The Cloisters]

## CHRIST BEFORE PILATE FROM A SERIES OF THE PASSION OF CHRIST

South Lowlands
1480–1500
Fairly smooth, reamy white glass with some imbedded impurities; silver stain; two shades of vitreous paint; back-painting
Diameter: 19 (7½)
Four breaks, leaded; paint considerably rubbed throughout; pitted corrosion on back
*Provenance:* Grosvenor Thomas, London; Roy Grosvenor Thomas, New York
*Bibliography:* Grosvenor Thomas Stock Book I, 6, item no. 41; unpublished.
32.24.11 [The Cloisters]

## ANGEL SUPPORTING A HERALDIC SHIELD

*Arms:* Argent two fleurs-de-lis or a bordure engrailed; on a canton, a column sable (unidentified); impaling barry gules and or, the bars gules, fretty argent dimidiated (unidentified)
South Lowlands
1490–1500
Fairly smooth, slightly reamy white glass; silver stain; two shades of vitreous paint; thin back-painting
Diameter: 18.5 (7 5/16)
Paint somewhat rubbed in areas
*Provenance:* Sir Thomas Neave, Dagnam Park, Essex; Grosvenor Thomas, London; Roy Grosvenor Thomas, New York
*Bibliography:* Grosvenor Thomas Stock Book I, 98, item no. 1046; unpublished.
32.24.12 [The Cloisters]

## AGONY IN THE GARDEN FROM A PASSION SERIES

South Lowlands, Ghent or Bruges ?
1490–1510
White, heavy and reamy glass with numerous minute bubbles; two hues of silver stain; two shades of vitreous paint
Diameter: 22.3 (8 3/4)
Unpainted diagonal line through center caused by a flaw in the glass; some scratches on unpainted surface; one large deep straw mark
*Provenance:* James R. Herbert Boone, Baltimore, MD; Trustees of Johns Hopkins University, Baltimore, MD
*Bibliography:* European Works of Art sale (1988), n. p., no. 60; Metropolitan Museum annual report (1988–1989), 33.
*Related Material:* Roundel, close, slightly weaker version, Musées Royaux d'Art et d'Histoire, Brussels (690)
1988.304.2 [The Cloisters]

## TWO KINGS FROM AN ADORATION GROUP

Germany, Lower Rhineland or Lowlands
1500–1510
Thin, smooth white glass; silver stain; two shades of vitreous paint; back-painting
Diameter: 21.6 (8 1/2)
Probably cut from panel of larger format; shatter crack and four other breaks, leaded; loss at upper right, stopgap; losses on both sides, restored; paint somewhat rubbed
*Provenance:* Grosvenor Thomas, London; Roy Grosvenor Thomas, New York
*Bibliography:* Grosvenor Thomas Stock Book I, 20, item no. 219; unpublished.
32.24.21 [The Cloisters]

## ST. MARY MAGDALENE KNEELING

After Albrecht Dürer
Germany, Nuremberg ?
1500–1510
Heavy, uneven white glass (Butzenscheibe) with several large bubbles in concentric pattern; silver stain; several shades of thin vitreous paint
Diameter: 9.5 (3¾)
Some abrasion on raised surfaces
*Provenance:* Bashford Dean, Riverdale, NY; George D. Pratt, Glen Cove, NY
Unpublished
*Related Material:* Woodcut, Albrecht Dürer, from the Small Passion series [Christ as a gardener appearing to Mary Magdalene] {Illustrated Bartsch 10:47}
30.73.2 [Medieval]

## ST. FRANCIS RECEIVING THE STIGMATA

After Albrecht Dürer
Germany, Nuremberg ?
1505–1515
Very uneven white glass with bubbles and impurities; two hues of silver stain; three shades of vitreous paint; back-painting
Diameter: 22.2 (8⅝)
Shatter crack and nine other breaks, leaded; small loss near center, restored; paint flaking along left edge
*Provenance:* Grosvenor Thomas, London; Roy Grosvenor Thomas, New York
*Bibliography:* Grosvenor Thomas Stock Book I, 64, item no. 803; unpublished.
*Related Material:* Woodcut, rectangular format, Albrecht Dürer {Illustrated Bartsch 10:110}; drawing, variant composition, Albrecht Dürer {Winkler, 1936, I, no. 212}; engraving, Marcantonio Raimondi after Albrecht Dürer {Illustrated Bartsch 27:642}
32.24.34 [The Cloisters]

## CHRIST TAKING LEAVE OF HIS MOTHER

After Hans Leonhard Schäufelein
Germany, Nuremberg
1507–c. 1515
Heavy uneven white glass with numerous bubbles and imbedded impurities; silver stain; two shades of vitreous paint
Diameter: 16.5 (6½)
Paint lifted off in areas, particularly along lower edge
*Provenance:* Sibyll Kummer-Rothenhäusler, Zurich; Ruth Blumka, New York; Dr. Louis Slattery, New York
*Bibliography: Songs of Glory: Medieval Art from 900–1500* [exh. cat., Oklahoma Museum of Art] (Oklahoma City, 1985), no. 116, ill.; *The Metropolitan Museum of Art, Annual Report for the Year 1985–1986* (New York, 1986), 33; Husband, in Raguin et al. (1987), 61, no. 24; Timothy Husband, "Hans Leonard Schäufelein and small-scale stained glass: A design for a quatrelobe and two silver-stained roundels in New York," in *Hans Schäufelein: Vorträge, gehalten anlässlich des Nördlinger, Symposiums im Rahmen der 7. Rieser Kulturtage in der Zeit vom 14. Mai bis 15. Mai 1988* (Nördlingen, 1990), 84–87, fig. 54.
*Related Material:* Woodblock, *Speculum Passionis Domini nostri Jhesu Christi* (Ulrich Pinder, Nuremberg, 1507)
1985.146 [The Cloisters]

### ST. MARK

North Lowlands
c. 1500
Smooth, slightly reamy white glass
with an imbedded impurity and a
large elliptical bubble; silver stain;
two shades of vitreous paint; back-
painting
Diameter: 23.5 (9¼)
Paint slightly flaked in spots;
scratches on back surface
*Provenance:* Bresset Frères, Paris
*Bibliography:* Metropolitan Museum
annual report (1980–1981), 42;
Hayward (1981), 30.
1980.223.1 [The Cloisters]

### ANNUNCIATION TO THE SHEPHERDS FROM A SERIES OF THE INFANCY OF CHRIST

North Lowlands, Haarlem ?
1500–1510
*Inscription:* gloria · in · excelsis · deo
Fairly smooth, very reamy white glass
with straw marks; several hues of
silver stain; several shades of vitreous
paint
Diameter: 21.6 (8½)
Paint rubbed in areas; some surface
scratches
*Provenance:* Grosvenor Thomas,
London; Roy Grosvenor Thomas,
New York
*Bibliography:* Grosvenor Thomas
Stock Book I, 22, item no. 226; Drake
(1913), pt. 2, 32, no. 174.
32.24.23

### CHRIST AND ZACCHAEUS FROM A SERIES OF THE LIFE OF CHRIST

North Lowlands
1500–1510
Very uneven white glass; three hues
of silver stain; two shades of
vitreous paint; back-painting
Diameter: 21.6 (8½)
Break, leaded; some surface scratches
*Provenance:* Grosvenor Thomas,
London; Roy Grosvenor Thomas,
New York
*Bibliography:* Grosvenor Thomas
Stock Book I, 34, item no. 354; Drake
(1913), pt. 2, 25, no. 128.
32.24.44 [The Cloisters]

**KING ARTHUR OR ALEXANDER THE GREAT FROM A SERIES OF THE NINE HEROES**

After the Master MG ?, perhaps the Master of the Death of Absalom ?
North Lowlands, Leiden ?
1500–1510
*Inscription:* connick kersten artus
Heavy, reamy white glass; silver stain; two shades of vitreous paint
Diameter: 17.7 (7)
Horizontal break, leaded; paint considerably rubbed
*Provenance:* William M. Dodson, Tilbury, Essex; Wilfred Drake, London; Grosvenor Thomas, London; Roy Grosvenor Thomas, New York
*Bibliography:* Grosvenor Thomas Stock Book I, 222, item no. 1315; A. E. Popham, "A Dutch Designer for Glass," *Mélanges Hulin de Loo* (Brussels and Paris, 1931), 276, n. 2; Wouter Nijhoff, *Nederlandsche Houtsneden* (s'Gravenhagen, 1933–1939), 5:152; Boon (1987), 1:192, no. 515.
*Related Material:* Fragment of a woodcut, based on, Master MG ? {Nijhoff, 1933–1939, 5:pl. 387 b}
32.24.58 [The Cloisters]

**SUSANNA LED TO JUDGMENT FROM A SERIES OF THE STORY OF SUSANNA**

*Arms:* on cushion: an imperial eagle displayed sable surmounted by a crown (Holy Roman Empire)
North Lowlands
c. 1510
*Inscription:* on hem of woman's robe: ROMSTEI OMO
Fairly smooth white glass with several large and many smaller elliptical bubbles and faint straw marks; silver stain; three shades of vitreous paint
Diameter: 21.8 (8⅝)
Two breaks, leaded; surface abrasion at upper center
*Provenance:* Grosvenor Thomas, London; Roy Grosvenor Thomas, New York
*Bibliography:* Grosvenor Thomas Stock Book I, 172, item no. 1053; Berserik (1982), no. 23, fig. 39.
*Related Material:* Roundel, somewhat earlier version, based on the same design but the composition reversed, formerly Thomas F. Flannery, Jr., collection {sale cat., Sotheby's, 1–2 December (London, 1983), lot no. 234}
32.24.59 [The Cloisters]

**JUSTICE**

North Lowlands
c. 1510
Fairly heavy white glass with bubbles and imbedded impurities; silver stain; two shades of vitreous paint
Diameter: 22.5 (8⅞)
Break through center, glued
*Provenance:* Sibyll Kummer-Rothenhäusler, Zurich
*Bibliography:* Metropolitan Museum annual report (1983–1984), 40; Timothy Husband, in *Notable Acquisitions 1983–1984, The Metropolitan Museum of Art* (New York, 1984), 19, ill. (image reversed).
*Related Material:* Roundel, close version, Christ Church, Llanwarne, Hereford and Worcester (sI 2a)
1983.418 [The Cloisters]

## DECEMBER: KILLING THE OX FROM A SERIES OF THE LABORS OF THE MONTHS

North Lowlands
c. 1510
*Inscription:* Dris Vossen hout vast /
Jan Somers slaet alst past / Mest
hebbyt ghenoeg ghetast
Heavy, uneven, slightly reamy white
glass with numerous small bubbles;
two hues of silver stain; three shades
of vitreous paint
Diameter: 22.9 (9)
Some surface abrasion; some chipping
around edge
*Provenance:* Sibyll Kummer-
Rothenhäusler, Zurich
*Bibliography:* Hayward (1971–1972),
144, 145 ill.
1970.323 [The Cloisters]

## ST. CATHERINE OF ALEXANDRIA

*Arms:* Hausmark (unidentified)
repeated in border
South Lowlands, Ghent or Bruges
c. 1500
*Inscription:* on border: ihs
maria
White glass; silver stain; vitreous
paint; white and pot metal glass
border with silver stain and vitreous
paint
Diameter: 20.5 (8¹/₁₆)
Paint rubbed in areas; border
composed of 15th- and 16th-century
glass; marked: [.]a[.]wiexes (on back)
*Provenance:* Pieter de Boer,
Amsterdam; J. Polak, Amsterdam
*Bibliography:* Metropolitan Museum
annual report (1984–1985), 44.
1984.338 [The Cloisters]

## ST. JOHN THE BAPTIST

South Lowlands, Ghent or Bruges
c. 1500
Uneven white glass; silver stain;
vitreous paint; back-painting
Diameter: 21.5 (8½)
Surface scratches; impurity fused to
surface at lower right; small chip at
upper left edge; modern border
*Provenance:* Pieter de Boer,
Amsterdam; A. Vecht, Amsterdam
*Bibliography:* Metropolitan Museum
annual report (1984–1985), 44.
1984.205 [The Cloisters]

## ST. MARY MAGDALENE

South Lowlands
c. 1500 or 20th century
Very heavy white glass with circular
bubbles; silver stain; vitreous
paint; back-painting
Diameter: 19.5 (7¹³/₁₆)
Some surface scratches; paint slightly
rubbed in areas
*Provenance:* Grosvenor Thomas,
London; Roy Grosvenor Thomas,
New York
*Bibliography:* Grosvenor Thomas
Stock Book II, 34, item no. 1798;
unpublished.
32.24.10 [The Cloisters]

*Related Material:* Drawing, design
for an earlier close variant, The
Queen's Collection, Windsor Castle,
Berkshire (12952); drawing, design in
rectangular format for a scene from a
close version of the same series
[Raphael departs Tobit and Tobias],
Kupferstichkabinett, Dresden (C
2232); roundel, slightly earlier version
based on the former drawing, Chapel
R, King's College Chapel, Cambridge,
Cambridgeshire (51C2); roundel,
contemporary version, Musées
Royaux d'Art et d'Histoire, Brussels
(567); roundel, similar version, church
of St. Michael, Begbroke, Oxfordshire
(n IV); two roundels, from a closely
related version of the same series
[Blinding of Tobit, Raphael with Tobit
and Tobias], Musées Royaux d'Art et
d'Histoire, Brussels (560 A, B);
roundel, replica of the former
[Blinding of Tobit], The Metropolitan
Museum of Art, The Cloisters
(37.120); roundel, later version,
church of St. Michael, Begbroke,
Oxfordshire (s I); roundel, from a
slightly later version of the same
series [Raphael departs Tobit and
Tobias, Death of Tobit], Musées
Royaux d'Art et d'Histoire, Brussels
(554, 555); roundel, from another
version of the series [Tobit comforts

Sarah], Schnütgen-Museum, Cologne
(M 613); three roundels, from a
somewhat earlier variant of the same
series [Departure of Rebekah,
Marriage of Rebekah, Healing of
Tobit], Victoria and Albert Museum,
London (1244–1855, 1245–1855,
1246–1855); roundel, version from a
series close to the latter [Rebekah
with Tobias], Rijksmuseum,
Amsterdam (NM 12561); three
roundels, from a version of the same
series [Healing of Tobit, Tobit
comforting Sarah, Raphael departs
Tobias], church of St. Mary, Glynde,
East Sussex; roundel, from a close
version of the latter series [Healing of
Tobit], church of St. John the
Evangelist, Rownhams, Hampshire;
roundel, close version of the latter,
church of St. Mary, Acton, Cheshire;
two roundels, from a version of the
same series [Tobias and Raphael,
Raphael departing Tobias], church of
All Saints, Earsham, Norfolk; roundel,
from a version of the same series
[Marriage of Tobias], Galilee Chapel,
Durham Cathedral, Durham, Durham
(nwl la); roundel, variant, based on a
series of the same designs [Raphael
departing Tobias], church of St. John,
Cranford, Northamptonshire
32.24.22 [The Cloisters]

## TOBIAS DRAWING THE FISH FROM THE WATER FROM A SERIES OF THE STORY OF TOBIT AND TOBIAS

South Lowlands, Ghent or Bruges ?
1500–1510
Heavy, uneven white glass with large
elliptical bubbles and imbedded
impurities; two hues of silver stain;
several shades of vitreous paint
Diameter: 21 (8¼)
Four breaks, leaded; paint rubbed in
areas; loss at lower left, restored;
surface scratches; mark etched in
back surface; back pitted
*Provenance:* Grosvenor Thomas,
London; Roy Grosvenor Thomas,
New York
*Bibliography:* Grosvenor Thomas
Stock Book I, 66, item no. 807;
unpublished.

## ANNUNCIATION TO THE VIRGIN

South Lowlands
1500–1510
*Inscription:* on banderol: Ave gratia plena
Thin, uneven white glass with several imbedded impurities and large blister on back surface; two hues of silver stain; two shades of vitreous paint
Diameter: 22.5 (8¹³/₁₆)
Some minor flaking of paint
*Provenance:* Sibyll Kummer-Rothenhäusler, Zurich
*Bibliography:* Metropolitan Museum annual report (1972–1973), 46.
1972.245.1 [The Cloisters]

## SOULS TORMENTED IN HELL

Adapted from Dierick Bouts
South Lowlands, Louvain ?
1500–1510
Very heavy, reamy white glass; two hues of silver stain; two shades of vitreous paint
Diameter: 22.2 (8¾)
Paint flaking in some areas; minor surface abrasion
*Provenance:* Grosvenor Thomas, London; Roy Grosvenor Thomas, New York
*Bibliography:* Grosvenor Thomas Stock Book I, 18, item no. 172; unpublished.
*Related Material:* Panel painting, adapted from, Dierick Bouts, Palais des Beaux-Arts, Lille; roundel, somewhat later replica, Museum Mayer van den Bergh, Antwerp (652); roundel, replica, Oudheidkundig Museum van de Bijloke, Ghent (9033); roundel, slightly later replica, formerly Peter Newton collection, York, Yorkshire; roundel, version, church of St. Mary, Stoke d'Abernon, Surrey; roundel, slightly earlier stronger replica, The Metropolitan Museum of Art, The Cloisters (1990.119.2)
32.24.43 [The Cloisters]

## SOULS TORMENTED IN HELL

Adapted from Dierick Bouts
South Lowlands, Louvain ?
c. 1500–1510
Moderately heavy, uneven white glass; two hues of silver stain; two shades of vitreous paint; back-painting
Diameter: 21.8 (8½)
Minor areas of abrasion; surface scratches
*Provenance:* Sibyll Kummer-Rothenhäusler, Zurich
*Bibliography:* Metropolitan Museum annual report (1989–1990), 29.
*Related Material:* Panel painting, adapted from, Dierick Bouts, Palais des Beaux-Arts, Lille; roundel, somewhat later replica, Museum Mayer van den Bergh, Antwerp (652); roundel, replica, Oudheidkundig Museum van de Bijloke, Ghent (9033); roundel, slightly later replica, formerly Peter Newton collection, York, Yorkshire; roundel, slightly later, weaker replica, The Cloisters (32.24.43); roundel, version, church of St. Mary, Stoke d'Abernon, Surrey
1990.119.2 [The Cloisters]

## ST. JOHN ON PATMOS

South Lowlands
1500–1510 or 19th–20th century
Very heavy, slightly reamy white
glass; silver stain; vitreous paint;
back-painting; marked VII on back
Diameter: 20.8 (8³⁄₁₆)
Several surface scratches; paint
somewhat rubbed in areas
*Provenance:* Grosvenor Thomas,
London; Roy Grosvenor Thomas,
New York
*Bibliography:* Grosvenor Thomas
Stock Book II, 10, item no. 1623;
unpublished.
32.24.24 [The Cloisters]

## ST. DUNSTAN OF CANTERBURY

Lowlands
1510–1520
Fairly heavy, smooth white glass; two
hues of silver stain; two shades of
vitreous paint
Diameter: 22.5 (8⁷⁄₈)
Two breaks, leaded; some surface
abrasion and flaking; loss of paint and
crizzling of glass at left side; some
corrosion and surface accretions on
back surface
*Provenance:* Grosvenor Thomas,
London; Roy Grosvenor Thomas,
New York
*Bibliography:* Grosvenor Thomas
Stock Book I, 2, item no. 9;
unpublished.
32.24.51 [The Cloisters]

## WILD MAN SUPPORTING A HERALDIC SHIELD

*Arms:* Argent a sheaf of wheat or
(unidentified); impaling in chief three
pales bendy in base sable a mullet of
six points (unidentified)
Lowlands
1510–1530
Fairly smooth, reamy white glass
with several large elliptical bubbles;
straw marks; two hues of stain; two
shades of vitreous paint
Diameter 21 (8¹⁄₄)
Numerous surface scratches
*Provenance:* Grosvenor Thomas,
London; Roy Grosvenor Thomas,
New York
*Bibliography:* Grosvenor Thomas
Stock Book II, 28, item no. 1755;
unpublished.
32.24.28 [The Cloisters]

## JOAB MURDERING ABNER

North Lowlands
1510–1520
Heavy, slightly reamy white glass
with bubbles and numerous
impurities; silver stain; two shades of
vitreous paint
Diameter: 21.7 (8⁹⁄₁₆)
Some minor surface abrasion in small
areas
*Provenance:* F. E. Sidney, Holly
House, Hampstead; Maurice Drake,
Exeter, Devonshire; Pieter de Boer,
Amsterdam; A. Vecht, Amsterdam
*Bibliography:* Bernard Rackham,
"Stained Glass in the Collection of
Mr. F. E. Sidney, II. Netherlandish
and German Medallions," *Old
Furniture: A Magazine of Domestic
Ornament* (1931), 14, fig. 2; *The
Collection of English and Continental
Furniture, Porcelain and Objects of
Art and Stained Glass formed by
F. E. Sidney, Esq.* [sale cat., Christie's,
9 December] (London, 1937), lot nos.
52, 53, or 75; Metropolitan Museum
annual report (1984–1985), 44; *Journal
of Glass Studies* 27 (1985), ill. cover
and frontispiece; Husband, in Raguin
et al. (1987), 64–65, no. 26, ill.
1984.206 [The Cloisters]

*Color illustration page 8*

## ADORATION

North Lowlands, Amsterdam ?
1510–1520
*Inscription:* on banderol: uit ganser
lief drin
Heavy, slightly uneven white glass
with numerous small bubbles and a
few imbedded impurities; two hues of
silver stain; three shades of vitreous
paint
Diameter: 22.2 (8¾)
Paint partially lifted by adhesive tape
in diagonal band across surface; some
surface scratches
*Provenance:* Sibyll Kummer-
Rothenhäusler, Zurich
*Bibliography:* Metropolitan Museum
annual report (1972–1973), 46.
*Related Material:* Roundel, version,
church of St. Peter Rendcombe,
Gloucestershire
1972.245.3 [The Cloisters]

## LAZARUS AT THE HOUSE OF
## DIVES

North Lowlands
c. 1510–1520
Uneven white glass with some
bubbles and impurities; two hues of
silver stain; two shades of vitreous
paint
Diameter: 22.2 (8¾)
Six breaks, leaded; loss at left edge
and another at bottom edge, restored;
paint flaking in areas
*Provenance:* Grosvenor Thomas,
London; Roy Grosvenor Thomas,
New York
*Bibliography:* Grosvenor Thomas
Stock Book I, 26, item no. 265;
unpublished.
*Related Material:* Roundel,
rectangular format, close version,
formerly F. E. Sidney collection, Holly
House, Hampstead {Bernard Rackham,
"Stained Glass in the Collection of
Mr. F. E. Sidney, II. Netherlandish
and German Medallions," *Old
Furniture: A Magazine of Domestic
Ornament* (1931), 17, fig. 10};
roundel, based on a design from the
same series [Death of Lazarus],
Stedelijk Museum De Lakenhal,
Leiden (7679)
32.24.37 [The Cloisters]

## ALLEGORY OF ROUT AND PILLAGE

North Lowlands
1510–1520
Uneven white glass with minute bubbles and impurities; two hues of silver stain; several shades of vitreous paint
Diameter: 24.7 (9¾)
Five breaks, glued; small loss at left edge, restored with polymer; losses along breaks in center, restored with polymer; chipping at lower left edge
*Provenance:* Grosvenor Thomas, London; Fine Arts Society, London
*Bibliography:* Maurice Drake, *A History of English Glass-painting, with Some Remarks upon the Swiss Miniatures of the Sixteenth and Seventeenth Centuries* (London, 1912), pl. 26, fig. 1.
12.137.7 [European Sculpture and Decorative Arts, at The Cloisters]

## VANITAS: DEATH WITH A PEASANT, A PRINCE, AND A POPE

North Lowlands
1510–1520
Slightly uneven white glass with straw marks; two hues of silver stain; three shades of vitreous paint; green and bluish green opaque enamel
Diameter: 22.3 (8¾)
Some flaking of enamel; paint slightly rubbed in areas; surface scratches
*Provenance:* Sibyll Kummer-Rothenhäusler, Zurich
*Bibliography: The Metropolitan Museum of Art, Annual Report for the Year* 1976–1977 (New York, 1977), 59.
*Related Material:* Roundel, version, Museum Mayer van den Bergh, Antwerp (651); roundel, slightly later version, formerly James R. Herbert Boone and the Trustees of the Johns Hopkins University, Baltimore, MD; roundel, later variant, church of St. Mary, Fawsley, Northamptonshire; roundel, later variant, formerly Peter Newton collection, York, Yorkshire
1977.89 [The Cloisters]

## BLINDING OF TOBIT FROM A SERIES OF THE STORY OF TOBIT AND TOBIAS

South Lowlands, Ghent or Bruges ?
c. 1510
Fairly even white glass with imbedded impurities; two hues of silver stain; three shades of vitreous paint
Diameter: 24.1 (9½)
Horizontal break, leaded; surface scratches; mark etched on front surface
*Provenance:* Canterbury ?; Grosvenor Thomas, London; Roy Grosvenor Thomas, New York, to 1927; Mrs. Charles Hofer, Cincinnati, OH; Philip Hofer, Cambridge, MA
*Bibliography:* Grosvenor Thomas Stock Book I, 42, item no. 505; unpublished.
*Related Material:* Roundel, replica, Musées Royaux d'Art et d'Histoire, Brussels (560 B); roundel, from the same series [Raphael with Tobit and Tobias], Musées Royaux d'Art et d'Histoire, Brussels (560 A); roundel, later version of the former, church of St. Michael, Begbroke, Oxfordshire (s I); drawing, design for an earlier close variant [Tobias drawing the fish from the water], The Queen's Collection, Windsor Castle, Berkshire (12952); drawing, design in rectangular format for a scene from a close version of the same series, [Raphael departs Tobit and Tobias], Kupferstichkabinett, Dresden (C 2232); roundel, slightly earlier version based on the former drawing, Chapel R, King's College Chapel, Cambridge, Cambridgeshire (51C2); roundel, contemporary version, Musées Royaux d'Art et d'Histoire, Brussels (567); roundel, similar version, church of St. Michael, Begbroke, Oxfordshire (n IV); roundel, from a slightly later version of same series [Raphael departs Tobit and Tobias, Death of Tobit], Musées Royaux d'Art et d'Histoire, Brussels (554, 555); roundel, from another version of the series [Tobit comforts Sarah], Schnütgen-Museum, Cologne (M 613); three roundels, from a somewhat earlier variant of the same series [Departure of Rebekah, Marriage of Rebekah, Healing of Tobit], Victoria and Albert Museum, London (1244–

1855, 1245–1855, 1246–1855); roundel, version from a series close to the latter [Rebekah with Tobias], Rijksmuseum, Amsterdam (NM 12561); three roundels, from a version of the same series [Healing of Tobit, Tobit comforting Sarah, Raphael departs Tobias], church of St. Mary, Glynde, East Sussex; roundel, from a close version of the latter series [Healing of Tobit], church of St. John the Evangelist, Rownhams, Hampshire; roundel, close version of the latter, church of St. Mary, Acton, Cheshire; two roundels, from a version of the same series [Tobias and Raphael, Raphael departing Tobias], church of All Saints, Earsham, Norfolk; roundel, from a version of the same series [Marriage of Tobias], Galilee Chapel, Durham Cathedral, Durham, Durham (nwl la); roundel, variant, based on a series of the same designs [Raphael departing Tobias], church of St. John, Cranford, Northamptonshire
37.120 [Medieval, at The Cloisters]

## ST. JOHN ON PATMOS

South Lowlands
c. 1510 ?
Fairly heavy white glass with one large imbedded impurity protruding from back surface; two hues of silver stain; two shades of vitreous paint; back-painting
Diameter: 21.9 (8⅝)
Paint rubbed in areas; abrasions on back surface
*Provenance:* William M. Dodson, Tilbury, Essex; Wilfred Drake, London; Grosvenor Thomas, London; Roy Grosvenor Thomas, New York
*Bibliography:* Grosvenor Thomas Stock Book I, 18, item no. 173; unpublished.
*Related Material:* Roundel, replica, church of St. Mary, Shrewsbury, Salop; roundel, reversed replica, chapel of St. Leonard, Blithfield Hall, Staffordshire; roundel, reversed variant, Arensberg window, Chapelle castrale, Enghien, Belgium
32.24.33 [The Cloisters]

## JUDGMENT OF SUSANNA FROM A SERIES OF THE STORY OF SUSANNA

After the Master of the Joseph Panels, Jacob van Lathem ?
South Lowlands, Ghent ?
1510–1515
Very uneven white glass; two hues of silver stain; two shades of vitreous paint
Diameter: 21.6 (8½)
Two shatter cracks and two other breaks, leaded; loss at bottom, restored; several deep scratches on back surface; paint rubbed
*Provenance:* William M. Dodson, Tilbury, Essex; Wilfred Drake, London; Grosvenor Thomas, London; Roy Grosvenor Thomas, New York
*Bibliography:* Grosvenor Thomas Stock Book I, 64, item no. 801; Berserik (1982), no. 14, fig. 24a.
*Related Material:* Roundel, slightly later replica, The Metropolitan Museum of Art, The Cloisters, New York (1984.339); roundel, replica of the latter, Christ Church, Llanwarne, Hereford and Worcester (sI 4b); roundel, later but close version, British Museum, London (1852.3–27.14); roundel, later version, Lincoln College, Oxford, Oxfordshire; roundel, reversed variant of the latter, Gemeente Museum, The Hague (HH 9–51)
32.24.56 [The Cloisters]

## ALLEGORICAL FIGURE: GOATHERDESS WITH DISTAFF AND SPINDLE

South Lowlands
c. 1510–1515
White, reamy glass with a few imbedded impurities; silver stain; vitreous paint
Diameter: 22.7 (8¹⁵⁄₁₆)
Some surface accretions on back; broken surface blister; some slight abrasion
*Provenance:* James R. Herbert Boone, Baltimore, MD; Trustees of the Johns Hopkins University, Baltimore, MD
*Bibliography: European Works of Art* sale (1988), n. p., no. 66; Metropolitan Museum annual report (1988–1989), 33.
1988.304.1 [The Cloisters]

*Color illustration on cover*

## MORDECAI OVERHEARS THE CONSPIRATORS BIGTHAN AND TERESH AND THE HANGING OF BIGTHAN AND TERESH FROM A SERIES OF THE STORY OF ESTHER

South Lowlands
1510–1520
Heavy, uneven white glass with numerous impurities; three hues of silver stain; two shades of vitreous paint
Diameter: 22.2 (8¾)
Some flaking of paint; rubbed in areas
*Provenance:* Grosvenor Thomas, London; Roy Grosvenor Thomas, New York
*Bibliography:* Grosvenor Thomas Stock Book I, 32, item no. 345; Drake (1913), pt. 2, 13, no. 52.
*Related Material:* Roundel, replica, Victoria and Albert Museum, London (5660–1859); drawing, design for a version of the same composition, The Metropolitan Museum of Art, New York (80.3.441); four roundels from the same series [Ahasuerus counseled to reject Vashti, Mordecai rides through the streets in the clothes of Ahasuerus, Esther's banquet for Ahasuerus and Haman, Greatness of Mordecai], Victoria and Albert Museum, London (5644–1859, 5656–1859, 5658–1859, 5654–1859); six drawings, later versions based on designs of the same series [Ahasuerus counseled to reject Vashti, Esther hears of the decree against the Jews, Mordecai rides through the streets in the clothes of Ahasuerus, Esther's banquet for Ahasuerus and Haman, Haman begs for his life, Greatness of Mordecai], The Metropolitan Museum of Art, New York (80.3.440, 80.3.438, 80.3.437, 80.3.439, 80.3.443, 80.3.435); drawing, later version based on a design from the same series [Ahasuerus crowns Esther], Städelsches Kunstinstitut, Frankfurt (5516); drawing, design from an earlier version of the series, Pseudo-Ortkens [Esther hears the decree against the Jews], {sale cat., F. Müller and Co., Amsterdam, 25 November 1958, lot 115}
32.24.41 [The Cloisters]

**JUDGMENT OF SUSANNA FROM A SERIES OF THE STORY OF SUSANNA**

After the Master of the Joseph Panels, Jacob van Lathem ?
South Lowlands, Ghent ?
1510–1520
Uneven white glass with a few bubbles; silver stain; two shades of vitreous paint; back-painting
Diameter: 22 (8⅝)
A few minor surface abrasions
*Provenance:* Sibyll Kummer-Rothenhäusler, Zurich
*Bibliography:* Metropolitan Museum annual report (1984–1985), 44.
*Related Material:* Roundel, replica, Christ Church, Llanwarne, Hereford and Worcester (sI 4b); roundel, slightly earlier replica, The Metropolitan Museum of Art, The Cloisters (32.24.56); roundel, slightly later version, British Museum (MLA 1852, 3–27, 14); roundel, later variant, Lincoln College, Oxford, Oxfordshire; roundel, reversed variant of the latter, Gemeente Museum, The Hague (HH 9–51)
1984.339 [The Cloisters]

**ADORATION**

After Hans Memling
South Lowlands, Brabant or Germany, Lower Rhineland
1500–1515
Heavy white glass with small bubbles throughout; silver stain; vitreous paint; back-painting
Diameter: 20 (7⅞)
Several broken surface blisters at bottom edge; some minor surface scratches
*Provenance:* Sibyll Kummer-Rothenhäusler, Zurich
*Bibliography:* Metropolitan Museum annual report (1983–1984), 40; Timothy Husband, in *Notable Acquisitions 1983–84, The Metropolitan Museum of Art* (New York, 1984), 19, ill.; Husband, in Raguin et al. (1987), 62–63, no. 25, ill.
*Related Material:* Panel painting, Hans Memling, center panel of the Adoration triptych, completed for the Hospital of St. John at Bruges in 1479; drawing, Cabinet des Dessins, Musée du Louvre, Paris (20.738); roundel, close version, Castle chapel, Cholmondeley, Cheshire
1983.235 [The Cloisters]

**NATIVITY**

South Lowlands, Louvain ?
1510–1520
Thin, smooth, fairly uneven white glass; silver stain; two shades of thin vitreous paint
Diameter: 21.3 (8⅜)
Paint considerably rubbed throughout; chip at right edge; surface scratches; slight abrasion on back surface
*Provenance:* Sibyll Kummer-Rothenhäusler, Zurich
*Bibliography: The Metropolitan Museum of Art, Annual Report for the Year 1976–1977* (New York, 1977), 59.
1977.40 [The Cloisters]

## HOLY TRINITY

South Lowlands ?
1510–1520
Fairly heavy, uneven white glass with one large elliptical and several smaller bubbles; two hues of silver stain; two shades of vitreous paint
Diameter: 21 (8¼)
Paint slightly rubbed and abraded in areas; front surface pitted
*Provenance:* Grosvenor Thomas, London; Roy Grosvenor Thomas, New York
*Bibliography:* Grosvenor Thomas Stock Book I, 22, item no. 224; Drake (1913), pt. 2, 18, 70.
32.24.61 [The Cloisters]

## ST. JOHN THE BAPTIST WITH A HERALDIC SHIELD

*Arms:* Quarterly, 1 and 4, or three scallops azure, 2 and 3, vert three martlets argent and two barrulets (van Schillperoot of Delft ?)
South Lowlands
c. 1510–1520
*Inscription:* ECCE ANGNUS / DEI
White glass with several large elliptical bubbles, blisters on back surface, and imbedded impurities; two hues of silver stain; two shades of vitreous paint
Diameter: 21.8 (8⅝)
Five breaks, leaded; loss at left side, restored; some surface scratches
*Provenance:* Grosvenor Thomas, London; Roy Grosvenor Thomas, New York
*Bibliography:* Grosvenor Thomas Stock Book II, 12, item no. 1637; unpublished.
32.24.27 [The Cloisters]

## ST. LAMBRECHT OF MAASTRICHT

South Lowlands
1510–1520
Very uneven, rippled white glass with numerous straw marks; two hues of silver stain; several shades of vitreous paint
Diameter: 22.2 (8¾)
Five breaks, glued; loss at left edge, restored; some chipping along break lines
*Provenance:* Grosvenor Thomas, London; Roy Grosvenor Thomas, New York
*Bibliography:* Grosvenor Thomas Stock Book I, 6, item no. 36; or I, 62, item no. 761; unpublished.
32.24.48 [The Cloisters]

## PANELS WITH THE ADORATION OF THE MAGI, STS. JOHN THE EVANGELIST AND CATHERINE OF ALEXANDRIA

A. Seated Virgin and Child with Melchior (1982.47.2)
B. St. John the Evangelist (1982.47.3a)
C. Fragment with St. Catherine of Alexandria and a Hausmark (1982.47.3b)
*Arms:* Or in chief a mullet between I and F, in base V and reversed over sable (unidentified Hausmark)
Germany, Cologne
c. 1515–1520
Heavy, fairly smooth white glass with imbedded impurities and large elliptical bubbles; three hues of silver stain; four shades of vitreous paint; back-painting
A. 37.5 x 32.3 (14¾ x 12¾)
B. 36.3 x 16.5 (14¼ x 6½)
C. 16.5 x 16.5 (6½ x 6½)
A. Panel(s) with other two kings missing; numerous surface paint somewhat rubbed in areas; large broken surface blister on back; back-painting pitted through in areas
B. Surface scratches, paint very rubbed in areas; three chips along lead line
C. Upper portion of figure missing; paint rubbed; numerous surface scratches, back surface pitted
*Provenance:* Sibyll Kummer-Rothenhäusler, Zurich
*Bibliography:* Herbert Rode in *Herbst des Mittelalters* [exh. cat., Kunsthalle] (Cologne, 1970), 73, no. 88, fig. 39 (A); *The Metropolitan Museum of Art, Annual Report for the Year 1981–1982* (New York, 1982), 38; Jane Hayward, in *Notable Acquisitions 1981–1982, The Metropolitan Museum of Art* (New York, 1982), 22–24, ill.; Checklist I, 140, ill. 1982.47.2, 3a, b [Medieval Department]

A

B

C

## CHRIST AND THE PILGRIMS AT EMMAUS

Germany
1520–1530 or 19th–20th century
Heavy, smooth, fairly reamy white glass; silver stain; two shades of vitreous paint
24.6 x 18.1 (9⁷/₁₆ x 7¹/₈)
Extensive and deeply pitted corrosion on back surface; flaking of paint
*Provenance:* George D. Pratt, Glen Cove, NY
Unpublished
28.46.1 [European Sculpture and Decorative Arts, at The Cloisters]

## ST. BASIL THE GREAT WITH A DONOR AND A SHIELD

*Arms:* Hausmark (unidentified)
Lowlands
c. 1515
Fairly smooth white glass with numerous impurities adhering to back surface; two hues of silver stain; three shades of vitreous paint; back-painting
Diameter: 21.6 (8¹/₂)
Break, leaded; loss of paint in lower right; surface scratches and some abrasion
*Provenance:* Grosvenor Thomas, London; Roy Grosvenor Thomas, New York
*Bibliography:* Grosvenor Thomas Stock Book I, 18, item no. 192; or Grosvenor Thomas Stock Book I, 6, item no. 36; unpublished.
32.24.39 [The Cloisters]

## CHRIST AS *SALVATOR MUNDI*

Lowlands
1520–1530
*Inscription:* Ick bij die wech der waerheijt en dat leve daer en mach nimant totte vad da alleijn doer mich johan x
Very heavy, uneven, reamy white glass with numerous bubbles of varying sizes and impurities; two hues of silver stain; three shades of vitreous paint
Diameter: 21.7 (8⁹/₁₆)
Three breaks, leaded; paint quite rubbed in areas; some surface scratches
*Provenance:* Grosvenor Thomas, London; Roy Grosvenor Thomas, New York
*Bibliography:* Grosvenor Thomas Stock Book I, 20, item no. 199; Drake (1913), pt. 2, 17, no. 64.
32.24.60 [The Cloisters]

**CHRIST BEFORE PILATE FROM A SERIES OF THE PASSION OF CHRIST**

North Lowlands, Amsterdam ?
1515–1520
*Inscription:* So zalt voortgae wat ghy bestaet ghy die volck ende lat regert, Hennt dat recht dat onrecht haet ende des wysheits licht anthiert
Heavy, uneven, very reamy white glass; two hues of silver stain; two shades of vitreous paint; back-painting
Diameter: 23.1 (9⅛)
Severe pitting around lower edge; some surface scratches
*Provenance:* Grosvenor Thomas, London; Roy Grosvenor Thomas, New York
*Bibliography:* Grosvenor Thomas Stock Book I, 298, item no. M-19; unpublished.
32.24.67 [The Cloisters]

**LAST SUPPER FROM A SERIES OF THE PASSION OF CHRIST**

North Lowlands, Amsterdam ?
1515–1525
Heavy, uneven white glass with a few imbedded impurities; silver stain; three shades of vitreous paint
Diameter: 19.4 (7⅝)
Four breaks, leaded; considerable flaking of paint; chipped at lower edge
*Provenance:* Grosvenor Thomas, London; Roy Grosvenor Thomas, New York
*Bibliography:* Grosvenor Thomas Stock Book I, 6, item no. 37; unpublished.
*Related Material:* Two roundels, from an earlier, variant series relying on a version of the same designs [Ecce homo, Carrying the cross], Oudheidkundig Museum van de Bijloke, Ghent (A.C.L. nos. 206537, 206540); woodcuts, 1511–1517, series on which the compositions of the latter rely, Jacob Cornelisz. van Oostsanen [Last supper, Agony in the garden, Betrayal, Scouring, Mocking, Flagellation, Crown of thorns, Ecce homo, Carrying the cross, Crucifixion, Lamentation, Resurrection], {Steinbart 1937, nos. 20–31; Illustrated Bartsch 13:1–12}
32.24.46 [The Cloisters]

## NUDE WOMAN SUPPORTING A HERALDIC SHIELD

*Arms:* (RIGHT) Sable a tree or, canton dexter quartered Brabant and Luxembourg (LEFT) Or three cauldrons sable (Magraeta Hendrick ?)
North Lowlands, North Brabant ?
1515–1530
*Inscription:* margraeta he indric va sarthoge bos
Fairly smooth white glass; silver stain; three shades of vitreous paint
Diameter: 24.1 (9½)
Shatter crack and four other breaks, leaded; two small losses in shatter crack, restored; some surface abrasion
*Provenance:* Grosvenor Thomas, London; P. W. French & Co., New York; Roy Grosvenor Thomas, New York
*Bibliography:* Grosvenor Thomas Stock Book I, 22, item no. 228; P. W. French & Co. stock sheet no. 19289; Drake (1913), pt. 2, 36, 204, ill.
32.24.35 [The Cloisters]

## CARRYING OF THE CROSS FROM A SERIES OF THE PASSION OF CHRIST

North Lowlands ?
c. 1520
Very heavy, uneven white glass; silver stain; four shades of vitreous paint
Diameter: 22.8 (9)
Star fracture and one break, leaded; two cracks, unmended; considerable flaking of paint over entire surface; some surface scratches
*Provenance:* William M. Dodson, Tilbury, Essex; Wilfred Drake, London; Grosvenor Thomas, London; Roy Grosvenor Thomas, New York
*Bibliography:* Grosvenor Thomas Stock Book I, 228, item no. 1343; Drake (1913), pt. 1, 18, no. 13.
*Related Material:* Roundel, from a variant, related series [Crucifixion], The Baltimore Museum of Art, (1941.399.1a)
32.24.50 [The Cloisters]

## DELILAH CUTTING THE HAIR OF SAMSON

North Lowlands
c. 1520–1525
Very heavy white glass with some impurities and bubbles; two hues of silver stain; two shades of vitreous paint
Diameter: 23.7 (10¼)
Three chips along lower right edge; several surface scratches
*Provenance:* Bresset Frères, Paris
*Bibliography:* Metropolitan Museum annual report (1980–1981), 42; Hayward (1981), 30.
*Related Material:* Roundel, later version, Dundalk church, County Louth, Ireland
1980.223.3 [The Cloisters]

## SORGHELOOS WITH LICHTE FORTUNE FROM A SERIES OF THE ALLEGORY OF SORGHELOOS

Probably North Lowlands, Leiden
c. 1520–1525
Fairly heavy, uneven white glass with several large impurities adhering to back surface and a few straw marks; two hues of silver stain; back-painting
Diameter: 23 (9¹/₁₆)
Abraded surface at left edge; flaking of paint along lower edge; surface scratches; mark etched on back surface in later hand
*Provenance:* Sibyll Kummer-Rothenhäusler, Zurich
*Bibliography: The Metropolitan Museum of Art, Annual Report for the Year 1975–1976* (New York, 1976), 53; Husband (1989), 24:173–188.
*Related Material:* Tondo, distemper on canvas, closely related reversed variant, Öffentliche Kunstammlungen, Basel (359); three tondi, from the same series [Sorgheloos attacked by Pover and Aermoede, Sorgheloos carrying Aermoede, Sorgheloos in poverty] Öffentliche Kunstsammlungen, Basel (360, 1578, 1579); roundel, contemporary version based on the Basel design, Toledo Museum of Art, Toledo, OH (57.49); later version of the same, Cranbrook Academy of Art Museum, Bloomfield Hills, MI (1939.57); fragment of roundel, another version of the latter two, Royal Museum and Free Library, Canterbury, Kent {Thornton, pl. ill. window in staircase}; roundel, probably based on a lost design from the same series [Sorgheloos dancing with Weelde], Stedelijk Museum De Lakenhal (7684); roundel, replica, Castle chapel, Cholmondely, Cheshire; drawing for a roundel, contemporary variant, Kestner Museum, Hannover (Z 81); tondo, oil on panel, later debased variant, formerly Albert Figdor collection, Vienna {sale cat., Giroux, 1954, lot no. 58}; roundel, replica, based on a design from the Basel series [Sorgheloos attacked by Aermoede and Pover], formerly James R. Herbert Boone and the Trustees of the Johns Hopkins University, Baltimore, MD; roundel, slightly later version, K. G.

Boon collection, Amsterdam; roundel, based on a design from the same series [Sorgheloos carrying Aermoede], Hessisches Landesmuseum, Darmstadt (31:35); roundel, replica, Christ Church, Llanwarne, Hereford and Worcester (sI a2); roundel, another replica, Christ Church, Llanwarne, Hereford and Worcester (sI c2); roundel, close version, Museum für angewandte Kunst (G1 2798); another close version with an inscribed border, Victoria and Albert Museum, London (66–1929); roundel, somewhat later version, private collection, Melksham Court, Wiltshire; roundel, based on a design from the same series [Sorgheloos in poverty], Christ Church, Llanwarne, Hereford and Worcester (sI c3); roundel, replica, private collection, Sussex; roundel, replica with an inscribed border, Victoria and Albert Museum, London (65–1929); drawing for a roundel, version, from a series based on same designs, Nationalmuseum Stockholm (Ankarsväld collection 432)
1976.47 [The Cloisters]

## TURKISH SOLDIER HOLDING AN ARROW AND SUPPORTING A SHIELD

*Arms:* Hausmark (unidentified)
Manner of Jan Swart van Groningen ?
North Lowlands
1520–1530
Heavy, uneven white glass with several large and numerous other bubbles, imbedded impurities, and diagonal ridged flaw; two hues of silver stain; two shades of vitreous paint
Diameter: 22.8 (9)
Break, leaded
*Provenance:* Sir Thomas Neave, Dagnam Park, Essex ?; Grosvenor Thomas, London; Roy Grosvenor Thomas, New York
*Bibliography:* Grosvenor Thomas Stock Book I, 98, item no. 1047; unpublished.
32.24.29 [The Cloisters]

## SACRIFICE IN THE TEMPLE

South Lowlands
1515–1525
Heavy, uneven white glass; two hues
of silver stain; two shades of
vitreous paint
Diameter: 23 (9¹/₁₆)
Slight loss of paint along lower left
edge; minor surface abrasion at top
edge
*Provenance:* Bresset Frères, Paris
*Bibliography:* Metropolitan Museum
annual report (1980–1981), 42.
1980.223.5 [The Cloisters]

## JOSEPH PRESENTING HIS FATHER JACOB TO THE PHARAOH FROM A SERIES OF THE HISTORY OF JOSEPH IN EGYPT

South Lowlands
1515–1530
Fairly uneven, rippled white glass;
silver stain; two shades of vitreous
paint
Diameter: 21.6 (8½)
Two breaks, leaded; two cracks,
unmended; paint flaked in areas;
some surface scratches
*Provenance:* Grosvenor Thomas,
London; Roy Grosvenor Thomas,
New York
*Bibliography:* Grosvenor Thomas
Stock Book I, 42, item no. 503;
unpublished.
*Related Material:* Roundel, variant,
church of St. Peter, Nowton, Suffolk
32.24.63 [The Cloisters]

## NUDE WOMAN SUPPORTING A HERALDIC SHIELD

*Arms:* A sword in pale argent hilted
or between two mullets of six points
or
Manner of Jan Gossaert
South Lowlands, Antwerp ?
c. 1515–1530
Fairly smooth white glass with
numerous bubbles of varying sizes;
three hues of silver stain; three
shades of vitreous paint
Diameter: 24 (9⁷/₁₆)
Two breaks, leaded
*Provenance:* Grosvenor Thomas,
London; Roy Grosvenor Thomas,
New York
*Bibliography:* Grosvenor Thomas
Stock Book I, 172, item no. 1050;
unpublished.
32.24.32 [The Cloisters]

## DANIEL SLAYING THE DRAGON

Style of the Pseudo-Ortkens
South Lowlands, Antwerp or Brussels
c. 1520
Quite smooth white glass with
several imbedded impurities and
innumerable small elliptical bubbles;
silver stain; three shades of vitreous
paint
Diameter: 21.6 (8½)
Two breaks, leaded
*Provenance:* Sir Thomas Neave,
Dagnam Park, Essex ?; Grosvenor
Thomas, London; Roy Grosvenor
Thomas, New York
*Bibliography:* Grosvenor Thomas
Stock Book I, 98, item no. 1045;
James L. Sturm, *Stained Glass from
the Medieval Times to the Present:
Treasures to Be Seen in New York*
(New York, 1982), 9, fig. 9.
32.24.49 [The Cloisters]

## JOSEPH ORDERING CORN TO BE STORED FROM A SERIES OF THE HISTORY OF JOSEPH IN EGYPT

South Lowlands
c. 1520
Fairly heavy uneven white glass with
some bubbles; two hues of silver
stain; two shades of vitreous paint
Diameter: 22.2 (8¾)
Two breaks, leaded; paint rubbed in
areas
*Provenance:* Sir Thomas Neave,
Dagnam Park, Essex; Grosvenor
Thomas, London; Roy Grosvenor
Thomas, New York
*Bibliography:* Grosvenor Thomas
Stock Book I, 172, item no. 1051;
unpublished.
32.24.47 [The Cloisters]

## SUSANNA AND THE ELDERS FROM A SERIES OF THE STORY OF SUSANNA

Based on a design of the Pseudo-
Ortkens
South Lowlands, Antwerp ?
c. 1520
*Inscription:* Exarserūt senes /
[. . .]los suos ut nō vide[. . .] /
Susanna et / in cōcupiscentiā /
declinaverūt ocū[. .] / [. . .]rēt celū
daniel 13
Moderately heavy, uneven white glass
with numerous impurities; two hues
of silver stain; two shades of vitreous
paint
*Provenance:* Sibyll Kummer-
Rothenhäusler, Zurich
*Bibliography:* Metropolitan Museum
annual report (1989–1990), 29.
*Related Material:* Roundel, version
without border, Dr. William Cole
collection, Hindhead, Surrey (148);
drawing, reversed version, Institut
néerlandais, Fondation Custodia, Paris
(6612); roundel, version, Institut
néerlandais, Fondation Custodia, Paris
(546a); roundel, somewhat later
version, The Baltimore Museum of
Art, Baltimore, MD (1941.399.2c);
roundel, slightly later variant with
inscribed border, Rijksmuseum,
Amsterdam (NM 16833); drawing,
slightly later version of the latter,
formerly Theodor Cremer collection,
New York, now on loan from
Vermeer Associates to the Fogg Art
Museum, Harvard University,
Cambridge, MA {Raguin et al. 1987,
59–60, no. 23 A}; two drawings from
the same series [Judgment of Susanna,
Stoning of the elders] {Raguin et al.
1987, 59–60, nos. 23 B-C}; drawing,
variant of the Fogg drawing, The
Pierpont Morgan Library; roundel,
based on Paris drawing, Victoria and
Albert Museum, London (5636–1859);
two roundels, earlier versions, from a
series based on the same designs
[Susanna and the elders, Daniel
condemns the elders], church of St.
Peter, Nowton, Suffolk; roundel,
version, from a series based on the
same design [Susanna led to
judgment], Victoria and Albert
Museum, London (5637–1859);
roundel, version of the latter, church
of St. Mary, Ickworth, Suffolk;
roundel, version with inscribed

border, from a series of the same design [Daniel judges the elders], Castle chapel, Cholmondeley, Cheshire; roundel, from a series close to the latter [Stoning the elders], church of St. Oswald, Malpas, Cheshire; roundel, another version of the latter, Long Stratton, Norfolk; roundel, later version, formerly Horace Walpole collection, Strawberry Hill, Middlesex; roundel, later and weaker variant [Susanna and the elders], Musée des Antiquités de la Seine Maritime, Rouen; roundel, later, weaker version, The Metropolitan Museum of Art (41.170.73)
1990.119.1

*Color illustration on frontispiece*

## CARRYING OF THE CROSS WITH ST. VERONICA

*Arms:* a banner or, an eagle displayed sable (unidentified)
South Lowlands, Antwerp ?
c. 1520
*Inscription:* on sleeve hem of figure supporting the cross: IOCHE[.]
Uneven white glass with innumerable minute bubbles; silver stain; two shades of vitreous paint; back-painting
Diameter: 22 (8⅝)
Front surface pitted; several surface scratches
*Provenance:* Bresset Frères, Paris
*Bibliography:* Metropolitan Museum annual report (1980–1981), 42.
*Related Material:* Roundel, replica, church of St. Peter, Nowton, Suffolk; roundel, version, church of St. Mary Magdalene, Norwich, Norfolk
1980.223.2 [The Cloisters]

## LAZARUS AT THE HOUSE OF DIVES, THE TORMENT OF DIVES, AND GOD RECEIVING THE SOUL OF LAZARUS

South Lowlands, Antwerp ?
c. 1520
*Inscription:* on hanging: ET EPVN[. . .] / MORTVS EST AT ET . DIV [. .] on parapet: PAVPERTAS
Slightly uneven white glass with innumerable small and medium-sized bubbles and some impurities; two hues of silver stain; two shades of vitreous paint
Diameter: 22 (8¹¹⁄₁₆)
Two breaks, leaded; chip at right edge; minor flaking of paint; a few surface scratches
*Provenance:* Grosvenor Thomas, London; Roy Grosvenor Thomas, New York
*Bibliography:* Grosvenor Thomas Stock Book I, 38, item no. 343; Drake (1913), pt. 2, 26, no. 130.
32.24.38 [The Cloisters]

## ST. CATHERINE OF ALEXANDRIA

South Lowlands
c. 1520 or 19th–20th century
Uneven white glass with straw marks; two hues of silver stain; three shades of vitreous paint
Diameter: 19.1 (7½)
Break, leaded; paint rubbed; surface scratches
*Provenance:* Grosvenor Thomas, London; Roy Grosvenor Thomas, New York
*Bibliography:* Grosvenor Thomas Stock Book I, 172, item no. 1065; unpublished.
32.24.45 [The Cloisters]

## ST. JEROME IN HIS STUDY

Style of the Pseudo-Ortkens
South Lowlands, Antwerp or Brussels
c. 1520
White, moderately heavy glass with several elliptical bubbles; two hues of silver stain; three shades of vitreous paint
Diameter: 22.8 (9)
Back surface at upper left marred in manufacture; slight surface scratches
*Provenance:* James R. Herbert Boone, Baltimore, MD; Trustees of the Johns Hopkins University, Baltimore, MD
*Bibliography: European Works of Art* sale (1988), n. p., no. 69; Metropolitan Museum annual report (1988–1989), 33; *The Metropolitan Museum of Art Bulletin* 47, no. 2 (1989), 18, ill.
1988.304.3 [The Cloisters]

## ST. JOHN THE BAPTIST

Style of the Pseudo-Ortkens
South Lowlands, Antwerp or Brussels
c. 1520 or 19th–20th century
Fairly heavy white glass with blisters on back surface; two hues of silver stain; two shades of vitreous paint; back-painting
Diameter: 20.8 (8³⁄₁₆)
Surface heavily pitted; some surface scratches
*Provenance:* Grosvenor Thomas, London; Roy Grosvenor Thomas, New York
*Bibliography:* Grosvenor Thomas Stock Book I, 4, item no. 26; unpublished.
32.24.26 [The Cloisters]

## ST. PETER WITH A HERALDIC SHIELD

*Arms:* Argent a fess or charged with three mounts sable hung by the guige (unidentified)
South Lowlands, Louvain ?
c. 1520
Reamy white glass with bubbles of varying sizes and numerous imbedded impurities; two hues of silver stain; two shades of vitreous paint; back-painting
Diameter: 24.8 (9¾)
Flaking and some loss of paint around edge
*Provenance:* Fine Arts Society, London
*Bibliography:* D. F[riedley]., "Stained Glass Panels," *Metropolitan Museum of Art Bulletin* 7 (November 1912), 213.
12.137.6 [The Cloisters]

## ST. JOHN ON PATMOS WITH APOCALYPTIC VISIONS

Manner of Dierick Vellert
South Lowlands, Antwerp ?
1520–1530
Thin, fairly smooth white glass with blister on back surface; silver stain; two shades of thin vitreous paint
Diameter: 22 (8⅝)
Eleven breaks, leaded; small loss at bottom edge, restored; paint rubbed in areas
*Provenance:* Grosvenor Thomas, London; Roy Grosvenor Thomas, New York
*Bibliography:* Grosvenor Thomas Stock Book II, item no. 1638; unpublished.
*Related Material:* Drawing, based on, Musée du Louvre, Cabinet des Dessins (18.998); drawing, close version of the latter, Musée du Louvre, Cabinet des Dessins, Edmond de Rothschild collection (588); roundel, later and simplified version, Arensberg window, Chapelle castrale, Enghien, Belgium
32.24.65 [The Cloisters]

## ST. JUDOCUS AND ST. CLARE OF ASSISI

South Lowlands
1520–1530
*Inscription:* S E
Fairly heavy, uneven white glass with one large and other elliptical bubbles; silver stain; two shades of vitreous paint
Diameter: 21.6 (8½)
One break, leaded; paint flaking along break; some surface scratches
*Provenance:* Grosvenor Thomas, London; Roy Grosvenor Thomas, New York
*Bibliography:* Grosvenor Thomas Stock Book I, 66, item no. 809; unpublished.
32.24.31 [The Cloisters]

## CHRIST AND THE WOMAN TAKEN IN ADULTERY

Manner of the Pseudo-Ortkens
South Lowlands, Antwerp or Brussels
c. 1525
Very smooth white glass with several
imbedded impurities and straw
marks; two shades of silver stain; two
shades of vitreous paint; back-
painting
Diameter: 22.2 (8¾)
Some minor surface scratches; paint
flaked in areas
*Provenance:* Sibyll Kummer-
Rothenhäusler, Zurich
*Bibliography:* Metropolitan Museum
annual report (1972–1973), 46.
1972.245.2 [The Cloisters]

## BEN-HADID AND THE SIEGE OF SAMARIA

South Lowlands, Antwerp ?
c. 1525
Uneven white glass with several large
elliptical bubbles and pronounced
straw marks; two hues of silver stain;
two shades of vitreous paint;
iridescence on back
Diameter: 21.6 (8½)
Shatter crack and four other breaks,
leaded; minor flaking of paint
*Provenance:* Grosvenor Thomas,
London; Roy Grosvenor Thomas,
New York
*Bibliography:* Grosvenor Thomas
Stock Book I, 6, item no. 29; Drake
(1913), pt. 1, 20, no. 33.
32.24.30 [The Cloisters]

## CRUCIFIXION WITH THE VIRGIN AND ST. JOHN

South Lowlands
c. 1525
Slightly uneven white glass with some large and other elliptical bubbles and straw marks; two hues of silver stain; three shades of vitreous paint; back-painting
Diameter: 25 (9⅞)
Paint rubbed in areas; iridescence on back
*Provenance:* Grosvenor Thomas, London; Roy Grosvenor Thomas, New York
*Bibliography:* Grosvenor Thomas Stock Book I, 22, item no. 225; unpublished.
32.24.53 [The Cloisters]

## VIRGIN AND CHILD IN A MANDORLA WITH A DONATRIX

South Lowlands
c. 1525 or 19th century
*Inscription:* on hem of Virgin's tunic: MAR[.]
Slightly uneven white glass with many minute bubbles and some impurities; three hues of silver stain; two shades of vitreous paint
Diameter: 21.6 (8½)
Paint rubbed in areas and flaking around edges; chip at lower right edge
*Provenance:* Grosvenor Thomas, London; Roy Grosvenor Thomas, New York
*Bibliography:* Grosvenor Thomas Stock Book II, 12, item no. 1636; unpublished.
32.24.64 [The Cloisters]

## ST. JOHN THE BAPTIST WITH A DONOR AND A DONATRIX

South Lowlands
c. 1525; border dated 1525
*Inscription:* on border: Petrus veestrepen Canonicus leodien Dns et magester anno dno 1525
Thin, uneven white glass; two hues of silver stain; three shades of vitreous paint; back-painting
Diameter: 22.9 (9); with border: 32.5 (12¾)
Crack in border; shield rubbed away; border apparently taken from 32.24.62
*Provenance:* Grosvenor Thomas, London; Roy Grosvenor Thomas, New York
*Bibliography:* Grosvenor Thomas Stock Book I, 22, item no. 229; unpublished.
32.24.68 [The Cloisters]

## ST. PETER AS POPE WITH CANON PETER VERSTREPEN OF LIÈGE AS A DONOR

South Lowlands, Liège ?
c. 1525
Heavy, slightly uneven white glass with minute bubbles; two hues of silver stain; two shades of vitreous paint; back-painting
Diameter: 22.2 (8¾)
Five breaks, leaded; paint severely rubbed in areas and flaking at lower edge; some chipping along breaks; back surface pitted; border belonging to this roundel erroneously attached to 32.24.68
*Provenance:* Grosvenor Thomas, London; Roy Grosvenor Thomas, New York
*Bibliography:* Grosvenor Thomas Stock Book I, 32, item no. 349; Drake (1913), pt. 2, 32, no. 173.
32.24.62 [The Cloisters]

## CRUCIFIXION WITH THE VIRGIN AND ST. JOHN

South Lowlands
c. 1525–1530
Thin, smooth white glass; two hues of silver stain; two shades of vitreous paint; back-painting
Diameter: 19.5 (7¹¹⁄₁₆)
Shatter crack and five other breaks, leaded; surface abrasion on back surface
*Provenance:* Grosvenor Thomas, London; Roy Grosvenor Thomas, New York
*Bibliography:* Grosvenor Thomas Stock Book I, 24, item no. 239.
32.24.66 [The Cloisters]

## LAZARUS AND THE RICH MAN

Manner of Lucas van Leiden
North Lowlands, Leiden ?
c. 1525–1535
White glass; silver stain; vitreous paint
Diameter: 25 (9¾); with border: 36.8 x 30 (14¼ x 12)
Numerous breaks, leaded; trimmed at top and bottom; modern border
*Provenance:* George D. Pratt, Glen Cove, NY
Unpublished
41.170.65 [European Sculpture and Decorative Arts on loan to the Mead Art Museum, Amherst, MA]

## SUSANNA AND THE ELDERS FROM A SERIES OF THE STORY OF SUSANNA

After the Pseudo-Ortkens
South Lowlands
1525–1550
White glass; silver stain; vitreous paint
Diameter: 21.6 (8½)
Paint rubbed in areas; some surface abrasion; glass pitted on back
*Provenance:* George D. Pratt, Glen Cove, NY
Unpublished
*Related Material:* Roundel, close but stronger version, Institut néerlandais, Fondation Custodia, Paris (546a); roundel, earlier variant, The Baltimore Museum of Art, Baltimore, MD (1941.399.2c); roundel; slightly later variant with inscribed border, Rijksmuseum, Amsterdam (NM 16833); roundel, reversed earlier variant with inscribed border, The Metropolitan Museum of Art, The Cloisters collection (1990.119.1); roundel, earlier, stronger version of the latter without border, Dr. William Cole collection, Hindhead, Surrey (148); drawing, earlier and stronger version, Institut néerlandais, Fondation Custodia, Paris (6612); drawing, slightly later version of the latter, formerly Theodor Cremer collection, New York, now on loan from Vermeer Associates to the Fogg Art Museum, Harvard University, Cambridge, MA (Raguin et al. 1987, 59–60, nos. 23 A); two drawings from the same series [Judgment of Susanna, Stoning of the elders] (Raguin et al., 1987, 59–60, nos. 23 B-C); drawing, variant of the Fogg drawing, The Pierpont Morgan Library; roundel, based on the Paris drawing, Victoria and Albert Museum, London (5636–1859); two roundels, earlier versions, from a series based on the same designs [Susanna and the elders, Daniel condemns the elders], church of St. Peter, Nowton, Suffolk; roundel, version, from a series based on the same design [Susanna led to judgment], Victoria and Albert Museum, London (5637–1859); roundel, version of the latter, church of St. Mary, Ickworth, Suffolk; roundel, version with inscribed border, from a series of the same

design [Daniel judges the elders], Castle chapel, Cholmondeley, Cheshire; roundel, from a series close to the latter [Stoning of the elders], church of St. Oswald, Malpas, Cheshire; roundel, another version of the latter, Long Stratton, Norfolk; roundel, later version, formerly Horace Walpole collection, Strawberry Hill, Middlesex; roundel, later and weaker variant [Susanna and the elders], Musée des Antiquités de la Seine Maritime, Rouen
41.170.73 [European Sculpture and Decorative Arts]

## BATTLE SCENE FROM THE SWISS-BURGUNDIAN WARS, POSSIBLY THE CAPITULATION OF THE TOWN OF GRANDSON TO CHARLES THE BOLD

*Arms:* on banners: Gules a saltire (Burgundy); flint and steel striking fire (badge of the dukes of Burgundy); a saltire argent (Switzerland)
After Jörg Breu the Elder ?
Germany, Augsburg
c. 1530
Heavy, smooth, uneven white glass with some imbedded impurities, minute bubbles, and several large elliptical bubbles; silver stain; two shades of vitreous paint; sanguine back-painting
Diameter: 25.7 (10⅛)
Break, leaded; black surface accretions near leads; paint slightly scratched in areas and somewhat rubbed near edges
*Provenance:* William H. Riggs, Paris
Unpublished
*Related Material:* Roundel, another scene based on a design from the same series, Wartburg, Eisenach (Schmitz 1913, 1:257, fig. 36a); roundel, replica (or identical with ?), Angermuseum-Museum für Kunst und Kunsthandwerk, Erfurt (Marita Steffens, in *Bulletin de l'association internationale pour l'histoire du verre* 7 (1973–1976) 73, pl. 75); roundel, another scene based on a design from the same series, Museum Carolino Augusteum, Salzburg (Fischer 1937, opp. 166, pl. 89)
25.135.170 [European Sculpture and Decorative Arts]

## SCENE OF A PUBLIC PUNISHMENT, POSSIBLY FROM THE *GESTA ROMANORUM*

*Arms:* Dimidiated per bend in chief an eagle displayed sable in base on a fess a rose; surmounted by a cardinal's hat (unidentified)
After Jörg Breu the Elder ?
Germany, Augsburg
c. 1530
Heavy, smooth, uneven white glass with some imbedded impurities; silver stain; two shades of vitreous paint
Diameter: 23.5 (9¼)
Paint flaked in places; surface scratched; paint somewhat rubbed in areas
*Provenance:* William H. Riggs, Paris
Unpublished
25.120.171 [European Sculpture and Decorative Arts]

## PRODIGAL BIDS FAREWELL FROM A SERIES OF THE PARABLE OF THE PRODIGAL SON

Germany, Cologne ?
c. 1530–1535
Uneven, white glass with several small bubbles; two hues of silver stain; two shades of vitreous paint
Diameter: 22.8 (9)
Minor flaking of paint around edges
*Provenance:* Grosvenor Thomas, London; Roy Grosvenor Thomas, New York
*Bibliography:* Grosvenor Thomas Stock Book I, 30, item no. 309; Lymant (1982), 232–235, fig. 149 h.
*Related Material:* Roundel, very close version with border and Hausmark, The Metropolitan Museum of Art, New York (41.190.446); seven roundels from the same series as the latter [Prodigal receives his share, Prodigal bids farewell, Prodigal gambles, Prodigal seeks work, Prodigal as a swineherd, Prodigal is given the best coat, Prodigal is banqueted], The Metropolitan Museum of Art, New York (41.190.442, 444, 441, 443, 445, 440, 439); roundel, missing scene from the latter series or a replica series with identical Hausmark and border [Prodigal returns], Schnütgen-Museum, Cologne (M670); roundel, slightly later version without Hausmark and border [Prodigal as a swineherd], The Metropolitan Museum of Art, The Cloisters, New York (32.24.42); roundel, later version based on the same series of designs without Hausmark and border [Prodigal gambles], The J. B. Speed Art Museum, Louisville, KY (44.31 [h]); two roundels, later versions without Hausmarks and border from a series based on the same designs [Prodigal receives the best coat, Prodigal is banqueted], private collection, Sion, Switzerland; two roundels, versions of the same or replica series as the latter two [Prodigal receives his share, Prodigal as a swineherd], private collection, Hillsborough, CA ([1014], [1015]); roundel, from a later, variant series [Prodigal is ejected from the brothel], Schnütgen-Museum, Cologne (597); two roundels, variants, from a later, related series [Prodigal receives his share, Prodigal as a swineherd], Castle chapel, Cholmondeley, Cheshire
32.24.55 [The Cloisters]

## PRODIGAL AS A SWINEHERD FROM A SERIES OF THE PARABLE OF THE PRODIGAL SON

Germany, Cologne ?
c. 1530–1535
Heavy, uneven white glass; two hues of silver stain; two shades of vitreous paint
Diameter: 24.3 (9%/₁₆)
Three breaks, leaded; some minor surface scratches
*Provenance:* Canterbury, Kent; Grosvenor Thomas, London; Roy Grosvenor Thomas, New York
*Bibliography:* Grosvenor Thomas Stock Book I, 42, item no. 504; Lymant (1982), 232–236, fig. 149 i.
*Related Material:* Roundel, close slightly earlier version with Hausmark and border, The Metropolitan Museum of Art, New York (41.190.445); seven roundels from the same series as the latter [Prodigal receives his share, Prodigal bids farewell, Prodigal sets out, Prodigal gambles, Prodigal seeks work, Prodigal is given the best coat, Prodigal is banqueted], The Metropolitan Museum of Art, New York (41.190.442, 446, 444, 441, 443, 440, 439); roundel, missing scene from latter series or a replica series with identical Hausmark and border [Prodigal returns], Schnütgen-Museum, Cologne (M 670); roundel, very close version without Hausmark and border [Prodigal bids farewell], The Metropolitan Museum of Art, The Cloisters, New York (32.24.55); roundel, later version based on the

same series of designs without Hausmark and border [Prodigal gambles], The J. B. Speed Art Museum, Louisville, KY; (44.31 [h]); two roundels, later versions without Hausmark and borders based on the same series of designs [Prodigal receives the best coat, Prodigal is banqueted], private collection, Sion, Switzerland; two roundels, versions from the same or replica series as the latter two [Prodigal receives his share, Prodigal as a swineherd], private collection, Hillsborough, CA ([1014], [1015]); roundel, from a later, variant series [Prodigal is ejected from the brothel], Schnütgen-Museum, Cologne (597); two roundels, variants, from a later related series [Prodigal receives his share, Prodigal as a swineherd], Castle chapel, Cholmondeley, Cheshire
32.24.42 [The Cloisters]

## EIGHT ROUNDELS FROM A SERIES OF THE PARABLE OF THE PRODIGAL SON WITH THE HAUSMARK OF JAN VAN HASSELT

A. Prodigal is banqueted (41.190.439)
B. Prodigal is given the best coat (41.190.440)
C. Prodigal gambles (41.190.441)
D. Prodigal receives his share (41.190.442)
E. Prodigal seeks work (41.190.443)
F. Prodigal sets out (41.190.444)
G. Prodigal as a swineherd (41.190.445)
H. Prodigal bids farewell (41.190.446)

*Arms:* A Hausmark (Jan van Hasselt) on a shield
Germany, Cologne ?
1532
*Inscription:* A. Jan : van : hasselt : Trynghen syn huisfrow Ao dm 1532
B, C, and E. Jan : van : hasselt : Tryngen : syn : Huijsfrow : Anno dm 1532
D. Jan : van : hasselt : Trynigen : syn : huisfrow Anno dm 1532
F. Jan : van : [ . . . ]lt : Trynghen : syn : huisfrow Ao dm 1532
G. Jan : van : hasselt : Tryngen : sy huisfrow Anno dm 1532
H. Jan : van : hasselt : Trynigen : syn : huisfrow Anno dm 1532
A–H. Thin to medium weight, smooth, uneven white glass with some imbedded impurities and numerous minute elliptical and several large bubbles; silver stain; four shades of vitreous paint; sanguine
Diameters: A and C–H: 26.4 (10³/₈); B: 26.7 (10¹/₂)
A. Some paint chipped along edge
B. Four breaks, leaded; three breaks, dutchmen; five breaks, unmended; some surface scratches; chips along break lines
C, D, G, and H. Some surface accretions
E. Some surface accretion and scratches
F. Loss at top edge, stopgap and leaded; two breaks at bottom, unmended; minor surface scratches
*Provenance:* Stadtisches Kunstmuseum, Cologne; Johann Baptist Hirn, Cologne; Christian Geerling, Cologne; Clavé von Bouhaben, Cologne; Eugen Felix,

A

B

Leipzig; George and Florence
Blumenthal, Paris and New York
*Bibliography:* Heinrich Oidtmann,
"Acht Scheiben Kölner Kleinmalerei
des XVI. Jahrhunderts," *Zeitschrift für
christliche Kunst* 23 (1910) cols. 363–
372, figs. 1–6(A-C, F-H); Schmitz
(1913), 68, fig. 110 (F); Schmitz (1923),
12, pls. 57 (B), 58 (E); Stella
Rubinstein-Bloch, *Catalogue of the
George and Florence Blumenthal
Collection* 3 (Paris, 1926), pls. 55–57;
Heinrich Oidtmann, *Rheinische
Glasmalereien vom 12. bis zum 16.
Jahrhundert II* (Düsseldorf, 1929), 345,
figs. 532–537 (A-C, F-H); Herbert
Rode, in *Herbst des Mittelalters:
Spätgotik in Köln und am
Niederrhein* [exh. cat., Kunsthalle]
(Cologne, 1970), 73–74, no. 89;
Lymant (1982), 232–236, figs. 149b-g
(A-D, F, G).

*Related Material:* Roundel, missing
scene from this or a replica series
with identical Hausmark and border
[Prodigal returns], Schnütgen-
Museum, Cologne (M 670); roundel,
very close version without Hausmark
and border [Prodigal bids farewell],
The Metropolitan Museum of Art,
The Cloisters, New York (32.24.55);
slightly later version without
Hausmark and border [Prodigal as a
swineherd], The Metropolitan
Museum of Art, The Cloisters, New
York (32.24.42); roundel, later version
based on the same series of designs
without Hausmark or border [Prodigal
gambles], The J. B. Speed Art
Museum, Louisville, KY (44.31 [h]);
two roundels, later versions without
Hausmark and border [Prodigal
receives the best coat, Prodigal is
banqueted], private collection, Sion,
Switzerland; two roundels, from the
same or replica series as the latter
two [Prodigal receives his share,
Prodigal as a swineherd], private
collection, Hillsborough, CA ([1014],
[1015]); roundel, from a later, variant
series [Prodigal is ejected from the
brothel], Schnütgen-Museum, Cologne
(597); two roundels, variants, from a
later related series [Prodigal receives
his share, Prodigal as a swineherd],
Castle chapel, Cholmondeley,
Cheshire
41.190.439–446 [European Sculpture
and Decorative Arts]

C

D

E

F

G

H

*Enlarged illustration of F page 192*

## TORMENT OF ST. ANTHONY ABBOT

*Arms:* Argent a cock or on a triple mount (Widman ?)
Germany, Swabia ?
1532
*Inscription:* Martinus Widman pfarrer cappel 1532/ 1532
Fairly heavy, reamy white glass; two hues of silver stain; two shades of vitreous paint; back-painting
Diameter: 20.3 (8)
Minor surface scratches; minor losses in back-painting; iridescence on back
*Provenance:* Sibyll Kummer-Rothenhäusler, Zurich
*Bibliography: The Metropolitan Museum of Art, Annual Report for the Year 1982–1983* (New York, 1983), 41; Timothy Husband, in *Notable Acquisitions 1982–1983, The Metropolitan Museum of Art* (New York, 1984), 25, ill.; Elizabeth Parker, ed., "Major Acquisitions of Medieval Art by American Museums," *Gesta* 23:1 (1984), 71, fig. 12.
1982.433.5 [The Cloisters]

## ADORATION OF THE MAGI

After Heinrich Aldegrever
Germany, Westphalia or Lower Rhineland
1535–1540
Thin, slightly uneven white glass; silver stain; three shades of vitreous paint; back-painting
Diameter: 32.7 (12⅞); with border: 40.5 (15¹⁵⁄₁₆)
Six breaks, leaded; circumference slightly trimmed; modern border
*Provenance:* Sir Thomas Neave, Dagnam Park, Essex; Grosvenor Thomas, London; Roy Grosvenor Thomas, New York
*Bibliography:* Grosvenor Thomas Stock Book I, 98, item no. 1044; unpublished.
*Related Material:* Drawing, reversed composition in rectangular format, Heindrich Aldegrever, Szépmüvészeti Müzeum, Budapest (5513–1955)
32.24.69 [The Cloisters]

## NETTING PARTRIDGE

After Augustin Hirschvogel
Germany, Nuremberg
1535–1545
Uneven white glass with one large elliptical and other smaller bubbles; two hues of silver stain; four shades of vitreous paint; two shades of back-painting; green translucent enamel
Diameter: 24.1 (9½)
Considerable loss of paint particularly at lower edge; flaking of paint in middle
*Provenance:* Edward R. Lubin, New York
*Bibliography:* Metropolitan Museum annual report (1980–1981), 41; Hayward (1981), 29, ill.
*Related Material:* Drawing, Augustin Hirschvogel, Szépmüvészeti Müzeum, Budapest (E 19–13A); twenty-five other drawings from the same series all representing hunting scenes, Augustin Hirschvogel, Szépmüvészeti Müzeum, Budapest; two roundels, based on designs from the same series [Hunting rabbit, Falconry], Bayerisches Nationalmuseum, Munich (G 750, G 746); roundel, based on a design from the same series [Hunting hare], formerly Kunstgewerbemuseum, Berlin {Jane S. Peters, "Frühe Glasgemälde von Augustin Hirschvogel," *Anzeiger des Germanischen Nationalmuseums*, 1980, 22, fig. 8}; roundel, based on a design from the same series [Hound with deer at bay], Burg Kreuzenstein near Vienna {*Kunst und Kunsthandwerk* 11 (1908), 20, ill.}; twenty-seven drawings, Augustin Hirschvogel, rectangular format, mostly reversed compositions of the circular series, Szépmüvészeti Müzeum, Budapest; roundel, rectangular format, based on a design from the latter series [Attack on a standing bear], dated 1537 {Jane S. Peters, "Early Drawings by Augustin Hirschvogel," *Master Drawings* 17:4 (Winter 1979), 375–376, fig. 27}
1979.185 [The Cloisters]

## ALLEGORY OF LAW AND GRACE WITH THE HAUSMARK OF HERMANN VON MEMMINGEN

*Arms:* A Hausmark between M and H
(Hermann von Memmingen)
Germany, Cologne
Dated: 1538
*Inscription:* Va syner vulle haebbe
wyr alle genome gnad um gnad da dar
gesatz ys dorch moisen gegeybbe die
genad und waerheyt durch jesu
christi. Joes I . Herman va Memige a
1538
Smooth white glass with numerous
small elliptical bubbles; two hues of
silver stain; two shades of vitreous
paint; back-painting
Diameter: 24.1 (9½)
Inscription, which is integral to
roundel, was executed on back surface
and therefore reads in reverse; minor
surface abrasion
*Provenance:* A. Pickaert, Nuremberg;
Eugen Felix, Leipzig; Dr. John E.
Stillwell, New York
*Bibliography:* A. von Eye and P. E.
Börner, *Die Kunstsammlung von
Eugen Felix in Leipzig* (Leipzig, 1880),
151; Schmitz (1913), 1:68–69, fig. 112;
*The Important Art Collection of Dr.
John E. Stillwell, part I* [sale cat.,
Anderson Gallery, 1–3 December]
(New York, 1927), lot no. 491, ill.;
*The Metropolitan Museum of Art
Bulletin* 23:2 (February 1928), 63;
Hayward (1971–1972), ill.; Lymant
(1982), 249, fig. 155a; Timothy
Husband in Raguin et al. (1987), 66–
67, no. 27, ill.
*Related Material:* Roundel, later
version dated 1551, Schnütgen
Museum, Cologne (M 695); roundel,
later variant with unidentified
Hausmark, Suermondt-Museum,
Aachen {Lymant (1982), 249,
fig. 155 b}
27.224.1 [European Sculpture and
Decorative Arts]

## ST. CHRISTOPHER

South Lowlands, Louvain ?
c. 1530
Reamy white glass with one large
elliptical blister and one large
imbedded impurity; two hues of silver
stain; two shades of vitreous paint
Diameter: 19.7 (7¾)
Horizontal break, leaded; arc etched
on back surface in later hand
*Provenance:* Grosvenor Thomas,
London; Roy Grosvenor Thomas,
New York
*Bibliography:* Grosvenor Thomas
Stock Book I, 30, item no. 320;
unpublished.
32.24.57 [The Cloisters]

## ANGEL SUPPORTING A HERALDIC SHIELD

*Arms:* Argent a stag lodged and
transfixed by an arrow (unidentified)
South Lowlands
c. 1530
Slightly uneven white glass with one
large imbedded impurity and
pronounced straw marks; two hues of
silver stain; vitreous paint
Diameter: 23.4 (9³/₁₆)
Paint somewhat rubbed in center;
several surface scratches
*Provenance:* Grosvenor Thomas,
London; Roy Grosvenor Thomas,
New York
*Bibliography:* Grosvenor Thomas
Stock Book II, 28, item no. 1754;
unpublished.
32.24.36 [The Cloisters]

## CRUCIFIXION SCENE WITH THE THREE MARIES AND ST. JOHN

South Lowlands
c. 1530–1540
Slightly uneven white glass with numerous elliptical bubbles of varying sizes; silver stain; two shades of vitreous paint
Diameter: 21.9 (8⅝)
Four breaks, leaded; loss at upper right, stopgap; a few surface scratches
*Provenance:* Grosvenor Thomas, London; Roy Grosvenor Thomas, New York
*Bibliography:* Grosvenor Thomas Stock Book I, 34, item no. 425; unpublished.
32.24.52 [The Cloisters]

## HANGING OF HAMAN FROM A SERIES OF THE STORY OF ESTHER

Manner of Jan Swart van Groningen
North Lowlands ?
c. 1530–1540
Very uneven white glass; two hues of silver stain; two shades of vitreous paint
Diameter: 22.2 (8¾)
Eight breaks, leaded; some surface scratches
*Provenance:* Grosvenor Thomas, London; Roy Grosvenor Thomas, New York
*Bibliography:* Grosvenor Thomas Stock Book I, 26, item no. 268; unpublished.
32.24.40 [The Cloisters]

## VIRGIN AND CHILD WITH A CARMELITE DONATRIX

South Lowlands
1530–1540
Rippled white glass with numerous small bubbles; two hues of silver stain; three shades of vitreous paint; sanguine
Diameter: 20.5 (8³⁄₁₆)
Four breaks, leaded; loss at right edge, stopgap; paint flaking in areas; two marks scratched on surface
*Provenance:* Grosvenor Thomas, London; Roy Grosvenor Thomas, New York
*Bibliography:* Grosvenor Thomas Stock Book I, 224, item no. 1328; unpublished.
32.24.54 [The Cloisters]

A

B

## JOSEPH REVEALS HIS IDENTITY TO HIS BROTHERS FROM A SERIES OF THE HISTORY OF JOSEPH IN EGYPT

After Jan Swart van Groningen ?
South Lowlands, Antwerp ?
1530–1540
Very heavy, uneven white glass with several imbedded impurities; two hues of silver stain; three shades of vitreous paint; sanguine
Diameter: 25.1 (9⅞)
Paint flaked in areas; paint much scratched and abraded
*Provenance:* Fine Arts Society, London
Unpublished
*Related Material:* Drawing, The Queen's Collection, Windsor Castle, Berkshire
12.137.10 [European Sculpture and Decorative Arts]

## PRODIGAL SON FEASTING FROM A SERIES OF THE PARABLE OF THE PRODIGAL SON

Manner of Pieter Coecke van Aelst
South Lowlands, Antwerp or Brussels ?
1530–1550
Thin, smooth, fairly even white glass with two large and other elliptical bubbles; two hues of silver stain; two shades of vitreous paint
Diameter: 25.4 (10)
Star fracture and one vertical break, leaded; another break, leaded; one crack, unmended; surface abraded; paint rubbed; chips along unmended edge
*Provenance:* George D. Pratt, Glen Cove, NY
Unpublished
*Related Material:* Roundel, close version, composition cut around edge, Victoria and Albert Museum, London (5649–1859)
28.46.4 [European Sculpture and Decorative Arts]

## ST. JAMES THE GREAT

Germany or South Lowlands
1550–1575
White glass; silver stain; vitreous paint
Diameter: 24.7 (9¼)
Star fracture, leaded; modern border
*Provenance:* George D. Pratt, Glen Cove, NY
Unpublished
*Related Material:* Roundel, version from the same series [St. Paul], formerly Sibyll Kummer-Rothenhäusler, Zurich (1985)
41.170.43
[European Sculpture and Decorative Arts on loan to the Mead Art Museum, Amherst, MA]

## ARCHITECTURA FROM A SERIES OF THE *SEPTEM ARTES MECHANICAE*

After Monogramist SZ based on a composition by Jörg Breu the Elder
Germany, Augsburg ?
After 1563
*Inscription:* on plaque: ARCHIE / CTVRA
Smooth, thin white glass with numerous straw marks; silver stain; two shades of vitreous paint; back-painting; sanguine; opaque enamel
Diameter: 22.2 (8¾)
Opaque enamel flaking; paint rubbed in areas; mark scratched on back
*Provenance:* Lewis V. Randall, Toronto; Blumka collection, New York
*Bibliography: The Metropolitan Museum of Art, Annual Report for the Year 1979–1980* (New York, 1980), 41; Hayward (1981), 30.
*Related Material:* Drawing, Monogramist SZ, dated 1563, after Jörg Breu the Elder, Albertina, Vienna (13.257); three drawings from the same series [Vestiaria, Metalaria, Mercatura], Albertina, Vienna (13.255, 13.256, 13.258); drawing, Jörg Breu the Elder, from the original series [Coquinaria], Staatliche Graphische Sammlung, Munich (19 441) roundel, based on latter drawing, Victoria and Albert Museum, London (604–1872); drawing, after Jörg Breu the Elder, from the same series [Milicia], Prentenkabinet der Rijksuniversiteit, Leiden (PK 2301); two roundels in pot metal glass [Vestiaria, Milicia], formerly Historisches Museum, Dresden {Otto Holtze, "Die Kunst Jörg Breu D. Ä.," *Pantheon* 1 (January 1940), 10–12, ill.}; roundel in pot metal glass from same series [Mercatura] {*Aus Schloss E. Sr. erlaucht des Grafen K. zu E. . . , Glasgemälde aus fürstlichem Besitz* [sale cat., Hugo Helbig, 21–23 June] (Frankfurt, 1932), 19, lot no. 210}; two drawings, Tobias Stimmer, dated 1558, variants, from a series of the same subject [Architectura, Vestiaria], British Museum, London (1899–1–20–56, 1899–1–20–57)
1979.186 [The Cloisters]

## JOSEPH AND POTIPHAR'S WIFE FROM A SERIES OF THE HISTORY OF JOSEPH IN EGYPT

*Arms:* Or a buck sable springing from a triple mount vert (Böck ?)
Southern Germany
Dated: 1565
*Inscription:* Potiphars Weib Josep Zwingen Wolt. Das Er Bey Ir Schloffen Solt. Im i Buch Mose am XXXVIIII / Martin Boger Anno 1565
Heavy, uneven white glass; pot metal glass; two hues of silver stain; two shades of vitreous paint; back-painting; back-painting with translucent enamels
Diameter: 23.2 (9⅛); with border: 17.2 (9⅞)
Arms and inscription are contemporary stopgaps; loss at lower edge, two breaks, leaded; one break in border, unmended
*Provenance:* Unknown
Unpublished
10.196.3 [European Sculpture and Decorative Arts]

## TWO PERSONIFICATIONS FROM A SERIES OF THE SEVEN LIBERAL ARTS

A. Arithmetic (41.170.8)
B. Logic (41.170.9)
After Jost Amman ?
Germany, Augsburg ?
1570–1590
*Inscriptions:* A. above seated figure: Arithmetica; on slate: [.] 12 24/ 3 12 36/ 4 12 48/ 5 12 [.]0; below seated figure: [. . .]phio per numerum / [. . .] sit proportio rerum
B. above seated figure: Logica; above other figure: Ari[. . .]; below seated figure: Myno concludo / [. . .]logiso sophisenata iudo
Thin, even white glass with imbedded frit and other surface flaws; silver stain; vitreous paint
17.8 x 11.5 (7 x 4½ ) each (approx.)
A and B. Cut down from larger format; loss at left side (A), right side (B) restored; breaks, leaded; filled out into rectangular panel with modern glass
B. Loss at bottom, stopgap
*Provenance:* George D. Pratt, Glen Cove, NY
Unpublished
*Related Material:* Roundel, rectilinear format, from this or a replica series [Astronomia], Institut néerlandais, Fondation Custodia, Paris (I 3959); roundel, rectilinear format, close version from a series based on the same designs [Geometria], Dr. William Cole collection, Hindhead, Surrey (147); drawing, from the same or a closely related series, attributed to Jost Amman [Astrologia], The Queen's Collection, Windsor Castle, Berkshire (12186)
41.170.8,9 [European Sculpture and Decorative Arts]

A

B

## COMPOSITE PANEL WITH FRAGMENTS OF TWO ROUNDELS

A. Jacob's dream
B. Samson and the Nemean lion
Lowlands
1550–1575
A. Heavy, fairly even white glass; two hues of silver stain; two shades of vitreous paint; back-painting with translucent enamels
B. Heavy, uneven white glass; silver stain; two shades of vitreous paint; back-painting with translucent enamels
A. 9.5 x 17.7 (3¾ x 6¾)
B. 11.2 x 14.6 (4⅜ x 5¾);
together with surrounds: 29.8 x 27.2 (11¾ x 107/8)
A. Lower portion lost; loss at lower right corner, stopgap; disparate surrounds
B. Composition trimmed; loss at right corner, stopgap; two breaks, unmended; paint very rubbed; disparate surrounds
*Provenance:* Mme. d'Olivera, Florence; Coudert Brothers
Unpublished
A and B: 88.3.87 [European Sculpture and Decorative Arts]

A

B

## BATTLE SCENE

North Lowlands ?
16th or 19th–20th century
Heavy, uneven white glass; two
shades of vitreous paint
17 x 22 (6¾ x 8⅝); with border: 27.5
x 32.5 (10⅝ x 12½)
Surface abraded; border composed of
fragments and modern glass·
*Provenance:* George D. Pratt, Glen
Cove, NY
Unpublished
41.170.11 [European Sculpture and
Decorative Arts]

## TWO PERSONIFICATIONS FROM A SERIES OF THE ELEMENTS

A. Earth (22.118.1)
B. Fire (22.118.2)
After Martin de Vos
South Lowlands, Brussels
1580–1620
*Inscriptions:* A. TERRA
B. IGNIS
White glass; silver stain; vitreous
paint; translucent enamels
20 x 27.6 (7⅞ x 10⅞) each (approx.)
A. Breaks at right edge, glued; two
losses, restored
B. Loss of right, restored and leaded;
some flaking of enamels
*Provenance:* Grosvenor Thomas,
London, to 1913; George D. Pratt,
New York
*Bibliography:* Drake (1913), pt. 1, 25,
no. 86 (B).
*Related Material:* Two engravings,
Johannes Sadeler I after Martin de
Vos, from a series representing the
Four Elements (Hollstein 530, 532);
two engravings, from the same series
[Air, Water], (Hollstein 529, 531)
22.118.1, 2 [European Sculpture and
Decorative Arts]

A

B

## THREE ROUNDELS FROM A SERIES OF VIEWS OF TOWNS AND OF THE MONASTERY OF ZEVENBURREN NEAR LOUVAIN

A. View of a walled town (48.149.1)
B. View of the monastery (48.149.2)
C. View of a village (48.149.3)
After Hans Collaert based on
Hans Bol
South Lowlands, Louvain ?
1600–1625
White glass; silver stain; vitreous paint; translucent enamels
16.5 x 21.6 (6½ x 8½) each (approx.)
A. Six breaks, leaded, cracks in center; some flaking of enamel
B. Numerous breaks, leaded; two further breaks; some flaking of enamel
C. Eight breaks, leaded; minor flaking of vitreous paint along lower edge
*Provenance:* George D. Pratt, Glen Cove, NY
Unpublished
48.149.1–3 [European Sculpture and Decorative Arts]

A

B

C

## PERSONIFICATION OF CHARITY FROM A SERIES OF THE VIRTUES AND VICES

After Hendrick Goltzius
Netherlands, Haarlem ?
1600–1625
Even white glass with one large elliptical bubble; silver stain; two shades of vitreous paint; sepia
22 x 16.5 (8⅝ x 6½)
Extensive flaking of paint; scratched surface; surface accretion
*Provenance:* George D. Pratt, Glen Cove, NY
Unpublished
*Related Material:* Engraving, Jacob Matham after Hendrick Goltzius, from a series of the Virtues and Vices (Illustrated Bartsch 4:266; rest of series 4:264–265, 267–277); roundel, variant, Rijksmuseum, Amsterdam (NM 10193); roundel, version, Rijksmuseum, Amsterdam (1635); roundel, variant in rectangular format, Rijksmuseum, Amsterdam (NM 10189); version, Frans Hals Museum, Haarlem; roundel, version, Old Church, Chelsea, London; roundel, version, Missenden Abbey, Buckinghamshire
28.46.3 [European Sculpture and Decorative Arts]

## TWO LEADED WINDOWS WITH SCENES FROM A SERIES OF THE SEVEN ACTS OF CHARITY AND ORNAMENT

A. Feeding the hungry (51.185.2)
B. Burying the dead (51.185.3)
After Maarten van Heemskerck
Netherlands, Haarlem ?
Dated: 1618
*Inscriptions:* A. on cartouche at top:
[.]an Jaco[.]sen DeeKen [.]nde / e[.] Neesker [. . .] Zyn huijsfrouw
on cartouche below scene: O Mensch gedulf enlt te Bew[.]t naer Godts Gebodt / want devraeck alleen ent oor hae[. .]oet dat doet ghij[.]odt / Anno 1618
B. on cartouche at top: Jonas Cornel [.]ssen Schouf Ende / En Maerijke Fa[. .]d Zijn huijsvrouw
on cartouche below scene: Den dorstijgen saeft minlij[. .] [.]oordeele mijt v Broeder teer / ondat v claer Godtrou[.]t deel reen toe comt de heer / Anno 1618
A and B: Thin, smooth, uneven white glass; silver stain; five shades of vitreous paint; sanguine; translucent enamels
A: 26 x 20 (10¼ x 8¼); with surrounds: 90.2 x 44 (35½ x 16⅞)
B: 26.3 x 20.6 (10⅛ x 8⅛); with surrounds: 90.2 x 42.9 (35½ x 16⅞)
A. Composition trimmed at bottom edge; four breaks, leaded: small loss at top, restored; some paint flaked; surface abraded in areas; twenty-one quarries with one or more breaks, leaded; upper quarry of left harpy reversed; enamel crizzled and rubbed in areas
B. Some minor flaking of paint along upper right edge; sixteen quarries with one or more breaks, leaded; three quarries with one or more breaks, unmended; enamel flaked in areas; some losses, restored
*Provenance:* Stanley Mortimer, New York
Unpublished
*Related Material:* Engravings, based on, from a series of the Seven Acts of Charity [Feeding the hungry, Burying the dead], Dierick Volbertsz. Cornhert after Maarten van Heemskerck (Hollstein 160, 161)
51.185.2, 3 [European and Decorative Arts]

A    *Enlarged illustrations page 218*

B    *Color illustrations page 21*

**TWO LEADED WINDOWS WITH ALLEGORICAL SCENES, ORNAMENT, AND THE ARMS OF GEERTIEN MATTHYS DE ENS AND HIS WIFE, VERONICA JOHANS DE HUBERT**

A. Romans executing their treasonous sons (21.87.3)
B. Exhorting the crowds to overthrow the tyrants (21.87.4)
*Arms:* A. On a lozenge, dexter, parted per pale or an eagle dimidiated sable sinister, per fess in chief argent a ball or B. on a lozenge, quarterly, 1 and 4 three herrings swimming argent crowned or (de Hubert of Zeeland); 2 and 3 azure a fess between three roses or (Vierling of Holland ?)
Monogrammed: ME (Jan Maertansz. Engelman van Hoorn ?)
Netherlands, Holland, Alkmaar ?
Dated: 1620
*Inscriptions:* A. O traghe nacomelinct weert doch de shan / hout onder u de Regering vant Landt, / Straft of iaacht wech die na hoocheit staen / Gelijck de Romeinen die hun Soons condemne / er van buels handen doen executeren, / om dat s slants Staet pooghen te verraan / Geertien Matthijs / d'Ens 1620

B. comt vrijgevochten volck enhelpt vankan / dees opgeworpen heer dees Dwingelant, / dre u vrouwen vercracht, u vrijhet schent / u Manschap vermoort doet vroomen verband / vervullend de maet der oude Tyrannen, / enbeveelt u staten het opper Regiment / Veronica Johans / De Hubert 1620/ ME (monogram)
A and B: Thin white glass; silver stain; several shades of vitreous paint; sanguine; translucent enamels; unpainted pot metal glass quarries 107.6 x 47.6 (42⅜ x 18¾) each with surrounds
A. Three breaks in roundel, leaded; seventeen ornamental panes with breaks, leaded; marked 323
B. One vertical break, leaded; eleven ornamental panes with breaks, leaded
*Provenance:* Uffculm House, Exeter, Devonshire; Durlacher Brothers, New York
*Bibliography:* C.O.C., "Rearrangement of Stained Glass Including Some Recent Acquisitions," *Bulletin of the Metropolitan Museum of Art* 16 (November 1921), 234 (A and B), ill. (B only); Hayward (1971–1972), 152, ill. (B)
21.87.3, 4 [European Sculpture and Decorative Arts]

**DUTCH BOYER**

Netherlands
Dated: 1645
*Inscription:* Frans de Kets / 1645
White glass; vitreous paint; enamels
Height: 23.5 (9¼)
Minor abrasion in areas
*Provenance:* Fine Arts Society, London
Unpublished
12.137.9 [European Sculpture and Decorative Arts]

A

B

*Enlarged illustrations page 226*

## TWO PANELS WITH WARSHIPS

A. Man of war firing on another ship
(41.170.19)
B. Man of war firing from starboard
side (41.170.20)
Netherlands
1650–1675
White glass; silver stain; vitreous
paint; translucent enamels
27.3 x 21.5 (10¾ x 8½) each (approx.)
*Provenance:* George D. Pratt, Glen
Cove, NY
Unpublished
41.170.19, 20 [European Sculpture and
Decorative Arts; B. on loan to the
Mead Art Museum, Amherst, MA]

A

B

## TWO LEADED WINDOWS WITH WARSHIPS

A. Man of war, starboard side
(41.170.2)
B. Man of war, port side (41.170.3)
Netherlands, Holland, Amsterdam ?
Dated: A. 1669; B. 1665
*Inscription:* A. on banderol at top:
Anno 1669
on cartouche below: D[e] Heer Jacob
de Wa[. .]erder / R[. . .]i oudt Schepen
en D[. .]kgrars / Anno 1669
B. on banderol at top: Anno 1665
on cartouche below: De Heer Joan
van Gent Hoog / Hee[. .]aet van de
Beemster en Geere / [. .]taris Ao 1665
White glass; silver stain; vitreous
paint; translucent enamels
49.5 x 32.3 (19½ x 12¾) each
(approx.)
A. Five panes with one break each,
leaded; another pane with one break,
glued
B. Two panes with one break each,
leaded
*Provenance:* George D. Pratt, Glen
Cove, NY
Unpublished
41.170.2,3 [European Sculpture and
Decorative Arts, on loan to the Mead
Art Museum, Amherst, MA]

A

B

**PANEL WITH A WARSHIP**

Netherlands, Holland
Dated: 1667
*Inscription:* Hollandts Glorij / 16 67
White glass; silver stain; vitreous
paint; translucent enamels
27.3 x 21.5 (10¾ x 8½)
Breaks through the middle, leaded;
modern border
*Provenance:* George D. Pratt, Glen
Cove, NY
Unpublished
41.170.17 [European Sculpture and
Decorative Arts, on loan to the Mead
Art Museum, Amherst, MA]

**PANEL WITH A WARSHIP**

Netherlands, Holland
Dated: 1670
*Inscription:* Hendrick Lucas de /
Craemersch. / 16 79
White glass; silver stain; vitreous
paint; translucent enamels
27.3 x 21.5 (10¾ x 8½)
Modern border
*Provenance:* George D. Pratt, Glen
Cove, NY
Unpublished
41.170.18 [European Sculpture and
Decorative Arts on loan to the Mead
Art Museum, Amherst, MA]

## NATIVITY

South Lowlands
c. 1480 or 19th century
Fairly heavy, even white glass with
straw marks and numerous minute
bubbles; silver stain; two shades of
vitreous paint; back-painting; white
and pot metal surrounds
Diameter: 19 (7½); with surrounds:
38.5 x 24.5 (15⅛ x 9⅝)
Modern surrounds composed of 17th-
and 19th-century glass
*Provenance:* Unknown
Unpublished
Unaccessioned

## ST. ANTHONY ABBOT

South Lowlands
1490–1510 or 19th century
Heavy, even white glass with
numerous minute bubbles, straw
marks and several surface flaws; two
hues of silver stain; two shades of
vitreous paint; back-painting
Diameter: 20.8 (8⅛); with surrounds:
35.8 x 24.5 (15⅛ x 9⅝)
Paint severely rubbed; numerous
surface scratches; modern surrounds
composed of 17th- and 19th-century
glass
*Provenance:* Unknown
Unpublished
Unaccessioned

## SEATED MADONNA AND CHILD

North Lowlands
c. 1520
White glass; two hues of silver stain;
two shades of vitreous paint
19 x 15 (7½ x 5⅞) (approx.)
Paint slightly rubbed; modern
surrounds composed of 15th-, 16th-,
17th-, and 19th-century glass
*Provenance:* Unknown
Unpublished
West Room

**ST. GEORGE**

South Lowlands
1520–1530 or 19th century
Very heavy, even white glass; two
hues of silver stain; two shades of
vitreous paint; back-painting
Diameter: 19.7 (7¾); with surrounds:
38.5 x 25 (15⅛ x 9⅞)
Numerous surface scratches; modern
surrounds composed of 17th- and
19th-century glass
*Provenance:* Emile Gaillard, Paris, to
1904
*Bibliography: Catalogue des Objets
d'Art et de Haute Curiosité . . . ,
Composant la Collection Emile
Gaillard* [sale cat., Paul Chevallier,
8–16 June] (Paris, 1904), 131, lot no.
625.
Unaccessioned

**ST. MARGARET**

South Lowlands
1520–1530 or 19th century
Heavy, even white glass with some
impurities and two parallel ridged
flaws; two hues of silver stain; three
shades of vitreous paint; white and
pot metal glass surrounds
Diameter: 19.5 (7⅛); with surrounds:
38.5 x 25.5 (15⅛ x 10¹/₁₆)
Minor surface abrasion; modern
surrounds composed of 17th- and
19th-century glass; panel
photographed from back
*Provenance:* Emile Gaillard, Paris, to
1904
*Bibliography: Catalogue des Objets
d'Art et de Haute Curiosité . . . ,
Composant la Collection Emile
Gaillard* [sale cat., Paul Chevallier,
8–16 June] (Paris, 1904), 131, lot no.
626.
Unaccessioned

**ST. GERMANUS OF AUXERRE**

South Lowlands
1540–1560
White glass; two hues of silver stain;
sanguine; two shades of vitreous paint
19 x 15 (7½ x 5⅞) (approx.)
Paint somewhat rubbed on left side;
modern surrounds composed of 15th-,
16th-, 17th-, and 19th-century glass
*Provenance:* Unknown
Unpublished
West Room

## CHARLEMAGNE

Germany
1600–1650
Uneven, rippled white glass; two hues
of silver stain; two shades of vitreous
paint; translucent enamels
33 x 14 (13 x 5½) (approx.)
Two breaks, leaded; loss at lower
right corner, stopgap; enamel flaked;
modern surrounds composed of 14th-,
15th-, 16th-, 17th-, and 19th-century
glass
*Provenance:* Unknown
Unpublished
West Room

## ST. PETER

Germany
1600–1650
*Inscription:* [.]ETRVS / Ic[.] [..]auben
in got[...]ter / All[.]echtigen schep
[..]r / Hi[.]mels und der e[..]e[.]
White glass; silver stain; four shades
of vitreous paint; translucent enamels
19 x 16 (7½ x 6¼) (approx.)
Two shatter cracks, leaded; two other
breaks, leaded; extensive flaking of
paint; modern surrounds composed of
15th-, 16th-, 17th-, and 19th-century
glass
*Provenance:* Unknown
Unpublished
West Room

## ST. MARTIN

North Lowlands
1660–1670 or 19th century
White glass; three shades of vitreous
paint
18 x 15 (7¹⁄₁₆ x 5⅞) (approx.)
Severely corroded surface; modern
surrounds composed of 15th-, 16th-,
17th-, and 19th-century glass
*Provenance:* Unknown
Unpublished
West Room

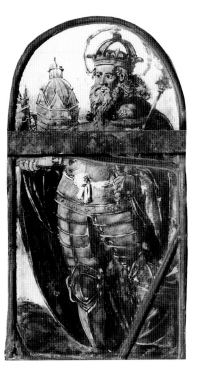

## ST. CATHERINE AND THREE CANONIZED NUNS

Wolfgang Spengler; signed: WSP
Southern Germany, Constance
1670–1679; dated 167[.]
*Inscription:* WSP Constanz; Sch: Maria
Catharina sch: M. Elizabet. sch: / M.
Johanna · sch: M: Ge[.]trut · Gesa = /
mptes Convendt · zu Weppach · /
hāb: die schiben mahlen lasen /
Anno: 167[.] ·
Heavy, fairly even white glass; two
hues of silver stain; two shades of
vitreous paint; back-painting in
translucent enamels
Diameter: 16.2 (6⅜); with border:
21 (8¼)
Five breaks, leaded; two other breaks,
glued; one break, partially leaded; one
other break, unmended; two losses
toward lower right, restored; surface
scratches; border probably modern
*Provenance:* Unknown
Unpublished
Unaccessioned

## VISION OF THE CRUCIFIXION WITH SAINTS AND A FRANCISCAN DONOR AND ARMS

*Arms:* (LEFT) Gules a tree vert
enfenced (Baumgartner ?); helmed and
crested a man holding a tree; (RIGHT)
Azure dimidiated with dexter three
mullets and sinister or a lion rampant
holding a star or (Kimin ?), helmed
and crested a lion rampant or holding
a star or
Wolfgang Spengler; signed: W von
Constanz
Germany, Constance
1670–1679; 167[.]
*Inscription:* W von Constanz; Joha[.]n
Fra[.]ciscu[.] / [.]aumgartner Caes:
/ Not: [.]us und s[.]cret = / arius dess
Go[. .]ha = / uses Müst[. .] = / lingen
und Ann[.] / Elizabet Kimin / sein [.]
gema[.] / Anno 167[.]
Heavy, fairly even white glass; silver
stain; two shades of vitreous paint;
back-painting in translucent enamels
Diameter: 22.5 (8⅞); with border: 29
(11⅜)
Star fracture, leaded; shatter crack,
leaded; several other breaks, leaded;
vitreous paint rubbed in areas; 19th-
century border
*Provenance:* Unknown
*Bibliography:* Checklist I, 185.
Unaccessioned

## BLUMKA COLLECTION

**TWO ROUNDELS FROM A SERIES OF A GENESIS CYCLE**

A. Isaac begs for the hand of Rebekah [1a]
B. Jacob blesses his sons [1b]
Manner of Adriaen Pietersz. or Dierick Pietersz. Crabeth
North Lowlands, Gouda ?
A. Dated: 1550
B. c. 1550
Uneven white glass; three hues of silver stain; sanguine; three shades of vitreous paint
Diameter: 25 (9⅞) each; with borders: 30 (11¹³⁄₁₆) each
A. Some surface abrasion
B. Two breaks, leaded
*Provenance:* Sibyll Kummer-Rothenhäusler, Zurich
Unpublished
*Related Material:* Roundel, from a replica series [Jacob blessing his sons], Corning Museum of Glass, Corning, NY; roundel, slightly later version based on the same series of designs [Isaac begs for the hand of Rebekah], formerly James A. Newton collection, San Antonio, TX
[1 a, b]

A

B

## ST. MARTIN AND THE BEGGAR

Germany, Middle Rhineland
1500–1510
Heavy, smooth white glass; two hues
of silver stain; two shades of vitreous
paint
Diameter: 19.8 (7⅞)
Break, leaded; surface scratches; chips
at upper and lower ends of break;
paint slightly rubbed and flaking in
areas
*Provenance:* Sibyll Kummer-
Rothenhäusler, Zurich; Ruth Blumka,
New York
Unpublished
80.1

## ST. GEORGE AND THE DRAGON

Style of the Master of the Johannes
Panels
North Lowlands, Leiden
1515–1520
Heavy, fairly smooth white glass; two
hues of silver stain; three shades of
vitreous paint
Diameter: 23.5 (8⅞)
Vertical break, glued; two small
losses along break, restored with
polymer; small shatter crack, glued
*Provenance:* Lady Chapel, Christ
Church Cathedral, Oxford,
Oxfordshire; Sir Esmond Ovey,
Culham Manor, Oxfordshire;
J. Goudstikker, Amsterdam; Pieter
de Boer, Amsterdam; J. Polak,
Amsterdam
*Bibliography:* Berserik (1982), part 2,
no. 18, fig. 28; *Works of Art from the
Collection of Sir Esmond Ovey* [sale
cat., Sotheby and Co., 13 March]
(London, 1936), lot no. 187, no. 7;
*Jeroen Bosch: Noord-Nederlandsche
Primitieven* [exh. cat., Museum
Boymans-van Beuningen, Rotterdam]
(Rotterdam, 1936), 115, no. 9.
85.6

## JACOB IN THE HOUSE OF LABAN FROM A SERIES OF THE STORY OF JACOB

North Lowlands, Leiden
1515–1525
Uneven white glass; two hues of silver stain; three shades of vitreous paint
Diameter: 22.8 (9)
Extensive shatter crack and other breaks, glued; small loss at lower left edge and another at center, restored with polymer; corrosion on back surface, particularly at upper and lower left fill
*Provenance:* Ruth Blumka, New York
Unpublished
81.3

## PYRAMUS AND THISBE

After Hans Leonhard Schäufelein
Germany, Nuremberg
c. 1515
Heavy, uneven white glass with ridges and a few imbedded impurities; two hues of silver stain; two shades of vitreous paint; back-painting
Diameter: 21.6 (8½)
Surface scratches on back and front; paint slightly rubbed in areas
*Provenance:* Sibyll Kummer-Rothenhäusler, Zurich
*Bibliography:* Timothy Husband, "Hans Leonard Schäufelein and small-scale stained glass: A design for a quatrelobe and two silver-stained roundels in New York," in *Hans Schäufelein: Vorträge, gehalten anlässlich des Nördlinger Symposiums im Rahmen der 7. Rieser Kulturtage in der Zeit vom 14. Mai bis 15. Mai 1988* (Nördlingen, 1990), 87–93, fig. 57.
*Related Material:* Woodcut, Hans Leonhard Schäufelein, reversing the composition (Illustrated Bartsch 11:95)
82.4

**EXECUTION OF SISAMNES FROM A SERIES OF THE JUDGMENT OF CAMBYSES**

Style of the Master of the van Groote Adoration
South Lowlands, Antwerp
1515–1525
Thin, uneven white glass; silver stain; three shades of vitreous paint; back-painting
24 x 19 (9⁷/₁₆ x 7¹/₂)
Minor surface abrasion; some pitting of back surface
*Provenance:* Sibyll Kummer-Rothenhäusler, Zurich; Ruth Blumka, New York
Unpublished
80.1

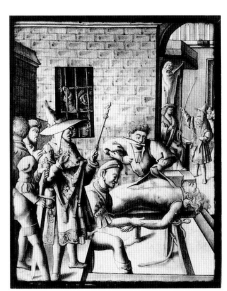

**JUPITER WITH POLLUX AND MERCURY ?**

Manner of Pieter Coecke van Aelst
South Lowlands, Brussels or Antwerp
1540–1560
Thin, uneven white glass; two hues of silver stain; three shades of vitreous paint
Diameter: 22 (8⁵/₈)
Parallel surface scratches on both sides; small areas of surface corrosion on both sides
*Provenance:* Closterman collection, Brussels; Sibyll Kummer-Rothenhäusler, Zurich
Unpublished
83.5

**PORTRAIT ROUNDEL OF GENERAL GUSTAVUS HORN**

Northern Germany or Sweden ?
1633
*Inscription:* Gustavus Horn Genera[.] under ihr Küningtlich Maiestet auf Schweden · Auff Gott sthet mein Hoffnung ANNO DOMINI 1633
White glass; silver stain; two shades of vitreous paint; Jean Cousin; translucent enamel
Diameter: 15 (5⁷/₈)
Three breaks, glued; enamel chipped in places along break lines; some surface accretions
*Provenance:* Galerie de Chartres, Chartres; private collection, Hillsborough, CA
*Bibliography: Vitraux-Tapisseries* sale (1989), 24, lot no. 1226, 1228, 1229, 1231–1236, or 1259–1257.
1990.7

*Color illustration page 10*

**FOUR PERSONIFICATIONS FROM A SERIES OF THE SEVEN LIBERAL ARTS**

A. Grammatica [1 a]
B. Rhetorica [1 b]
C. Arithmetica [1 c]
D. Geometria [1 d]
After Cornelis Cort based on Frans Floris
South Lowlands, Antwerp
after 1565
*Inscription:* A. on writing tablet on floor in front of children: (monogram); on hem of Grammatica's dress: A B C D E F G H I J K L M N O P Q R S T V
B. on book at Rhetorica's feet: [. . .]nia
C. on edge of chair: Jacob de Gheyn; on piece of paper under easel: (monogram); on writing board on back wall: 140 / 16 / 150 / 4; on strip of paper hanging from edge of table: 1670 / 123 / 4; on tablet held by Arithmetica: 8567 / 67
A-D. Thin, fairly uneven white glass; three shades of vitreous paint

28 x 23.5 (11 x 9¼); (with border) 35.5 x 31.7 (14 x 12½)
A. One break and a shatter crack, unmended; other smaller breaks; some surface abrasion and flaking of paint
B. One crack, unmended; surface slightly rubbed
C. One crack, unmended; minor surface abrasion
D. Some surface accretions
A-D. Plated with plexiglass; borders probably 19th century
*Provenance:* Unknown
Unpublished
*Related Material:* Seven paintings, series of the Seven Liberal Arts, Frans Floris, 1555 for Nicolaas Jongelinck (lost); engravings, from a series based on Frans Floris, Cornelis Cort, published by Hieronymus Cock, 1565 {Hollstein 224, 227, 225, 229}; roundel, rectangular format, earlier version based on the same series of designs [Rhetorica], Frans Hals Museum, Haarlem
[1 a-d]

C

D

A

B

# WESTCHESTER
*VICTORIA AND ERIC STERNBERG COLLECTION*

**ANGEL HOLDING A HERALDIC SHIELD**

*Arms:* Argent in chief a bull's head caboshed paly of four or (unidentified)
South Lowlands
c. 1520–1530
White glass; two hues of silver stain; three shades of vitreous paint
Diameter: 22.8 (9); with border: 29.2 (11¼)
Shatter break, leaded; other breaks, leaded; paint rubbed in areas; some surface abrasion
*Provenance:* James W. Newton, San Antonio, TX
Unpublished
[4]

**ANGEL HOLDING A HERALDIC SHIELD**

*Arms:* Argent two leopards rampant guardant combatant sable surmounted by a fleur-de-lis or (unidentified)
South Lowlands
c. 1530–1540
Heavy, flat, and smooth glass with some minute bubbles; silver stain; two shades of vitreous paint
Diameter: 22.8 (9); with border: 29.2 (11¼)
One break, leaded; some sections of border reversed; paint somewhat rubbed; surface scratched
*Provenance:* James W. Newton, San Antonio, TX
Unpublished
[3]

**VISION OF ST. HEBERT OR EUSTACE**

South Lowlands
c. 1530–1540
Smooth white glass with some bubbles and pot metal glass; two hues of silver stain; two shades of vitreous paint; back-painting
Diameter: 22.8 (9); with border: 31.8 (12½)
Nine breaks, leaded; some chips along break lines; some surface abrasion; border composed of stopgaps and modern glass, some sections reversed
*Provenance:* James W. Newton, San Antonio, TX
Unpublished
[2]

## CHRIST AS A GARDENER APPEARING TO MARY MAGDALENE

Germany ?
c. 1550
Smooth, moderately heavy glass with numerous bubbles and imbedded impurities; silver stain; two shades of vitreous paint
24.7 x 19 (9¾ x 7½); with surrounds: 39.3 x 31.7 (15½ x 12½)
Loss at top, stopgap; some surface scratches; minor flaking of paint; shatter crack in border, leaded; another break in border, leaded; breaks in two sections, unmended; lower left and right vertical sections of border are modern; border composed of 16th- and 19th- or 20th-century glass
*Provenance:* Stiesel collection, Litchfield, CT
Unpublished
[1]

## CHRIST AND THE DINNER AT EMMAUS

South Lowlands
1540–1560
Fairly heavy, uneven white glass with some elliptical bubbles and imbedded impurities; three hues of silver stain; three shades of paint
Diameter: 22.5 (8⅞)
Loss at lower left, stopgap; seven breaks, leaded; paint rubbed in areas; surface scratches; one chip along break line
*Provenance:* James W. Newton, San Antonio, TX
Unpublished
[7]

**MALE HEAD IN PROFILE**

North Lowlands, Leiden or Germany,
North Rhineland-Westphalia ?
1520–1530
Smooth, slightly uneven white glass
with several imbedded impurities;
two hues of silver stain; three shades
of vitreous paint
8 x 8 (3⅛ x 3⅛)
Probably cut down from larger format
*Provenance:* Sibyll Kummer-
Rothenhäusler, Zurich
Unpublished
[1]

**CIRCUMCISION OF CHRIST**

Southern Germany
c. 1540
White glass; silver stain; vitreous
paint
Diameter: 9.7 (3¹³⁄₁₆)
Two inadvertent runs of silver stain
on the surface; some minor surface
abrasion
*Provenance:* Sibyll Kummer-
Rothenhäusler, Zurich
Unpublished
[2]

## ADORATION

Style of Hans Sebald Beham
Germany, Nuremberg ?
1530–1540
White glass; silver stain; vitreous
paint
Diameter: 10.1 (4); with border: 12
(4⅞)
Border probably modern
*Provenance:* Sibyll Kummer-
Rothenhäusler, Zurich; Michael
Ward, New York
*Bibliography: Form and Light* (1985),
no. 8.
[1]

## MOTHER AND CHILD WITH FOUR PUTTI

Style of Hans Sebald Beham
Germany, Nuremberg ?
1530–1540
White glass; silver stain; vitreous
paint
Diameter: 10.1 (4); with border: 12
(4⅞)
Border probably modern
*Provenance:* Sibyll Kummer-
Rothenhäusler, Zurich; Michael
Ward, New York
*Bibliography: Form and Light* (1985),
no. 8.
[2]

## TRIUMPHAL PROCESSION OF PUTTI

Style of Hans Sebald Beham
Germany, Nuremberg ?
1530–1540
White glass; silver stain; vitreous
paint
Diameter: 10.1 (4); with border: 12
(4⅞)
Modern border
*Provenance:* Sibyll Kummer-
Rothenhäusler, Zurich; Michael
Ward, New York
*Bibliography: Form and Light* (1985),
no. 8.
[3]

**Prodigal Sets Out.** *See pages 165–166.*

# NORTH CAROLINA

# DURHAM
*DUKE UNIVERSITY MUSEUM OF ART*

**STS. PETER AND ANDREW**

Germany
1510–1520
White glass; silver stain; vitreous paint
Diameter: 18.7 (7⅜); with border: 20 (7⅞)
Originally a rectangular panel with a central vertical lead, cut and filled out at sides to form a roundel; several cracks in left portion; border probably modern
*Provenance:* Polak and Winternitz, Vienna; Joseph Brummer, New York; Mrs. Ernest Brummer, New York
Unpublished
1978.20.6

# GREENSBORO
*DR. HENRY HOOD COLLECTION*

**FLIGHT INTO EGYPT FROM A SERIES OF THE INFANCY OF CHRIST**

After the Master of the Seven Acts of Charity, Pieter Cornelisz. Kunst ?
North Lowlands, Leiden ?
1515–1525
Heavy, uneven white glass; two hues of silver stain; three shades of vitreous paint; back-painting
Diameter: 23 (9 1/16); with border: 29.2 (11 1/2)
Severe shatter crack, sandwiched between plate glass; three minor losses near center, stopgaps; large chip at right edge; numerous smaller chips along break lines; modern white glass border
*Provenance:* Michael Fiorillo, Philadelphia
Unpublished
*Related Material:* Roundel, slightly earlier reversed replica, Detroit Institute of Arts, Detroit, MI (36.97); roundel, based on a design from a version of the same series [Visitation], Bruce J. Axt collection, Altadena, CA
[16]

## SEATED COUPLE WITH MUSICAL INSTRUMENTS AND A SHIELD WITH A HAUSMARK

*Arms:* Hausmark (unidentified)
South Lowlands or Germany, Lower Rhineland
1520–1530
Thin, uneven white glass with straw marks and numerous elliptical bubbles; silver stain; three shades of vitreous paint
Diameter: 23.3 (9⅛)
Star fracture and further break, leaded; paint somewhat abraded
*Provenance:* Joseph Binder, New York; Michael Fiorillo, Philadelphia
*Bibliography: The Binder Collection of English, Flemish, Dutch, Swiss and German Stained Glass of the XIVth to the XVIIth Century Formed by the Noted Experts Joseph Binder, Father and Son* [sale cat., Anderson Galleries, 17 November] (New York, 1927), 28, no. 78, ill.
[17]

## FRAGMENT OF ORNAMENT

South Lowlands
1530–1550
Smooth, uneven white glass with a few small bubbles and imbedded impurities; two hues of silver stain; two shades of vitreous paint
8.3 x 10.7 (3¼ x 4⅝)
Background or border ornament from leaded panel; surface accretions along edges
*Provenance:* Michael Fiorillo, Philadelphia
Unpublished
[18]
(not illustrated)

## ARCHANGEL MICHAEL AND A CLERIC DONOR

*Arms:* Hausmark between the letters I and C (unidentified)
South Lowlands, Antwerp ?
1550–1560
Fairly heavy white glass with minute bubbles and a few imbedded impurities; two hues of silver stain; three shades of vitreous paint; sanguine
Diameter: 25.2 (9⅞); with border: 31.2 (12¼)
Four breaks, leaded; some surface abrasion; mark etched on surface by later hand; modern white glass border
*Provenance:* Michael Fiorillo, Philadelphia
Unpublished
[19]

## SEATED MALE FIGURE

*Arms:* (LOWER LEFT) Per pale sable a fleur-de-lys or countercharged (unidentified); (LOWER RIGHT) Or, a key plate argent, a mullet of six points and a loaf of bread or (unidentified)
South Lowlands
1550–1560
Thin, slightly uneven white glass with some large and numerous minute bubbles; two hues of silver stain; two shades of vitreous paint
12 x 10.5 (4¾ x 4⅛); with border: 25.5 x 23.2 (9⅝ x 9⅛)
Probably cut from larger format; one small break, leaded; lower right section of border and lower coats-of-arms are 16th-century; rest of surrounds composed of 19th- or 20th-century glass
*Provenance:* Dealer, London
Unpublished
[20]

# REIDSVILLE

*CHINQUA-PENN PLANTATION*

## PAIR OF COMPOSITE PANELS WITH DONORS

A. Kneeling cleric with hunting scene above (2a)
B. Kneeling young nobleman with inscription above (2b)
France
A. 16th century
B. 1537
*Inscription:* A. O SALVATOR[.] HOSTIA ORA
B. ANNO 1537 STE HUBERTE BEATE ET GLORIOSISSIME ORA PRO NOBIS
A and B. Heavy, uneven, bubbled white glass with large imbedded impurities; two hues of silver stain; three shades of vitreous paint
58 x 20 (22⅞ x 8) each (approx.)
A. Three breaks in upper scene, leaded; lower section of upper panel lost, restored; paint of middle section severely rubbed; lower section cut along upper edge; the whole is a composite
B. Two breaks in upper section, leaded; paint of upper section much abraded; loss at top, restored; two breaks in border section, leaded; the whole is a composite
*Provenance:* Thomas Jefferson Penn, Reidsville, NC
Unpublished
[2a, b]

A                    B

## SICK AND INFIRM AT A SHRINE WITH HOLY WATER FOUNTAIN

Southern Germany ?
1520–1530; section of surrounds
dated: M·L·VI
*Inscription:* on section of lower
surrounds: ML VI; on shield: IHS
Fairly heavy, uneven white glass; two
hues of silver stain; two shades of
vitreous paint; back-painting
23.5 x 19 (9½); with surrounds:
33.5 x 24 (13³⁄₁₆ x 9³⁄₈)
Paint rubbed; some surface scratches;
modern surrounds composed of
stopgaps and modern glass
*Provenance:* Thomas Jefferson Penn,
Reidsville, NC
Unpublished
[1]

## PRODIGAL BIDS HIS FATHER FAREWELL FROM A SERIES OF THE PARABLE OF THE PRODIGAL SON

Southern Germany or Switzerland
1620–1640; dated: 1583
*Inscription:* on fragment of cartouche:
Klaus Bernh[. . .] / [. . .]ahts Loblich /
Ruswijl un[.] / [.]nno [. . .]
in lower section of surrounds: 1583
Thin, even white glass; two hues of
silver stain; three shades of vitreous
paint; translucent enamels
27.4 x 19 (10¾ x 7½)
Some loss of enamel; paint somewhat
rubbed; two losses at right side and
upper left corner; numerous stopgaps
in surrounds; loss at bottom, restored;
numerous breaks in surrounds,
leaded; surrounds composed of
stopgaps and modern glass
*Provenance:* Thomas Jefferson Penn,
Reidsville, NC
Unpublished
[4]

# OHIO

# CINCINNATI

*CINCINNATI ART MUSEUM*

### ST. JOHN AND THE EAGLE

After Agostino Veneziano
Lowlands
1550–1600
Fairly smooth, reamy white glass
with straw marks; two hues of silver
stain; three shades of vitreous paint
Diameter: 21.6 (8½); with border:
23.8 (9 3/5)
Break, leaded; loss at left side,
restored; modern border
*Provenance:* K. Demirdjian ?
Unpublished
*Related Material:* Engraving, reversed,
Agostino Veneziano after Guilio
Romano, 1518, from the series of the
four evangelists (Illustrated Bartsch
26:93); roundel, reversed composition,
church of Saint-Julien, Pruillé-
L'Éguillé, Maine {Grodecki et al. in
*Recensement des vitraux anciens de
la France* 2, CVMA (Paris, 1981),
264}; roundel, rectangular format,
from a version of the same series [St.
Matthew and the angel], private
collection, Charlestown, MA
1934.291

# CLEVELAND

*THE CLEVELAND MUSEUM OF ART*

**JUDGMENT OF PARIS**

South Lowlands
1510–1520
Moderately heavy white glass; silver
stain; vitreous paint
Diameter: 22.2 (8¾)
Several breaks, glued, filled, and
inpainted; small loss at left edge,
restored
*Provenance:* Sibyll Kummer-
Rothenhäusler, Zurich; Michael
Ward, New York
*Bibliography: Form and Light* (1985),
no. 2.
85.148 John L. Severance Fund

# TOLEDO
*THE TOLEDO MUSEUM OF ART*

### SORGHELOOS AND LICHTE FORTUNE FROM A SERIES OF THE ALLEGORY OF SORGHELOOS

Probably South Lowlands, Antwerp
1520–1525
White glass; silver stain; vitreous paint
Diameter: 27 (10⅝)
Several breaks, leaded; two small losses in upper right; stopgaps; modern border
*Provenance:* Adalbert von Lanna, Prague; von Pannwitz, Hartekamp; Rosenberg and Stiebel, New York
*Bibliography: Sammlung des Freiherrn Adalbert von Lanna, Prag* [sale cat., Rudolph Lepke's, 21–28 March] (Berlin, 1911), pt. 2, 97, no. 799, pl. 65; Otto von Falke, *Die Kunst Sammlung von Pannwitz* [sale cat.] (Munich, 1926), pt. 2, no. 114; "Accession of American and Canadian Museums," *Art Quarterly* 21 (1958), 92, ill.; J. Bruyn, "Lucas van Leiden en zijn Leidse tijdgenoten in hun relatie tot Zuid-Nederland," *I.Q. Regeteren Altena* (Amsterdam, 1969), 44–47, ill. 263, fig. 3; *Toledo Museum News* 3, no. 3 (1960), 50, ill.; *Art in Glass, A Guide to the Glass Collections*, Toledo Museum of Art (Toledo, 1969), 53, ill.; Husband (1989), 173–175, 184, ill.
*Related Material:* Tondo, distemper on canvas, replica based on same design, Öffentliche Kunstsammlung, Basel (360); three tondi from same series [Sorgheloos attacked by Aermoede and Pouer, Sorgheloos carrying Aermoede, Sorgheloos in poverty], Öffentliche Kunstsammlung, Basel [359, 1579, 1578]; fragment of roundel, close version, Royal Museum

and Free Library, Canterbury, Kent
{Thornton, 1899, pl. ill. window on
staircase}; roundel, contemporary
reversed variant, The Metropolitan
Museum of Art, The Cloisters
Collection, New York (1976.47);
drawing for a roundel, variant,
Kestner Museum, Hannover (Z 81);
roundel, later and weaker version,
based on a design from the same
series, Cranbrook House, Cranbrook
Educational Community, Bloomfield
Hills, MI (1939.57); tondi, oil on
panel, later, debased version, formerly
Albert Figdor collection, Vienna {sale
cat., Giroux, 1954, lot no. 58};
roundel, slightly later variant based
on the same series of designs
[Sorgheloos attacked by Aermoede
and Pouer], formerly James R. Herbert
Boone and Trustees of the Johns
Hopkins University, Baltimore, MD;
roundel, slightly later variant of the
latter, K. G. Boon collection,
Aerdenhout; roundel, probably based
on a lost composition from the same
series [Sorgheloos dancing with
Weelde], Stedelijk Museum "De
Lakenhal," Leiden (7684); roundel,
based on a design from the same
series [Sorgheloos carrying Aermoede],
Hessisches Landesmuseum,
Darmstadt (31:35); roundel, replica,
Christ Church, Llanwarne, Hereford
and Worcester (sI c2); another replica,
Christ Church, Hereford and
Worcester (sI a2); roundel, slightly
later replica, Österreiches Museum
für angewandte Kunst, Vienna (Gl
2798); another slightly later replica
with an inscribed border, Victoria and
Albert Museum, London (66–1929);
roundel, somewhat later version,
private collection, Melksham Court,
Wiltshire; roundel, earlier version
based on a design from the same
series [Sorgheloos in poverty], private
collection, Sussex; roundel, replica,
Christ Church, Llanwarne, Hereford
and Worcester (sI c3); roundel,
slightly later replica with an inscribed
border, Victoria and Albert Museum,
London (65–1929); drawing for a
roundel, variant, Nationalmuseum,
Stockholm (collection Anckarsvärd
432)
57.49

## TEMPLE OF VIRTUE

North Lowlands, Haarlem or Leiden
1525–1535
*Inscription:* above upper three
Virtues: FIDES · CHARITAS · SPES
center: PRVDENTIA / IVSTICIA / VIRTVS
/ FORTITVDO / TEMPERACIA
White glass; silver stain; vitreous
paint
Diameter: 32.4 (12¾)
Modern border
*Provenance:* von Pannwitz,
Bennebroek, Munich; Rosenberg and
Stiebel, New York
*Bibliography:* Otto von Falke, *Die
Kunst Sammlung von Pannwitz* [sale
cat.] (Munich, 1926), pt. 2, no. 112;
"Accession of American and
Canadian Museums," *Art Quarterly*
21 (1958), 92, ill. 88.
57.48

**Scenes from the Story of Esther (details).** *See page 58.*

# PENNSYLVANIA

# NARPERTH
*MRS. ISABELL HARDY COLLECTION*

**YOUNG MAN BESEECHING A
KNEELING LADY (UNIDENTIFIED
SECULAR SCENE)**

South Lowlands
c. 1530
White glass; three hues of silver stain;
three shades of vitreous paint
Diameter: 20.6 (8½)
Horizontal break, unmended; small
chips along break; paint slightly
rubbed
*Provenance:* Said to have come from
Westminster Abbey, London
Unpublished
[1]

# PHILADELPHIA

*PHILADELPHIA MUSEUM OF ART*

### CORONATION OF THE VIRGIN

South Lowlands
1550–1575
White glass; silver stain; vitreous
paint; translucent enamels
Diameter: 24.4 (9⅝)
Loss of upper left portion, replaced
with stopgap; modern border
*Provenance:* Grosvenor Thomas,
London; Roy Grosvenor Thomas,
New York, to 1924; Mr. and Mrs.
FitzEugene Dixon, Ronaele Manor,
Elkins Park, PA
*Bibliography:* Grosvenor Thomas
Stock Book I, 84, item no. 910;
Eden (1927), 90–91.
52–90–59 Gift of Mrs. Widener Dixon

### MAN OF WAR

North Lowlands
1580–1600
White glass; silver stain; vitreous
paint; translucent enamels
13.3 x 9.8 (5¼ x 3⅞)
Breaks, leaded; modern surrounds
*Provenance:* From an Elizabethan
house in Topsham; Grosvenor
Thomas, London; Roy Grosvenor
Thomas, New York, to 1924; Mr. and
Mrs. FitzEugene Dixon, Ronaele
Manor, Elkins Park, PA
*Bibliography:* Grosvenor Thomas
Stock Book I, 84, item no. 975; Eden
(1927), 87.
52–90–62 Gift of Mrs. Widener Dixon
(not illustrated)

### MAN OF WAR

North Lowlands
1580–1600
White glass; silver stain; vitreous
paint; translucent enamels
24.1 x 21.6 (9½ x 8½)
Several breaks, leaded
*Provenance:* From an Elizabethan
house in Topsham; Grosvenor
Thomas, London; Roy Grosvenor
Thomas, New York, to 1924; Mr. and
Mrs. FitzEugene Dixon, Ronaele
Manor, Elkins Park, PA
*Bibliography:* Grosvenor Thomas
Stock Book I, 84, item no. 978a; Eden
(1927), 85–87.
52–90–67 Gift of Mrs. Widener Dixon

## MAN OF WAR WITH TWELVE GUNS

North Lowlands
1580–1600
White glass; silver stain; vitreous paint; translucent enamels
13.3 x 10.2 (5¼ x 4)
Breaks, leaded; modern surrounds
*Provenance:* From an Elizabethan house in Topsham; Grosvenor Thomas, London; Roy Grosvenor Thomas, New York, to 1924; Mr. and Mrs. FitzEugene Dixon, Ronaele Manor, Elkins Park, PA
*Bibliography:* Grosvenor Thomas Stock Book I, 84, item no. 977; Eden (1927), 87.
52–90–64 Gift of Mrs. Widener Dixon
(not illustrated)

## TWO-MASTED SCHOONER

North Lowlands
1580–1600
White glass; silver stain; vitreous paint; translucent enamels
13 x 9.8 (5⅛ x 3⅞)
Breaks, leaded; modern surrounds
*Provenance:* From an Elizabethan house in Topsham; Grosvenor Thomas, London; Roy Grosvenor Thomas, New York, to 1924; Mr. and Mrs. FitzEugene Dixon, Ronaele Manor, Elkins Park, PA
*Bibliography:* Grosvenor Thomas Stock Book I, 84, item no. 978; Eden (1927), 87.
52–90–65 Gift of Mrs. Widener Dixon
(not illustrated)

## WHALING BOAT

North Lowlands
1580–1600
White glass; silver stain; vitreous paint; translucent enamels
13.3 x 9.8 (5¼ x 3⅞)
Breaks, leaded; modern surrounds
*Provenance:* From an Elizabethan house in Topsham; Grosvenor Thomas, London; Roy Grosvenor Thomas, New York, to 1924; Mr. and Mrs. FitzEugene Dixon, Ronaele Manor, Elkins Park, PA
*Bibliography:* Grosvenor Thomas Stock Book I, 84, item no. 976; Eden (1927), 87.
52–90–63 Gift of Mrs. Widener Dixon
(not illustrated)

## MERCHANT SHIP

North Lowlands
Dated: 1595
*Inscription:* Schipper Zachala Felix Van Slanerdon   1595
White glass; silver stain; vitreous paint; translucent enamels
24.7 x 22.3 (9¾ x 8½)
Three breaks, leaded
*Provenance:* Mrs. FitzEugene Dixon (Eleanor Widener Dixon), Ronaele Manor, Elkins Park, PA
*Bibliography:* Eden (1927), 87.
52–90–66 Gift of Mrs. Widener Dixon

## FIVE PANELS REPRESENTING THE ELEMENTS

A. Water (52–90–68)
B. Fire (52–90–69)
C. Air (52–90–70)
D. Air (52–90–71)
E. Earth (52–90–72)
North Lowlands
1620–1640
*Inscription:* B. Ignis; C. Air; D. Air;
E. Terra
White glass; silver stain; vitreous
paint; translucent enamels
Breaks, leaded
*Provenance:* From an Elizabethan
house in Topsham; Grosvenor
Thomas, London; Roy Grosvenor
Thomas, New York, to 1924; Mr. and
Mrs. FitzEugene Dixon, Ronaele
Manor, Elkins Park, PA
*Bibliography:* Grosvenor Thomas
Stock Book I, 86, item nos. 987–989
and 88m item nos. 990–991; Eden
(1927), 92–93.
52–90–68 to 52–90–72
Gift of Mrs. Widener Dixon
(A and C not illustrated)

A

B

C

D

E

## SEVEN PANELS REPRESENTING MONTHS

A. January (52–90–73)
B. February (52–90–74)
C. March (52–90–75)
D. April (52–90–76)
E. September (52–90–77)
F. October (52–90–78)
G. November (52–90–79)
England
1660–1680
*Inscription:* A. January; B. February;
C. Merty; D. Aprillis; E. September;
F. October; G. November
White glass; silver stain; vitreous
paint; translucent enamels
A-G: 13.3 x 10.1 (5¼ x 4)
Several breaks each panel, leaded
*Provenance:* From an Elizabethan
house in Topsham; Grosvenor
Thomas, London; Roy Grosvenor
Thomas, New York to 1924; Mr. and
Mrs. FitzEugene Dixon, Ronaele
Manor, Elkins Park, PA
*Bibliography:* Grosvenor Thomas
Stock Book I, 84, item no. 979; 86,
item nos. 980–982, 984–986; Eden
(1927), 96–98.
52–90–73 to 52–90–79
Gift of Mrs. Widener Dixon
(C only illustrated)

# PITTSBURGH
*THE CARNEGIE MUSEUM OF ART*

**HOLY KINSHIP (ANNASELBDRITT) WITH ST. BARBARA AND KNEELING DONATRIX**

*Arms:* Hausmark (unidentified)
North Lowlands
1550–1560
*Inscription:* K H
White glass; two hues of silver stain; three shades of vitreous paint
Diameter: 25.3 (10); with border: 30.7 (12.8)
Paint somewhat rubbed; surface scratches; modern border
*Provenance:* Richard M. Scaife, Pittsburgh
Unpublished
83.102.2

# UNIVERSITY OF PITTSBURGH
## UNIVERSITY ART GALLERY

**JOSEPH SOLD INTO SLAVERY FROM A SERIES OF THE HISTORY OF JOSEPH IN EGYPT**

*Arms:* on saddle bag: (LEFT) Hausmark (unidentified); (RIGHT) Hausmark (unidentified)

South Lowlands, Ghent or Bruges
1490–1500

Heavy, uneven white glass; three hues of silver stain; three shades of vitreous paint

Diameter: 22 (9⅝); with both borders: 36 (14⅛)

Two breaks, leaded; modern borders, one of red pot metal, the other old and modern white glass

*Provenance:* Mary Blair, Pittsburgh, to 1926; P. W. French & Co., to 1928; E. S. Bayer, New York; Richard Beatty Mellon, Pittsburgh; Mrs. Alan Magee Scaife, Pittsburgh

*Bibliography:* P. W. French & Co. Stock Sheet no. 14198; Walter Read Hovey, "Stained Glass Windows: Gift of Mrs. Alan M. Scaife," *Pitt Magazine* 49 (1953), 18.

1140–65

# RHODE ISLAND

# NEWPORT
*PRIVATE COLLECTIONS*

### ST. STEPHEN

France
1550–1600
Fairly heavy white glass with numerous minute bubbles and some imbedded impurities; silver stain; two shades of vitreous paint
19 x 17.7 (7½ x 7)
One break, leaded; some surface abrasion; paint rubbed in areas; words etched at top: [. .]or peut [. . .] / ra si bon quand . le [. . .]en su[. .] /1605
*Provenance:* Stuart Duncan, New York and Newport
Unpublished
Window XVII 2b

### ST. CHRISTOPHER CARRYING THE CHRIST CHILD

Southern Germany
1530–1540
Uneven white glass with silver stain; two shades of vitreous paint
Diameter: 19.7 (7¾)
Losses on left and right sides; paint rubbed and flaked in areas
*Provenance:* Edson Bradley, Washington, DC, and Newport
Unpublished
Stairwell window c4

### ST. MARY MAGDALENE IN THE WILDERNESS

Southern Germany ?
c. 1550
White glass; silver stain; three shades of vitreous paint; translucent enamels
Diameter: 23.5 (9¼)
*Provenance:* Edson Bradley, Washington, DC, and Newport
Unpublished
Stairwell window c8

## PEASANT COUPLE

North Lowlands
1550–1575
Very heavy, uneven white glass with imbedded impurities; two shades of vitreous paint; back-painting
13 x 9.6 (5¼ x 3¾)
Two breaks, leaded; small loss at left edge; one crack mended
*Provenance:* Stuart Duncan, New York and Newport
Unpublished
Window XVIII a

## PERSEUS AND ANDROMEDA

South Lowlands
1515–1550
Uneven white glass with some minute bubbles; two hues of silver stain; two shades of vitreous paint; back-painting
Diameter: 22.2 (8¾)
Two breaks, leaded; one crack, unmended; two runs, unmended; paint rubbed in areas; surface accretions around edge
*Provenance:* Stuart Duncan, New York and Newport
Unpublished
Window IV 1c

## PIETÀ

South Lowlands or Germany
1520–1530
White glass; silver stain; vitreous paint
Diameter: 14.7 (5¾)
Losses at top, stopgap; four breaks, leaded; surface accretions
*Provenance:* Edson Bradley, Washington, DC, and Newport
Unpublished
Room 207

## PILGRIM SAINT

South Lowlands
1540–1560
White glass with imbedded impurities; two hues of silver stain; vitreous paint
Diameter: 22.2 (8)
Loss at left sides; paint rubbed; surface covered with adhesive tape; paint largely lost
*Provenance:* Edson Bradley, Washington, DC, and Newport
Unpublished
Stairwell window c4

## HARROWING OF HELL FROM A SERIES OF THE PASSION OF CHRIST

South Lowlands
1550–1560
Heavy, uneven white glass; vitreous paint; sanguine applied on reverse; back-painting
14 x 10.8 (5½ x 4¼)
Paint scratched and rubbed in areas; marked 16
*Provenance:* Stuart Duncan, New York and Newport
Unpublished
Window XXII

## ALLEGORICAL FIGURE: PITY

South Lowlands
1550–1575
*Inscription:* PITIE
Heavy and uneven white glass with imbedded frit and some minute bubbles; silver stain; two shades of vitreous paint; sanguine
19.6 x 19.3 (7¾ x 7⅝)
Four breaks, leaded; loss at upper corner, restored; paint scratched in areas; some surface abrasion; paint rubbed
*Provenance:* Stuart Duncan, New York and Newport
Unpublished
Window XVIIIB

## VIRGIN AND CHILD

South Lowlands
1580–1600
Heavy, uneven white glass; silver stain; two shades of vitreous paint
20.3 x 19.7 (8 x 7¾)
*Provenance:* Stuart Duncan, New York and Newport
Unpublished
Window XVII 1b

## EMBLEMATIC PANEL: COUNTRY COOK

Netherlands
1600–1625
Heavy, uneven white glass; vitreous paint
13 x 10.2 (5¼ x 4)
One break, leaded; surface abrasion on back; surface scratches; paint rubbed in areas
*Provenance:* Stuart Duncan, New York and Newport
Unpublished
Window XVIII

# PROVIDENCE

*RHODE ISLAND SCHOOL OF DESIGN, MUSEUM OF ART*

**SCENE FROM THE LEGEND OF AN UNIDENTIFIED WARRIOR SAINT**

North Lowlands
1520–1540
White glass; silver stain; vitreous paint
Diameter: 23.5 (9¼)
Numerous breaks, leaded; surface scratches
*Provenance:* A. Vecht, Amsterdam; anonymous donor, Providence
Unpublished
62.076

*Enlarged illustration page 222*

**ROUNDEL WITH A COAT OF ARMS**

*Arms:* Gules a grozing iron and an ax in saltire and a bit in pale argent (Käser)
Switzerland
1550
*Inscription:* Karl Käser / Gläser alhie
White glass; translucent and opaque enamels; flashed pot metal glass
Diameter: 13.5 (5⁵⁄₁₆)
Shatter cracks in upper portion, unmended; enamels flaked along some break lines
*Provenance:* Anonymous gift
*Bibliography:* Checklist I, 210.
22.117

**Scenes from a series of the Seven Acts of Charity and Ornament.** *See page 175.*

# SOUTH CAROLINA

# GREENVILLE

*BOB JONES UNIVERSITY COLLECTION OF SACRED ART*

**EIGHT ROUNDELS WITH
PORTRAIT PROFILES**

A. Bearded male with helmet
(753/1A)
B. Female with pleated collar
(753/1B)
C. Male with head band (753/2A)
D. Female with headdress and
chinstrap (753/2B)
E. Male with helmet and yellow
feather (753/1C)
F. Female with black headdress
(753/1D)
G. Male with helmet and white
feather (753/2C)
H. Female with gray headdress
(753/2D)
South Lowlands
1580–1600 or 19th–20th century
White glass; silver stain; vitreous
paint
Diameter: A–H: 8.4–9.5 (3¹⁵⁄₁₆–3¾)
Paint rubbed in some areas
*Provenance:* Unknown
Unpublished
753/1A, B; 753/2A, B; 753/1C, D;
753/2C, D

A

B

E

F

C

D

G

H

**Scene from the Legend of an Unidentified Warrior Saint.** *See page 217.*

# TENNESSEE

# MEMPHIS
*WALTER R. BROWN/RICHARD K. TANNER COLLECTION*

**THREE DOMESTIC SCENES**

A. Couple in a landscape [1a]
B. Couple and a gardener before a house [1b]
C. Interior with two women and a man at a table [1c]
Netherlands
1680–1700
White glass; two shades of vitreous paint; translucent enamels
A: 15.9 x 20.3 (6½ x 8)
B: 15.3 x 20.3 (6 x 8)
C: 14 x 20.3 (5½ x 8)
A. Four breaks; enamel flaking and abraded in areas; border cut at left and bottom
B. Surface scratches; some flaking of enamel; border cut at bottom
C. Vertical break; flaking of enamel; border cut on four sides
*Provenance:* Dealer, London
Unpublished
[1 a-c]

A

B

C

# NASHVILLE

*VANDERBILT UNIVERSITY, VANDERBILT ART COLLECTION*

## ST. BARBARA

South Lowlands
c. 1520–1530
Uneven, moderately heavy, smooth
white glass with straw marks and
elliptical bubbles; two hues of silver
stain; two shades of vitreous paint;
back-painting
Diameter: 24.5 (9⅝); with surrounds:
25.5 x 25.5 (10¹/₁₆ x 10¹/₁₆)
Three breaks, leaded; numerous
scratches and some surface abrasion;
set in square panel with 16th-century
and modern surrounds
*Provenance:* Thomas F. Flannery, Jr.,
Chicago; Edward R. Lubin, New York
*Bibliography: The Thomas F.*
*Flannery, Jr., Collection: Medieval*
*and Later Works of Art* [sale cat.,
Sotheby's, 1–2 December] (London,
1983), 162, lot no. 238, ill.; Edward R.
Lubin, *European Works of Art: A*
*Selection from the Gallery* (New
York, n. d.), no. 61.
1985.12

**Allegorical Scenes (details).** *See page 176.*

# VIRGINIA

# RICHMOND

*VIRGINIA MUSEUM OF FINE ARTS*

**CHRIST CARRYING THE CROSS**

Germany, Upper Rhineland
1480–1500
White glass; silver stain; vitreous
paint
Minor surface abrasion
Diameter: 18.4 (7¼)
*Provenance:* John Hunt, Dumleck
Bailey, Ireland
Unpublished
69.12

**HOLY KINSHIP (ANNASELBDRITT)**

Germany
1510–1520
White glass; silver stain; vitreous
paint
17.8 x 10.2 (7 x 4)
Three breaks, leaded
*Provenance:* Grosvenor Thomas,
London, to 1913; Roy Grosvenor
Thomas, New York; George D. Pratt,
Glen Cove, NY; The Metropolitan
Museum of Art, New York, to 1968
*Bibliography:* Drake (1913), pt. 1,
no. 179.
68.9.9

# WISCONSIN

# MADISON

*UNIVERSITY OF WISCONSIN–MADISON, ELVEHJEM MUSEUM OF ART*

### BAPTISM OF CHRIST FROM A SERIES OF THE LIFE OF CHRIST

South Lowlands ?
c. 1520
*Inscription:* hic est filius meus dilectu[.]
White glass; silver stain; vitreous paint; sanguine
Diameter: 22.2 (8)
One break, leaded; some loss of paint; surface rubbed
*Provenance:* Carol L. Brewster, Madison, WI
Unpublished
1972.87 Gift of Mrs. Carol L. Brewster

### FEMALE SAINT WITH A PHOENIX

South Lowlands ?
1656
*Inscription:* M W / 1656
White glass; silver stain; vitreous paint; translucent enamels
19.7 x 14 (7¾ x 5½)
Three breaks, leaded; some loss of paint; surface slightly rubbed
*Provenance:* Dr. Hugo Oelze, Amsterdam; Carol L. Brewster, Madison, WI
*Bibliography: Highly Important Objects of Art Forming the Collection of the Late Dr. M. Hugo Oelze* [sale cat., Paul Brandt, 23–26 April] (Amsterdam, 1968), 43, lot no. 85.
1972.84 Gift of Mrs. Carol L. Brewster

### ST. JOHN THE BAPTIST

South Lowlands
1671
*Inscription:* ORA PRO DONATORE 1671
White glass; silver stain; vitreous paint; sanguine
19.7 x 14 (7¾ x 5½)
Two breaks, leaded; paint somewhat rubbed in areas
*Provenance:* Dr. Hugo Oelze, Amsterdam; Carol L. Brewster, Madison, WI
*Bibliography: Highly Important Objects of Art Forming the Collection of the late Dr. M. Hugo Oelze* [sale cat., Paul Brandt, 23–26 April] (Amsterdam, 1968), 43, lot no. 85.
1972.84 Gift of Mrs. Carol L. Brewster

# ADDENDUM

**Medallion with Arms and a border.** *See page 241.*

# CALIFORNIA

# HILLSBOROUGH

*PRIVATE COLLECTION*     M.H.C.

**Note**: This collection has been forming very rapidly. The following entries represent additions made between February 1987 (see Checklist III, 95–122) and December 1989 and a few panels overlooked before. The glass will be installed shortly in a house now under construction. A separate index for these leaded panels is provided at the end of this volume.

Among these acquisitions are two of the windows from the Hearst collection that disappeared from scholarly view after the Gimbel's sale in 1941 (nos. 1020–1021). Other rediscoveries are a Swiss Welcome panel from the Lewis collection, deaccessioned in 1947/1954 from the Pennsylvania (now Philadelphia) Museum of Art (no. 935), and a Swiss Friendship panel from the Sudeley collection unaccounted for since the 1911 sale. The origin of a late French decorative cusp (no. 1067) remains unknown, but the figures are in the same style as two tracery light angels in the Axt collection, Altadena (see Checklist III, 45).

## HERALDIC PANEL WITH THE ARMS OF DE MORGAN

*Arms:* Argent a griffon rampant sable (De Morgan)
England
14th–15th centuries and 19th century
Pot metal and flashed red glass
50.2 x 43 (19¾ x 16¹⁵/₁₆)
Probably made up from different sources; borders heavily restored, upper left quadrant of shield a replacement, the rest heavily overpainted; mending leads
*Provenance:* Sir Thomas Neave, Bart., Dagnam Park, Essex ?; Grosvenor Thomas, London; Roy Grosvenor Thomas, London and New York, to 1923; S. Vernon Mann, Great Neck, NY, to 1932; Sotheby's New York, to 1986, unidentified owner
*Bibliography:* Grosvenor Thomas Stock Book I, 110–111, item no. N-92; *Fine English Furniture, Early English Stained Glass, English & Chinese Porcelains, Georgian Silver Collected by S. Vernon Mann* [sale cat., American Art Association–Anderson Galleries, 29–30 January] (New York, 1932), 67, no. 251; *European Works of Art* sale (1986), n. p., no. 180.
A 335 a

## HERALDIC BADGE OF JANE SEYMOUR, QUEEN 1536–1537

*Badge:* A round tower of two stages, above the port a hawthorn tree crowned, and on the mound above a crowned phoenix rising from flames between one red rose, one white rose, and two gillyflowers
England
1536–1553
*Inscription:* HENRY/ DOWTE NOT
White glass with silver stain; flashed red glass; pot metal stopgaps
51.3 x 30.3 (20¼ x 11⅞)
Crown and badge do not look of the same facture; many stopgaps, including top of crown, fill at edges. Etched on green glass below the left column: William Holton, July 15, 1725

*Provenance:* Nonsuch Palace ?; R. C. Lucas, near Chilworth ?; Grosvenor Thomas, London; Roy Grosvenor Thomas, London and New York, to 1923; S. Vernon Mann, Great Neck, NY, to 1932; Sotheby's New York, to 1986, unidentified owner .
*Bibliography:* Grosvenor Thomas Stock Book I, 34–35, item no. 367; *Fine English Furniture, Early English Stained Glass, English & Chinese Porcelains, Georgian Silver Collected by S. Vernon Mann* [sale cat., American Art Association–Anderson Galleries, 29–30 January] (New York, 1932), 68, no. 252; *European Works of Art* sale (1986), n. p., no. 180.
*Related Material:* Cambridge, King's College Chapel, Side-Aisle Chapel I, window 27 a2; noted in Hilary Wayment, *King's College Chapel Cambridge: The Side-Chapel Glass* (Cambridge, 1988), 68.
A 335 b

## A FINIAL WITH TWO PUTTI

France or Low Countries
c. 1540
Pot metal; white glass with silver stain and Jean Cousin; flashed red glass
39 x 28.4 (15⅜ x 11¼)
Paint rubbed
*Provenance:* Jean & Jean-Pierre Lelievre, Galerie de Chartres, 1989
*Bibliography: Ventes aux enchères publiques* [sale cat., Galerie de Chartres, 30 September–1 October, 7–8 October] (Chartres, 1989), 34, no. 1231–1236.
106/

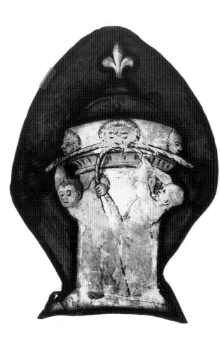

## THREE HERALDIC PANELS FOR GUILD HALLS

A. Arms of Ottel
*Arms:* Azure upon a triple mount vert a mullet of six points or (Ottel); crest: on a closed helm to sinister a demi-woman garbed parti of the colors between two buffalo horns the charge above her head; mantling of the colors
B. Arms of Werle with the scene of the Judgment of Solomon
*Arms:* Azure a wheel in chief two mullets of six points or (Werle); crest: on a closed helm to dexter between two buffalo horns the charge as in the shield (Werle); mantling of the colors
C. Arms of Wurmser with a scene of Jacob's Ladder
*Arms:* Per fess sable and or in chief two crescents argent (Wurmser); crest: on a barred helm affronté a coronet issuant a demi-woman bearing the charge of the colors between two buffalo horns; mantling of the colors
Ateliers of Swiss origin working in Alsace
France, Strasbourg, guild hall(s)
A. 1575
B. 1595
C. 1611
*Inscriptions:* A. Hans Ottel· Pfleger/ ·15· 75·
B. with woman: [.]au Sch[.]
in cartouche: Philipp Werle/ Pfleger, M.DXCV
C. Claus Jacob/ Wurmser Pf =/ leger 1611

A

A. Pot metal; white glass with silver stain, enamels, and Jean Cousin; flashed red glass
B. White glass with silver stain and enamels; flashed and abraded red glass
C. Pot metal; white glass with silver stain and enamels; flashed and abraded red glass
A. 31.8 x 23 (12½ x 9⅛)
B. 34 x 22.8 (13½ x 9)
C. 34 x 21.4 (13⅜ x 8⅜)
All have cracks and mending leads; in B there is a replacement in the crest and the figure to right is a stopgap.
*Provenance:* Sibyll Kummer-Rothenhäusler, Zurich, to 3/10/1989
Unpublished
A. 932
B. 933
C. 934

B

C

## TWO WINDOWS WITH GOTHIC CANOPIES

A. Christ before Caiphas ?
B. St. Catherine ? professing her faith
*Arms:* In lower panel (1) Azure a bend or between [charges effaced] impaling or a bend purpure between [charges effaced]
Germany, Rhineland
Mid-15th and 19th century
Pot metal; white glass with silver stain
A. 1. 59.5 x 73 (23⅜ x 28¾);
2. 36 x 73 (14³⁄₁₆ x 28¾); 3. 58 x 73.5 (22¾ x 29)
B. Almost the same as A
A. Largely modern, but with the following significant old fragments:
1. (base), purple dalmatic and shield (charges deliberately effaced); 2. (center), three heads, some repainted green pieces
B. One notable fragment with clerical heads (left panel 2)
*Provenance:* Demotte, Inc., Paris, to 11/16/1929; William Randolph Hearst, to 1944; Bishop Schremb ? of Cleveland Catholic Diocese; Archbishop Eduard Hoban, Bratenahl, OH; Raymond N. Ferreri, M.D., Bratenahl, OH, to 1989
*Bibliography:* C. W. Post Catalogue (1939), lot no. 178, art. no. 3; *Hearst sale* (1941), 133, no. 178–3

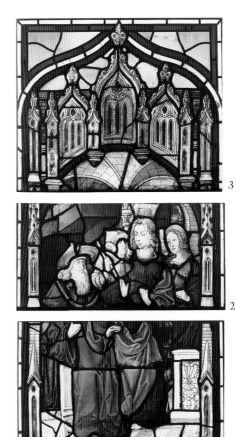

3

2

A

(A. identified as "St. Giles and His First Disciples"); *Important 18th and 19th C. European and English Furniture and Decorative Arts* [sale cat., Wolff's Auction, 30 September] (Cleveland, OH, 1989), 28, lot no. 413.
A. 1020
B. 1021

2

B

## WEDDING PANEL

*Arms:* Or three crickets proper
(unidentified)
Southern Germany
c. 1530
White glass with silver stain; flashed
and abraded pink, blue, and green
glass
34.0 x 23.5 (13⅜ x 9¼)
Spandrels and thighs of halberdier are
replacements; some mending leads
*Provenance:* Sibyll Kummer-
Rothenhäusler, Zurich, to 7/14/1989
Unpublished
1009

## HERALDIC MARRIAGE ROUNDEL

*Arms:* (LEFT) Argent a stag rampant
contourné langed and horned argent,
surmounted by a barred helm to
sinister crowned or (? von Kruft);
crest: issuant from a coronet a demi-
stag rampant or holding an orb argent,
mantling of the colors
(RIGHT) Argent three flabella [or
broom-heads ?] argent (sic),
surmounted by a barred helm to
dexter (? Schlossgen); crest: two vols
affronté charged as the shield;
mantling of the color
(BELOW) or a housemark sable
(unidentified)
Germany, Lower Rhineland ?
1572
*Inscription:* Martin von kruft / genant
krudener derol/ Rechten doctor /
S. Jacop elisabeth /und / Schlossgens /
sein husfraw . / Ao dñi 1·5·7·2
White glass with silver stain
Diameter: 32.9 (12¹⁵⁄₁₆)
Shatter crack, string-leaded; despite
sequential numbering of inscription
pieces in paint (1a–8a) at least two are
out of order; inscription may not
identify arms
*Provenance:* Sibyll Kummer-
Rothenhäusler, Zurich, to 4/7/1989
Unpublished
990

## HERALDIC PANEL OF PARISH PRIESTS WITH SECULAR SCENES

*Arms:* (CENTER) Argent a boar's head
sable langued gules, toothed and
crested or (von Reuschach); crest: a
barred helm to dexter surmounted by
a boar's head argent langued gules;
mantling of the colors
clockwise from top right:
1. Per pale or and argent a housemark
counterchanged; crest: a wine cask
proper (Spach)
2. Gules a cart wheel or; crest: on a
closed helm to dexter a demi-man
holding a baton garbed parti or and
argent; mantling of the colors (Pflu.?)
3. Or a falcon proper beaked, crested
and armed argent (Harkh)
4. Gules a grozing tool and a soldering
iron crosswise argent; crest: three
*Noppenbecher* (glasses) or (Sebel)
Germany
1574
*Inscription:* upper right: Ich Bedarff /
Wermets / [. . .]tlin thu[. . .]/ [. . .]
hoch zuo / heu. Katzbeiss / die mauss
/aus Beis/ mich nit/
on table edge: Rus Vom Vogel
on shields: 1. Iohannes Spach Pfarherr
zur obern Schweing[.] oben
2. Jerg Pflu[.]/ geistlicher ver[. . .]lter
uber Bau[.]/ pfarhe[.]
3. Jerg Hackh Der Allt Vogt [. . .] herr
Anno Dni. 15.74.
4. [.]ohannes Sebel pfarherr zuo
hechlen
on cartouche: Hanns Rafahel Von/
Reuschach zur Atzach./ 15.74

Pot metal; white glass with silver stain and Jean Cousin; flashed and abraded red
44.6 x 33 (17⁹/₁₆ x 13)
Two replacements, a few small stopgaps; edge-mended cracks and mending leads
*Provenance:* Unidentified owner, Dorotheum, 1922; V. M. Walton, Durham, England, to 1927; James R. Herbert Boone, Baltimore, MD; Trustees of Johns Hopkins University, Baltimore, MD
*Bibliography: Wertvolle Italienische Skulpturen des XIV. bis XVII. Jahrhunderts, Alte Gemälde, Kunstgewerbe, Schweizer Glasscheiben, Englische Farbstiche* [sale cat., Dorotheum, 8 April] (Vienna, 1922), 23, ill.; *Rugs, Textiles, Furniture, Paintings, Silver, Porcelain, Pewter, Arms, Bronzes, Miniatures, Snuff Boxes & Other Objets d'Art. . .from the Collections of Mrs. William Faversham, New York City; Mr. V. M. Walton, Durham, England; Mrs. Gardiner Washburn, Brookline, Mass. & the Stock of the Horn of Plenty* [sale cat., Anderson Galleries, 5–7 May] (New York, 1927), 109, lot no. 654; *European Works of Art* sale (1988), n. p., no. 51, ill.
905

## HERALDIC PANEL OF JOHANN THOMAS VON SPAUR, BISHOP OF BRIXEN

*Arms:* Quarterly: 1 gules a lamb trippant argent nimbed or, holding a pennant argent a cross or (Abbey of Brixen); 2 and 3 quarterly argent a lion rampant gules holding a mazer or and per band argent and gules a mullet of six points counterchanged (von Spaur); 4 argent a griffon displayed queue forché armed or and charged with a crozier or fesswise (Brixen Domkapitel); surmounted by a bishop's mitre, crozier and orphreys argent and or
Attributed to an Augsburg atelier
Southern Germany
1580
*Inscription:* IOHANN THOMAS VON GOTTES GENADEN BISCHOFFE ZV BRICHSEN
1580
White glass with silver stain and enamel; flashed and abraded red glass
Diameter: 31 (12³/₁₆)
Some mending leads and repaired cracks
*Provenance:* Fritz Dold, Zurich, to 4/7/1989
Unpublished
992

## ARMS OF MICHEL BRACKENHOFER WITH A SCENE OF THE ANNUNCIATION

*Arms:* Azure upon a triple mount or a hound argent collared and langued or (Brackenhofer); crest: on a closed helm to sinister a demi-hound charged as the shield; mantling of the colors
Southern Germany, Waldsee
1586
*Inscription:* on scroll at top: Ave/ Maria Gra[. . .]/ plena do/ tecum
in cartouche: Michel Bracken[.]of/ er dieser Zeit Ampt/ man dess Gotsshaus/ Waldseze 1586
White glass with silver stain, enamels, and Jean Cousin; flashed and abraded red glass
34 x 21.7 (13³/₈ x 8⁹/₁₆)
Mending leads
*Provenance:* Sibyll Kummer-Rothenhäusler, Zurich, to 3/10/1989
Unpublished
955

## ARMS OF HANS NEUSCHELLER WITH A BATTLE SCENE

*Arms:* Per fess, in chief per pale or and azure a demi-man counterchanged holding in his dexter hand a bell or and in his sinister hand a napping brush, in base barry of three sable or and azure (Neuscheller); crest: on a closed helm to dexter a demi-man charged as the shield; mantling of the colors
Germany, Reutlingen
1591 ?
*Inscription:* Hans Neuscheller der/ zeitt der tuocher altmaister./ 1591. (essentially modern)
White glass with silver stain, enamels, and Jean Cousin; flashed red and pink glass
30.7 x 21.5 (12½ x 8½)
All but "z" and "1" of inscription replaced; some cracks; mending leads
*Provenance:* Sibyll Kummer-Rothenhäusler, Zurich, to 3/10/1989
Unpublished
962

## ARMS OF SIMON WEINMAN BETWEEN LIFE AND DEATH, WITH A SCENE OF MUSICIANS PLAYING

*Arms:* Per fess sable and or on a triple mount or a demi-man holding a billhook (Weinman); crest: a closed helm to dexter surmounted by a charge as the field between two buffalo horns; mantling of the colors
Germany, Heilbronn
1598
*Inscription:* above shield: MORTALIS IM MORTALIS
in cartouche: ·VIVE DIV. SED DEO·/ Simon Weinman der/ Jünger Burger und des / Kleinen Raths zu/ Hailbron· 1598.
White glass with silver stain, enamels, and Jean Cousin; flashed and abraded red glass
31 x 21.7 (12³⁄₁₆ x 8½)
Cracks and mending leads elsewhere
*Provenance:* Sibyll Kummer-Rothenhäusler, Zurich, to 3/10/1989
Unpublished
952

## HERALDIC ROUNDEL WITH THE CREST OF THE CITY OF COLOGNE

*Crest:* A closed helm to sinister with a coronet ermine surmounted by a lion passant or, langued gules, holding a crest gules charged with three crowns or, plumed vert; mantling gules and argent (City of Cologne)
Germany, Cologne
16th–17th century
White glass with silver stain, Jean Cousin, and enamels
Diameter: 21.5 (8½)
*Provenance:* Sibyll Kummer-Rothenhäusler, Zurich, to 4/1987
Unpublished
*Related Material:* A similar roundel illustrated in *Aus Schloss E. Sr. Erlaucht des Grafen K. zu E., Glasgemälde aus Fürstlichem Besitz, Nachlass Dr. H. Wagner, Bad Soden/ Nachlässe R . . . u. S . . . , Jüdische Kultgegenstände, Moderne gemälde eines Frankfurter Sammlers und Anderer Besitz* [sale cat., Hugo Helbing, 21–23 June] (Frankfurt am Main, 1932), 19, no. 220, ill.
405

## HERALDIC ROUNDEL OF JOHANN FABER

*Arms:* Per fess argent and gules, in chief a ? thunderbolt azure in base a housemark sable between two mullets or (Faber ?); crest: on a helm affronté a bear sejent holding a forked pennant of the colors; mantling of the colors

Southern Germany
Early 17th century
*Inscription:* IOHANN CHRISTIAN FABER / P T VIERMANN I.27
White glass with silver stain and enamels
Diameter: 15 (5⅞)
Mending leads
*Provenance:* Sibyll Kummer-Rothenhäusler, Zurich, to 8/1988
Unpublished
916

## A LESSON IN FAMILY UNITY: AESOP'S FABLE OF THE BOUND STICKS

*Arms:* (LEFT) Azure in chief two mullets of six points or, on a pile inverted or a triple mount vert surmounted by talons and a cross azure [? or a cross rising from four talons], (unidentified); crest: on a closed helm to sinister a demi-man; mantling of the colors
(RIGHT) As the first (replaced)
Nüscheler atelier from Switzerland
Germany, Munich
1621
*Inscription:* above: Kein besser ding uff erd man findt/ Dan wan dbrüder ein muthiga sind/ Durch zwidrachtaber gond sy zgrund / Wies uns die gchichten machend kund
below: Hans Heinrich Zäller diener/ der Kilchen Schwamendinger/ und profisor der Latinsch schul zür/ ich und Staffen-Zäller beid gebrüd/ und Hans Riva [.]alt Bürger Zürich / ·1621·
Pot metal; white glass with silver stain, enamels, and Jean Cousin; flashed and abraded red glass
33 x 22.5 (13 x 8⅞)
Right shield replaced
*Provenance:* Sibyll Kummer-Rothenhäusler, Zurich, to 8/2/1989
Unpublished
1002

## HERALDIC ALLIANCE ROUNDEL OF VON IMHOFF AND LÖFFELHOLTZ

*Arms:* (LEFT) Gules a *Seelöwe* queue forché or (von Imhoff)
(RIGHT) Quarterly 1 and 4 or a lamb trippant argent langued tenné; 2 and 3 argent on a bend azure an artillary piece ? argent (Löffelholtz)
Germany, Nuremberg
1640 or 1646
*Inscription:* .I.I.H./ .164?.
White glass with silver stain, enamels, and Jean Cousin
Diameter: 24.3 (9⁹⁄₁₆)
Mending leads
*Provenance:* Sibyll Kummer-Rothenhäusler, Zurich, to 10/11/1987
Unpublished
*Related Material:* A related von Imhoff alliance roundel is in the Claire Mendel collection, Miami Beach, FL (Checklist II, 45; Checklist III, 310). The paired arms belong to Haller of Hallerstein.
677

## HERALDIC MARRIAGE PANEL

*Arms:* (LEFT SHIELD) Or a chevron argent between three oak branches leafed and fructed vert two and one (unidentified); (RIGHT OVAL) Or three bells argent two and one (unidentified); crest: above a barred helm to dexter a cross argent; mantling of the colors
North Lowlands
c. 1680
*Inscription:* R[. . .] [. . .]e
White glass with silver stain and enamels
58 x 55.3 (22¾ x 21¾)
Cracks; mending leads; inscription missing
*Provenance:* Sotheby's Amsterdam, unidentified owner
*Bibliography: Decorative Arts, Including a Private Collection of Liègeois Furniture and Automata and Mechanical Instruments* [sale cat., Sotheby Mark Van Waay B.V., 11–12 May] (Amsterdam, 1987), 26, no. 117.
578

## MEDALLION WITH THE ARMS OF LEUW, HORUTTINER AND ?YLER, AND A BORDER OF WINE-MAKING BEARS

*Arms:* (TOP) Azure a lion rampant or (Leuv); (LOWER LEFT) Or a demi-bear sable rampant contourné on two mounts holding a housemark sable (Horutener); (LOWER RIGHT) Gules on a triple mount vert a plowshare argent (?yler)
Switzerland, St. Gallen or Appenzell
16th century, early
*Inscription:*
marte·leuw·Iacob·horüttiner· hanss·[. .]yler.
Pot metal; white glass with silver stain; flashed and abraded blue and red glass
Diameter: 23.2 (9⅛)
One stopgap; pitting on front surface
*Provenance:* Sibyll Kummer-Rothenhäusler, Zurich, to 3/10/1989
Unpublished
954

*Enlarged illustration page 232*

## WELCOME PANEL WITH ARMS OF THE SCHWYZER FAMILY

*Arms:* Gules a fish naiant in chief a cross argent (Schwyzer)
Attributed to Brandolph Roter of Lucerne
Switzerland
16th century, early
*Inscription:* 1537
Pot metal; white glass with silver stain; flashed and abraded red glass
34 x 23.3 (13⅜ x 9⅛)
Shield a replacement; inscription may be stopgap; some mending leads
*Provenance:* Dr. F. W. Lewis; Mary Lewis; Pennsylvania Museum of Art ('07.55), to 1947/1954; Sibyll Kummer-Rothenhäusler, Zurich, to 3/10/1989
*Bibliography:* Charles E. Dana, "Stained Glass (First Part)," *Pennsylvania Museum Bulletin* 19 (July 1907), 41–45; Arthur E. Bye, *Catalogue of the Collection of Stained and Painted Glass in the Pennsylvania Museum* (Philadelphia, 1925), 64–65, no. 41, ill.
935

## CRUCIFIXION WITH MARY AND ST. JOHN, AND A SCENE OF CATTLE HERDING

*Arms:* Gules a cross argent (unidentified)
Switzerland, central region
1550 ?
*Inscription:* on cross: INRI; below: Hanns Moss/ Anno Dni 1550
Pot metal; white glass with silver stain; flashed and abraded blue and red glass
32.8 x 21.6 (12⅞ x 8½)
The inscription may not belong with the scene(s)
*Provenance:* Sibyll Kummer-Rothenhäusler, Zurich, to 7/14/1989
Unpublished
1003

## WELCOME PANEL WITH A SCENE OF THE ANNUNCIATION

*Arms:* (LEFT) Argent an arrow piercing a pretzel and a crescent or (unidentified)
(RIGHT) Sable bordered or a pitchfork between, in chief, a fleur-de-lys or and a cross argent (unidentified)
Switzerland, central region
16th century, second half
*Inscription:* scroll, top left: AVE MARIA GRAT PLENA DNS TEC
Pot metal; white glass with silver stain; flashed and abraded red glass
33.2 x 23 (13¹/₁₆ x 9)
Minor replacements to sides, stopgap between shields; cracks; mending leads; corrosion on interior surface
*Provenance:* Sibyll Kummer-Rothenhäusler, Zurich, to 7/14/1989
Unpublished
937

## HERALDIC ROUNDEL

*Arms:* Per fess or and sable, in chief a cock sable wattled and beaked or (unidentified), in base a demi-wheel or (unidentified); crest: over a closed helm to sinister a cock between two buffalo horns; mantling of the colors
Germany, Nuremberg ?
c. 1550–1570
White glass with silver stain; pot metal and white glass with enamels in the surround do not belong with the roundel
25 x 20.8 (9⅞ x 8¼)
*Provenance:* Sibyll Kummer-Rothenhäusler, Zurich, to 3/10/1989
Unpublished
947

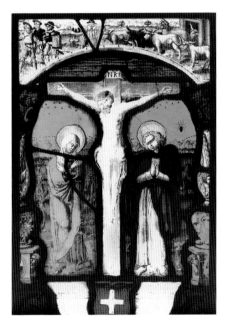

## ARMS OF JAGGY WITH A SCENE OF THE SACRIFICE OF ISAAC

*Arms:* Azure on a mount vert the letter I twice repeated in chief a mullet of six points or (Jaggy)
Switzerland
1570
*Inscription:* Jacob·Jagy·1570
Pot metal; white glass with silver stain and enamels; flashed red glass
33.6 x 22.2 (13¼ x 8¾)
Cracks; mending leads
*Provenance:* H. C. Honegger, New York and Feldbach; private collection; Sibyll Kummer-Rothenhäusler, Zurich
*Bibliography:* Silvia Klöti-Grob, *Katalog Glasmalerien Sammlung H. C. Honegger, New York/Feldbach* (Zurich, 1971), no. 4, ill; Paul Bösch, "Schweizerische Glasgemälde un Ausland, Privatsammlung von Herrn H. C. Honegger in New York," in *Archives Héraldiques Suisses, Annuaire* (Lausanne, 1953), 3–4, no. 10.
978

## TWO PANELS WITH SCENES FROM THE LIFE OF JACOB AND THE ARMS OF BALDTNER

A. Jacob wrestling with the angel and the arms of Ambrose Baldtner
B. Jacob's dream of the ladder and the arms of Hanns Baldtner
*Arms:* A. Or a housemark sable in chief an annulet (Baldtner)
B. Or a housemark sable in chief two annulets (Baldtner)
Switzerland
1574
*Inscriptions:* A. on Saint's desk: AMBROS/ IUS·
on arch: geb gott glück mitt freydenn
on cartouche: AMBROSY · BALDTNER/ ·ANNO··1574·
B. on arch: gott Verhütt mein Vnglück
on cartouche: ·HANNS··BALDTNER/ ·ANNO·II··1574·
White glass with silver stain, enamel, and sanguine
33 x 22.2 (13 x 8¾) each
*Provenance:* Sibyll Kummer-Rothenhusler, Zurich, to 3/10/1989
Unpublished
A. 938
B. 939

A

B

**BAPTISM OF CHRIST AND SCENES
OF JOHN THE BAPTIST AND JOHN
THE EVANGELIST WITH THE
ARMS OF WUSCHT**

*Arms:* Azure a housemark between
two mullets of six points or (Wuscht)
Switzerland, St. Gallen (Rhineland)
1582
*Inscription:* A[..]mo Johannes Wuscht
+ 1582
White glass with silver stain and
enamels; flashed and abraded red glass
31.8 x 22.8 (12½ x 9)
Cracks; mending leads; part of
inscription is replaced
*Provenance:* Sibyll Kummer-
Rothenhäusler, Zurich, to 3/10/1989
Unpublished
966

**WELCOME PANEL WITH THE
ARMS OF LIENERT AND A SCENE
OF MILLERS AT WORK**

*Arms:* Azure a plowshare argent
(Lienert)
Northeastern Switzerland
1583
*Inscription:* Jacob Lienertt Und Anna
Grienert Sin ee frouw 1583
Pot metal; white glass with silver
stain, enamels, and Jean Cousin;
flashed red glass
32.5 x 22.2 (12¾ x 8¾)
Some mending leads
*Provenance:* Sibyll Kummer-
Rothenhäusler, Zurich, to 8/2/1989
Unpublished
1004

**WELCOME PANEL**

*Arms:* Or a housemark sable
(unidentified)
Switzerland, central region
1584
*Inscription:* Fry· im· wald: und ana
Bi[...]/ ·1·5·8·4· sein ee fraw. ist
Pot metal; white glass with silver
stain, flashed red glass
32.3 x 22.3 (12¾ x 8¾)
Lower corners appear to be
replacements; a few cracks and
mending leads
*Provenance:* Sibyll Kummer-
Rothenhäusler, Zurich, to 3/10/1989
Unpublished
940

## CLOTHING THE NAKED, ONE OF THE ACTS OF MERCY, WITH ARMS OF GUILD MEMBERS

*Arms:* from left: 1. Gules upon a triple mount vert a barred helm surmounted by a crescent and a mullet of six points or (Ryter)
2. Gules upon a triple mount vert a tau cross or (Trichtinger)
3. Gules upon a triple mount a hammer and an arrow crosswise surmounted by three bezants or (Threchsler)
4. Or upon a triple mount vert a cross issuant from its base two leaves over all a vine sable (Balber)
Switzerland, Zurich
1585
*Inscriptions:* cartouche above:
Nakend und bloss bist du har kom/ hast nüt mit dir in dwelt gnan/ Drum thū kein kleid armen sparer/ Nakend und bloss müst wider faren
above shields: 1. Hanns Rytte[.]
2. o[.] Thrich[.]inger·
3. Caspar Threchsler·
4. A[.]dres Balber· 1585·
White glass with silver stain and enamels; flashed and abraded red glass
31.7 x 21.5 (12½ x 8½)
Cracks; mending leads; shield of Ryter is replacement
*Provenance:* Sibyll Kummer-Rothenhäusler, Zurich, to 7/14/1989
Unpublished
936

## FRIENDSHIP PANEL OF FRYE AND GRÜNDELER WITH A SCENE OF COW HERDING

*Arms:* (LEFT) Or a kettle sable (Frye)
(RIGHT) Gules a butcher's knife argent (Gründler)
Eastern Switzerland
1593
*Inscription:* Jacob Frye Heinrych Gründeler 1593
Pot metal; white glass with silver stain; flashed and abraded red glass
35 x 23 (13¾ x 9)
Replacements left and right in top scene, which may not belong
*Provenance:* Sibyll Kummer-Rothenhäusler, Zurich, to 3/10/1989
Unpublished
941

## DOUBLE WELCOME PANEL WITH ARMS OF ZIENDEL AND BRÄNWALD

*Arms:* (LEFT) Or a housemark sable (Ziendel)
(RIGHT) Gules a billhook argent and or within a circle sable (Bränwald)
Switzerland
1593
*Inscription:* Jacob Ziendel Kilch[..] iger/ und Hans Bränwald 1593
White glass with silver stain, enamels, and Jean Cousin; flashed red and pink glass
31.2 x 22.2 (12⅛ x 8¾)
Cracks; mending leads
*Provenance:* Sibyll Kummer-Rothenhäusler, Zurich, to 3/10/1989
Unpublished
942

## ADORATION OF THE MAGI WITH SCENES FROM THE INFANCY OF CHRIST

Switzerland
1596
*Inscription:* above: Die wisse komendtt uss morgeland/ [...] büttlehem gar unbekandt/ zu suchen das kind jesum cristt/ Der ein kunig der Jude gebore 1st
on cartouche: Casperr Romanus Bässller allt/ ter landvogt in ober vnd nider/ durgeuw · frouw margretta ·mul/lerin sin· egmachell 1·5·9·6· / HK (unidentified monogram)
Pot metal; white glass with silver stain and enamels; flashed and abraded red glass
38 x 27.5 (15 x 10⅞)
Stopgaps in place of shields, lower left and right and in Virgin's skirt; lower inscription may not belong
*Provenance:* Sotheby's, London, to 1988
*Bibliography: European Works of Art, Armour, Furniture and Tapestries* [sale cat., Sotheby's, 25 November] (New York, 1988), lot no. 221.
728

## WELCOME PANEL OF OFFRION WICK

*Arms:* Or a housemark sable (WicK)
Switzerland
1599
*Inscription:* Offrion Wick Selhafft zu/ Buts[.]vgl und Toyna Hugentobleri / Sin Ehgemahel 1599
Pot metal; white glass with silver stain, enamels, and Jean Cousin
33 x 22.3 (13 x 8¾)
Some mending leads and cracks
*Provenance:* Sibyll Kummer-Rothenhäusler, Zurich, to 3/10/1989
Unpublished
976

## SUSANNA AND THE ELDERS WITH THE ARMS OF STOLL AND UEBERLIN

*Arms:* (LEFT) Or a stag's antler sable impaled by sable three mullets of six points or 1 and 2 (Stoll)
(RIGHT) Vert upon a triple mount a ? demi-gourd or in chief a cross argent (Uberlin)
Switzerland
16th century
*Inscription:* scroll left: Heinrich Stoll
scroll center: Und
scroll right: Susan[.] Uberlin sin huss frouw
White glass with silver stain and enamels; flashed red, green, and blue glass
33.2 x 23.5 (13⅛ x 9¼)
Cracks; mending leads; some replacements
*Provenance:* Sibyll Kummer-Rothenhäusler, Zurich, to 3/10/1989
Unpublished
951

## ARMS OF VON HALLWYL AND RUTNER AND A HUNTING SCENE

*Arms:* (LEFT) Or two vols affronté (von Hallwyl); crest: on a barred helm to sinister two vols argent; mantling of the colors
(RIGHT) Azure bordered gules and or escalloped a crescent or (Rutner); crest: on a barred helm to dexter a crescent issuant a demi-man in armor; mantling of the colors; a fish hauriant and a hooded falcon perched on an amice with a sword in saltire hung by a guige above
Switzerland
1600
*Inscription:* Hans Caspar von und zu Hallwyl und Frouw/ Susana von Hallwyl ein geborne Rutnere/ von Wyl sin Elicher Gemahell.1600.
Pot metal; white glass with silver stain, enamels, and Jean Cousin; flashed and abraded red glass
32 x 22.4 (12⅝ x 8¾)
A few mending leads
*Provenance:* Sibyll Kummer-Rothenhäusler, Zurich, to 10/11/1987
Unpublished
672

## MARRIAGE PANEL OF FRIEDRICH FRIES AND REGULA TEUCHER

*Arms:* (LEFT) Gules on a triple mount a demi-stag rampant or (Fries); crest: on a closed helm to sinister a charge as the shield (modern); mantling of the colors
(RIGHT) Sable in chief two mullets of six points or, on a pile inverted ? or a horseshoe sable surmounted by a cross argent (Teucher)
AR monogram; attributed to the Murer workshop
Switzerland ?
1605
*Inscription:* [.]ans heinrich fries dis ser[...] H Wyrtt Alt/ [...] zur Lindenn und Regula Teucherin / Syn Egemehell Anno 1605 AR
Pot metal; white glass with silver stain, enamels, and Jean Cousin; flashed and abraded red glass
31.8 x 22 (12½ x 8⅞)
Some replacements, including left crest and lower corner
*Provenance:* Sibyll Kummer-Rothenhäusler, Zurich, to 7/14/1989
Unpublished
1001

## A FAMILY WITH THEIR ARMS AND A SCENE OF THE CRUCIFIXION

*Arms:* Gules a housemark sable (unidentified)
Central Switzerland
1608
*Inscription:* Den Schiltt Git Fräst [.]anall und Syn huss frou/ Drina Steineri Dem Joss Zum Källerr ·1608·
White glass with silver stain and Jean Cousin; flashed and abraded red glass
36 x 28.5 (14¼ x 11¼)
Repaired cracks; mending leads
*Provenance:* Private collection, France, to 1924; Sibyll Kummer-Rothenhäusler, Zurich, to 3/10/1989
Unpublished
943

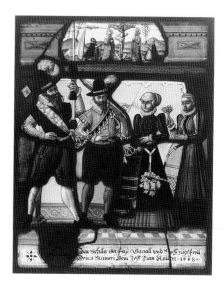

## HERALDIC PANEL WITH THE ARMS OF NICHOLAS KILCHBERGER OF NIDAU

*Arms:* Azure on a triple mount vert a church argent roofed gules; crest: a closed helm to dexter surmounted by a charge as the shield between two buffalo horns; mantling of the colors
Switzerland, Canton of Bern
1610
*Inscription:* H. Niclaus Kilchberger disser Zitt Landtvogt zu Nidouw.
1610:
White glass with silver stain, enamel, and Jean Cousin; flashed and abraded red glass
29 x 20 (11⅜ x 7⅞)
Edge-mended cracks; mending leads
*Provenance:* Sibyll Kummer-Rothenhäusler, Zurich, to 3/10/1989
Unpublished
944

## WELCOME PANEL OF LUDWIG PFISTER, WITH SCENES OF MILKING AND CHEESE MAKING

*Arms:* (LEFT) Or a triple mount vert surmounted by a flensing knife ? argent (Pfister ?) (RIGHT) Or a plough share argent (unidentified)
Switzerland
1610 ?
*Inscription:* Ludwig Pfister au Salberg und anna ho[. . .]ry sin E[. . .] 16[. . .]
Pot metal; white glass with silver stain, enamels, and Jean Cousin; flashed red glass
33.6 x 20.3 (13¼ x 8)
Many stopgaps; repaired breaks
*Provenance:* Sibyll Kummer-Rothenhäusler, Zurich, to 7/14/1989
Unpublished
1005

## THE FOUNDING OF SWITZERLAND AND WILLIAM TELL AIMING AT THE APPLE ON HIS SON'S HEAD WITH THE ARMS OF BELICKAN AND HAFFNER

*Arms:* (LEFT) Azure a fess argent in chief a mullet of six points or in base a mullet of six points argent (Belickan); crest: a demi-angel to sinister garbed in the colors (RIGHT) Azure on a triple mount vert a housemark or (Haffner); crest: a demi-angel garbed or
Switzerland, Zurich
1625
*Inscriptions:* above: Die Drey hand Eyn Bispiel gäben/ Dem Sollen nach ir al sampt läben/ Euch zamen Halten in den Dingen/ Dass gmeiner nutz Er thuo[.] Bringen
below: Cunradt Belickan / und Froneg Haff/nerin sein Ehgmah/el
·Anno·1625·
Pot metal; white glass with silver stain, enamels, and Jean Cousin; flashed red glass
33 x 22.5 (13⅛ x 8⅞)
Corrosion and some paint loss in the lower half; many mending leads
*Provenance:* Sibyll Kummer-Rothenhäusler, Zurich, to 3/10/1989
Unpublished
974

## FRIENDSHIP PANEL OF THE SCHUOLER BROTHERS WITH A SCENE OF TANNING

*Arms:* Or a housemark sable in chief a tanners knife argent and or (Schuoler)
Central Switzerland
1631
*Inscription:* Peter und Hans/ Schuoler gebrieder· 1631
White glass with silver stain, enamels, and sanguine; flashed red glass
34.2 x 20.6 (13½ x 8⅛)
*Provenance:* Lord Sudeley, Toddington Castle, Gloucestershire, to 1911; Sibyll Kummer-Rothenhäusler, Zurich, to 3/10/1989
*Bibliography:* Hans Lehman, *Sammlung Lord Sudeley, Toddington Castle, Schweizer Glasmalereien vorwiegend des XVI. und XVII. Jahrhunderts* [sale cat., Galerie Helbing, 4 October] (Munich, 1911), 76, no. 101.
945

## ALLIANCE PANEL WITH THE ARMS OF WYSS AND ERNI

*Arms:* (LEFT) Quarterly; 1 and 4 or a fleur-de-lys azure; 2 and 3 azure a mullet of six points or; crest: a closed helm to sinister issuant a demi-man garbed parti of the colors holding a fleur-de-lys and a mullet (Wyss); mantling of the colors
(RIGHT) Argent on a triple mount vert two roses leafed proper flowered purpure seeded or (Erni); crest: on a closed helm to dexter a demi-man belted or holding a rose in each hand; mantling argent and purpure
Attributed to the Nüscheler workshop
Switzerland, Trogen (Appenzell)
1636
*Inscriptions:* beside Time: Schick dich zur/ hinfart
in cartouche: H. Ha[...] Melchior [.]uss/ burge[.] Zurich gewessner[.]/ Pfa[...] Zu [.]att und Ell[.]/ [...]and Glarus 1630/ [.]er zeit Pfarer zu/ Trogen in Unseren Rode/ dess lands Appenzell/ Fr. Elssbetha Ern[.]n/ sein Ehlicher gemahel/ ANNO 1636
Pot metal; white glass with silver stain, enamels, and Jean Cousin; flashed and abraded red glass
29.2 x 20.3 (11½ x 8)
Upper part of panel missing; cracks; mending leads
*Provenance:* Sibyll Kummer-Rothenhäusler, Zurich, to 3/10/1989
Unpublished
967

## UNIDENTIFIED ARMS WITH THE FIGURES OF JUSTICE AND FORTITUDE AND CLAUDE CASTELLA AND HIS WIFE

*Arms:* Quarterly, 1 and 4 sable in base the letter B fesswise or in chief a cross argent (unidentified); 2 and 4 or a bull's head sable, ringed or, between two mullets of six points or (unidentified); crest: on a closed helm affronté a crown issuant a demi-fool bearing upon his breast a bend sinister sable charged with a crescent between two mullets of six points or; mantling of the colors
Switzerland, Fribourg
1638 and 19th century
*Inscription:* CLAVDE CASTELLA LIEV/ TTENANT DALBEUVE ET/ CATHERINE SA FEMME· / 1638
Pot metal; white glass with silver stain, enamels, and Jean Cousin; flashed and abraded red glass
33.8 x 28.2 (13⁵⁄₁₆ x 11⅛)
Arms do not correspond to donors and may not belong; cracks; mending leads; upper part of panel missing
*Provenance:* Unidentified owner, Dorotheum, 1922; V. M. Walton, Durham, England, to 1927; James R. Herbert Boone, Baltimore, MD; Trustees of Johns Hopkins University, Baltimore, MD
*Bibliography:* *Wertvolle Italienische Skulpturen des XIV. bis XVII. Jahrhunderts, Alte Gemälde, Kunstgewerbe, Schweizer*

*Glasscheiben, Englische Farbstiche* [sale cat., Dorotheum, 8 April] (Vienna, 1922), 23, ill.; *Rugs, Textiles, Furniture, Paintings, Silver, Porcelain, Pewter, Arms, Bronzes, Miniatures, Snuff Boxes & other Objets d'Art. . .from the Collections of Mrs. William Faversham, New York City; Mr. V. M. Walton, Durham, England; Mrs. Gardiner Washburn, Brookline, Mass. & the stock of the Horn of Plenty* [sale cat., Anderson Galleries, 5–7 May] (New York, 1927), 109, lot no. 654; *European Works of Art* sale (1988), n. p., no. 52, ill.
907

## THE ANNUNCIATION, WITH DEATH AND ST. FRIDOLIN, ST. SEBASTIAN, AND THE ARMS OF SCHALCH

*Arms:* Azure a mill wheel or (Schalch)
Switzerland, Tuggen, Canton Schwyz
1642
*Inscription:* Fridly Schalch von Duggen/ und Anna Maria Bruheni/ Sin Egemahel ·Anno ·1·6·4·2·/ S.R (? monogram)
Pot metal; white glass with silver stain, enamels, and Jean Cousin; flashed and abraded red glass
33 x 22 (13 x 8⅜)
*Provenance:* Sibyll Kummer-Rothenhäusler, Zurich, to 3/10/1989
Unpublished
975

## FRIENDSHIP PANEL WITH A SCENE OF A KING RETELLING THE FABLE OF THE BOUND STICKS TO HIS SONS

*Arms:* (LEFT) Azure a fleur-de-lys or (Casper Laser ?); (RIGHT) Or a phoenix displayed sable, in chief H L (Hans Laser ?)
Switzerland
1647
*Inscription:* Caspar L[. . .] und / Hans La[. . .] [. . .]brud / [. . .] zu Lu[. . .] sch[. . .] / [. . .] 1647
Pot metal; white glass with silver stain, enamels, and Jean Cousin; flashed red glass
32.7 x 24 (13³⁄₁₆ x 9⁷⁄₁₆)
Left shield may be replacement; many mending leads
*Provenance:* James R. Herbert Boone, Baltimore, MD; Trustees of Johns Hopkins University, Baltimore, MD
*Bibliography:* European Works of Art sale (1988), n. p., no. 48.
*Related Material:* Duplicate panel in Los Angeles County Museum, 45.21.50 (Checklist III, 79)
900

## MARRIAGE PANEL OF MEYER AND WYDLER, WITH FAITH, HOPE, AND CHARITY

*Arms:* (LEFT) Purpure three potted flowers argent leaved vert and a pitchfork argent (Meyer ?); (RIGHT) Gules ? in base a demi-mill wheel in chief a ladder per fess surmounted by a tripple mount vert (Wydler ?)
Signed W
Switzerland
1656
*Inscriptions:* above: Er kumdt zum Vatterlnt unt gnad / vor Gott unn dir ich grundigt hab / gar willig er int als ver gab
below: Christoffel Mey-/er und fr. Marg-/reta Wydleri sein / Ehegmachel 1656 / W
Pot metal; white glass with silver stain and enamels; flashed red glass
21 x 16.2 (8¼ x 6⅜)
Two stopgaps; repaired cracks
*Provenance:* Sibyll Kummer-Rothenhäusler, Zurich, to 7/14/1989
Unpublished
1007

## HERALDIC PANEL OF VON WATTENWYL AND STEIGER WITH A SCENE OF DAVID FIGHTING GOLIATH

*Arms:* Gules three vols argent 2 and 1 (von Wattenwyl); impaled gules a triple mount or issuant a demi-goat rampant horned and hoofed or (Steiger); crest: (dexter) upon a barred helm to sinister a demi-woman crowned between two vols, (sinister) upon a barred helm to dexter a charge as the shield; mantling of the colors
Switzerland, Bern
1664
*Inscription:* Jr. Vincentz Ma/ ximilian von Wat/ tenwyl und F. Magdale/ na Steiger syn Ehg : 1664
White glass with silver stain and enamels; flashed and abraded red glass
27.5 x 19 (10⅞ x 7½)
Stopgaps bottom right; cracks, mending leads; upper scene retouched
*Provenance:* Sibyll Kummer-Rothenhäusler, Zurich, to 3/10/1989
Unpublished
946

## WELCOME PANEL OF MULLER AND LANDER WITH ST. GEORGE SLAYING THE DRAGON

*Arms:* (LEFT) Purpure a housemark between the letters I and M or (Muller); (RIGHT) Azure on a triple mount vert a pretzel or (Lander)
Wolfgang Spengler (active c. 1624–1678)
Switzerland
1666
*Inscription:* w.sp / Jorg Muller und Mad/ lenna Landerin sein/ Ehelich usfrauw · 1666
White glass with silver stain, enamels, and Jean Cousin
33.8 x 22.8 (13⁵⁄₁₆ x 8⅞)
Cracks; mending leads
*Provenance:* Sibyll Kummer-Rothenhäusler, Zurich, to 3/10/1989
Unpublished
956

## JOSEPH SOLD BY HIS BROTHERS WITH THE ARMS OF BURGSTALLER AND BOSSERT

*Arms:* (LEFT) Azure on a triple mount vert a castle argent surmounted by a mullet of six points or (Burgstaller); crest: on a barred helm to dexter a triple mount surmounted by a mullet of six points or; mantling azure and gules; (RIGHT) Or a bull's head affronté sable horns or (Bossert); crest: above a closed helm to dexter a vol sable; mantling of the colors
Switzerland
1681
*Inscription:* Beniam Burgstaller/ des Grichts zu Wald/ kirch Wirt und gast/ geb zu Brucken und/ Leutenambt instruben/ [.]ell Fr: Aña maria Bossert/ sein Ehe Fr . 1681
White glass with silver stain and enamels
34.0 x 23 (13⅜ x 9)
Cracks; some mending leads
*Provenance:* Sibyll Kummer-Rothenhäusler, Zurich, to 1989
Unpublished
958

## A MAN ON HORSEBACK WITH THE ARMS OF SCHÜRCH

*Arms:* Azure bordered vert a pliers and a hammer crossed in saltire through a horseshoe or (Schürch) Switzerland, Alpine region of the canton of Bern
1685
*Inscription:* Hanns Schurch/ und Ursu = la Vetter sein/ Ehegemahel. Anno 1685.
White glass with silver stain and enamels
29 x 21 (11⅜ x 8¼)
Some stopgaps in white ground; mending leads
*Provenance:* Sibyll Kummer-Rothenhäusler, Zurich, to 7/14/1989
Unpublished
1006

## WELCOME PANEL WITH PLOWING SCENE

*Arms:* (LEFT) Azure a cross argent in base two flowers argent stemed vert in chief two quatrefoils or (unidentified); (RIGHT) Purpure a wall argent (Mur)
Switzerland
17th century
*Inscription:* Her[.] schult[.]es Lienhartt [. . .]/ Des ratts zu Schwytz und frouw/ Dorathea uf der Mur sin ehe/ gmahel
Between shields: 1614
White glass with silver stain and enamel
34.2 x 22.2 (13½ x 8¾)
Cracks; mending leads; stopgaps between figures; cartouche with date and shields are a replacement
*Provenance:* Sotheby's, London, unidentified owner
*Bibliography: European Works of Art* sale (1988), lot no. 220.
730

## SPIES WITH THE GRAPES FROM ESCHOL, WITH A PLOUGHING SCENE AND SHIELDS

*Arms:* (LEFT) Azure two roses ? in an urn surmounted by a mullet of six points argent (unidentified); (RIGHT) Argent a lily proper azure and vert between A and N (unidentified)
Switzerland
17th century
*Inscription:* Genesis 17 (modern)
White glass with silver stain, enamels, and Jean Cousin
32 x 21.8 (12⅝ x 8⅝)
Assemblage, but figural pieces belong together; devitrification and damage to paint and enamels; shattered and mended
*Provenance:* Sibyll Kummer-Rothenhäusler, Zurich, to 8/1988
Unpublished
914

## JOSEPH SOLD BY HIS BROTHERS

Switzerland
17th century and modern
*Inscription:* (LEFT) IOH.IACOB.FRISIUS
. / M.D.ET./ POLIATER
(RIGHT) IOH.IACOB.LAVATER / M.D.ET.
/ POLIATER
Pot metal; white glass with silver
stain, enamels, and Jean Cousin;
flashed and abraded red glass
31.5 x 22 (12¼ x 8¾)
Many replacements by Bruce Mahr,
1989, including arms; stopgaps;
inscription may not belong
*Provenance:* Sibyll Kummer-
Rothenhäusler, Zurich, to 8/1988
Unpublished
923

## THE FOUNDING OF SWITZERLAND

Switzerland
17th century
*Inscription:* Ein bös Tironis /
Regment mag mit beston nimbt bald
ein end
Pot metal; white glass with silver
stain and Jean Cousin; flashed red
glass
32.8 x 22.2 (13 x 8¾)
Stopgaps in inscription; mending
leads and unrepaired cracks; paint
abraded
*Provenance:* Fritz Dold, Zurich
Unpublished
1012

## ARMS OF MAXIMILIAN PHILIPS GRAF OF LICHTENSTEIN

*Arms:* Quarterly 1 and 4 gules a lion
rampant argent countercompony, 2
and 3 argent a lion gules erased
countercompony; an inescutcheon
azure a pile argent overall; crest:
(dexter) on a barred helm to sinister a
coronet issuant a demi-lion rampant
argent langued and armed gules,
(sinister) on a barred helm to dexter
a coronet issuant a demi-lion argent
gloved gules backed by ostrich
feathers, (center) on a helm affronté
a coronet issuant a pile with seven
ostrich feathers argent
Swiss painter working for an Austrian
patron
Austria/Switzerland
17th century
*Inscription:* on scroll: a mullet of six
points or between A and H
on cartouche: Max[.]milian Philips
Graff[...]/ Liech[..]stein fryher zu
Castelhorn[.]/ [.] S?[...]
Pot metal; white glass with silver
stain and enamels; flashed and
abraded red glass
41.5 x 32.5 (16¼ x 12¾)
Stopgaps at top and lower right
corner; surface corrosion and paint
loss; cracks; mending leads
*Provenance:* Sibyll Kummer-
Rothenhäusler, Zurich, to 3/10/1989
Unpublished
964

# FRAGMENTS

In addition, there are a number of panels of fragments in the collection, including:

Seraph's head, French ?, 15th century (1032)

Quarries and an unpainted red cusp, English, 13th–15th century (632)

Four quarries, English 15th and 16th centuries, with the white rose and crown, the initials M R (for Queen Mary Stuart), and the arms of England (396)

Shield-shaped panel made up of enameled cartouche fragments, Lowlands or England, late 16th century, from Christie, Manson, and Woods, Ltd., London, 1987 {*The Nineteenth Century: European Ceramics, Furniture, Sculpture and Works of Art* [sale cat., Christie, Manson & Woods, Ltd., 14 May] (London, 1987), 78, no. 191} (576 C)

Figure of a man, Swiss, 16th century (his left hand a stopgap), from Wigley, London, 1987 (558)

Composite panel, Swiss, 16th century, with six shields: 1. Azure a heart proper pierced by a two handled saw and two swords, inscribed above: H.B.H.; 2. Azure two lions rampant facing one another holding swords, inscribed above: M.D.H.; 3. Gules in base a shoe proper in chief two cobblers tools, inscribed above: G.B.;

4. Azure inescutcheon argent a house proper between two mullets of six points or, inscribed above: Bartli Kü[. . .]zler/ Waltzen[. . .]husen; 5. Azure a housemark or; 6. Or a doubleheaded ax blade azure, inscribed above: Joachim Mu[. . .]/ Hoffaman, and below: Sebastion Er/ hartt. Other inscriptions are (right): [.]er hanssThoma/ Schürff; Hanns Urscheller/ Altt Ama, and (center) Ein dreüer dienes/ ist liebund werdt./ Wan er dienet-/ Wie manss begertti. From Fritz Dold, Zurich, 3/10/1989 (926).

Friendship panel with scene of cattle husbandry, Swiss, 16th and 17th centuries, with the inscription: Hans Jorg Wirtt Der/ zit Binne[.]ier und Ene/ger zud Lichtenstaig und Susanna feder[..]/ sein Eliche Hus[.] 1540. From Fritz Dold, Zurich, 3/10/1989 (925).

Saint Thomas with a T-square, Flemish 17th century (part of a roundel) in a made-up panel with the inscription: F.Pierre Du Rieu/ Prieur d[. . .] Chartreuse / de la V[. . .]incte / A[. . .]o9, and a heavily restored Annunciation of the Death of the Virgin, Swiss, 16th century, from Sotheby's, New York, 11/25/1986 (427 c).

558

926

1032

576 C

925

427 C

# KEY TO ABBREVIATED REFERENCE CITATIONS

Berserik (1982)    C. J. Berserik, "Niet-monumentaal gebrandschilderd glas en ontwerpen uit Leiden, ca. 1480–1545, een catalogus" (Ph.D. diss., University of Leiden, 1982).

Boon    K. G. Boon, *Catalogue of the Dutch and Flemish Drawings in the Rijksmuseum II, Netherlandish Drawings of the Fifteenth and Sixteenth Centuries*, 2 vols. (The Hague, 1987).

Caviness et al. (1978)    Madeline H. Caviness et al., *Medieval and Renaissance Stained Glass from New England Collections* [exh. cat., Busch-Reisinger Museum of Harvard University, Cambridge, MA] (Medford, MA, 1978).

Checklist I    "Stained Glass before 1700 in American Collections: New England and New York (Corpus Vitrearum Checklist I)," *Studies in the History of Art* 15 (1985).

Checklist II    "Stained Glass before 1700 in American Collections: Mid-Atlantic and Southeastern Seaboard States (Corpus Vitrearum Checklist II)," *Studies in the History of Art* 23 (1987).

Checklist III    "Stained Glass before 1700 in American Collections: Midwestern and Western States (Corpus Vitrearum Checklist III)," *Studies in the History of Art* 28 (1989).

C. W. Post Catalogue (1939)    Greenvale, NY, C. W. Post Center of Long Island University, Special Collections Library, ms. "Catalogue of the Collections of William Randolph Hearst" [International Studio Art Corp., index compiled 2/18/1939], Stained Glass.

Douglass (1972)    George A. Douglass, Jr., "Personal Inventory," 1972.

Drake (1913)    Maurice Drake, *The Grosvenor Thomas Collection of Ancient Stained Glass*, pts. 1 and 2 [exh. cat., Charles Gallery] (New York, 1913).

Eden (1927)    F. Sydney Eden, *The Collection of Heraldic Stained Glass at Ronaele Manor, Elkins Park, Pennsylvania, the Residence of Mr. and Mrs. FitzEugene Dixon* (London, 1927).

*European Works of Art* sale (1986)    *European Works of Art, Armour, Furniture and Tapestries* [sale cat., Sotheby's, 25 November] (New York, 1986).

*European Works of Art* sale (1988)    *European Works of Art, Arms and Armour, Furniture and Tapestries* [sale cat., Sotheby's, 22–23 November] (New York, 1988).

Fischer    Josef Ludwig Fischer, *Handbuch der Glasmalerei* (Leipzig, 1937).

*Form and Light* (1985)    *Form and Light: Four Hundred Years of European Glass* [exh. cat., Michael Ward, Inc., New York] (New York, 1985).

Geisberg    Max Geisberg, *The German Single-Leaf Woodcut 1500–1550*, ed. Walter L. Strauss, 4 vols. (New York, 1974).

| | |
|---|---|
| Giroux catalogue (1954) | *Tableaux Anciens et Modernes, Antiquités* [sale cat., Georges Giroux, 18–19 June] (Brussels, 1954). |
| Grosvenor Thomas Stock Book | Norwich, private library of Dennis King, Roy Grosvenor Thomas Stock Books, unpublished. |
| Hayward (1971–1972) | Jane Hayward, "Stained-Glass Windows," *Metropolitan Museum of Art Bulletin* 33, no. 3 (December 1971–January 1972). |
| Hayward (1981) | Jane Hayward, in *Notable Acquisitions 1980–1981, The Metropolitan Museum of Art* (New York, 1981). |
| Hearst ms. (1943) | William Randolph Hearst, ms. A5141, "Personal Inventory," 1943 (Los Angeles County Museum). |
| *Hearst* sale (1941) | Hammer Galleries, *Art Objects and Furnishings from the William Randolph Hearst Collection* [sale cat., Gimbel Brothers, Saks Fifth Avenue] (New York, 1941). |
| Helbig | J. Helbig, *De Glasschelderkunst in Belgie, Repertorium en Documenten II* (Antwerp, 1951). |
| Hollstein | *F. Hollstein's German Engravings, Etchings and Woodcuts 1400–1700*, multiple volumes and various editors (Amsterdam, 1954– ). |
| Husband (1989) | Timothy B. Husband, " 'Ick Sorgheloose . . .': A Silver-Stained Roundel in The Cloisters," *Metropolitan Museum of Art Journal* 24(1989): 173–188. |
| Illustrated Bartsch | *The Illustrated Bartsch*, ed. Walter L. Strauss (New York, 1980). |
| Kieslinger | Franz Kieslinger, *Dutch and Flemish etchings, engravings and woodcuts, ca. 1450–1700* (Amsterdam, 1949– ). |
| *LACMA Quarterly* (1945) | "The William Randolph Hearst Collection of Medieval and Renaissance Stained and Vitreous Painted Glass," *Los Angeles County Museum Quarterly* 4, nos. 3, 4 (Fall–Winter 1945). |
| Lehrs | Max Lehrs, *Geschichte und Kritischer Katalog des deutschen, Niederländischen und Französischen Kupfersticks im XV Jahrhundert*, 9 vols. (New York, 1970). Collectors Editions reprint. |
| Lymant (1982) | Brigitte Lymant, *Die Glasmalerien des Schnütgen-Museums: Bestandskatalog* (Cologne, 1982). |
| Metropolitan Museum annual report (1972–1973) | *The Metropolitan Museum of Art, Annual Report for the Year 1972–1973* (New York, 1973). |
| Metropolitan Museum annual report (1980–1981) | *The Metropolitan Museum of Art, Annual Report for the Year 1980–1981* (New York, 1981). |
| Metropolitan Museum annual report (1983–1984) | *The Metropolitan Museum of Art, Annual Report for the Year 1983–1984* (New York, 1984). |

| Metropolitan Museum annual report (1984–1985) | *The Metropolitan Museum of Art, Annual Report for the Year 1984–1985* (New York, 1985). |
| --- | --- |
| Metropolitan Museum annual report (1988–1989) | *The Metropolitan Museum of Art, Annual Report for the Year 1988–1989* (New York, 1989). |
| Metropolitan Museum annual report (1989–1990) | *The Metropolitan Museum of Art, Annual Report for the Year 1989–1990* (New York, 1990). |
| Musée van Stolk catalogue (1912) | *Catalogue des Sculptures, Tableaux, Tapis, etc. formant la Collection d'Objets d'Art du Musée van Stolk* (The Hague, 1912). |
| *Nineteenth Century* sale (1987) | *The Nineteenth Century: European Ceramics, Furniture, Sculpture and Works of Art* [sale cat., Christie, Manson & Woods, Ltd., 14 May] (London, 1987). |
| P. W. French & Co. Stock Sheets | Santa Monica, CA, J. Paul Getty Center for the History of Art and the Humanities, Photoarchives, ms. P. W. French & Co. stock sheets. |
| Raguin et al. (1987) | Virginia C. Raguin et al., *Northern Renaissance Stained Glass: Continuity and Transformations* [exh. cat., College of the Holy Cross, Iris and B. Gerald Cantor Art Gallery, 2 February–8 March] (Worcester, MA, 1987). |
| Schmitz (1913) | Hermann Schmitz, *Die Glasgemälde der Königlichen Kunstgewerbemuseums in Berlin*, 2 vols. (Berlin, 1913). |
| Schmitz (1923) | Hermann Schmitz, *Deutsche Glasmalereien der Gotik und Renaissance: Rund- und Kabinettscheiben* (Munich, 1923). |
| *Sneyd* sale (1924) | *Old English and French Furniture, Porcelain and Objects of Art being a portion of the Sneyd Heirlooms removed from Keele Hall, Staffordshire* [sale cat., Christie's, 26 June] (London, 1924). |
| Steinbart | Kurt Steinbart, *Das Holzschnittwerk des Jakob Cornelisz von Amsterdam* (Burg b. Magdeburg, 1937). |
| Thornton | W. Pugin Thornton, *Catalogue of Two Old Dutch Painted and Stained Windows in the Royal Museum and Free Library of Canterbury* (Canterbury, 1899). |
| *Strawberry Hill* sale (1842) | *The Valuable Contents of Strawberry Hill* [sale cat., George Robbins, 21 May (24th day's sale)] (Strawberry Hill, Middlesex, England, 1842). |
| *Vitraux-Tapisseries* sale (1989) | *Vitraux-Tapisseries, Broderies* [sale cat., Galerie de Chartres, 8 October] (Chartres, 1989). |
| *Whitelaw Reid* sale (1935) | *Art Treasures and Furnishings of Ophir Hall, Residence of the Late Mrs. Whitelaw Reid* [sale cat., American Art Association, Anderson Galleries, Inc., 14–18 May] (Purchase, NY, 1935). |
| Winkler | Friedrich Winkler, *Die Zeichnungen Albrecht Dürers*, 4 vols. (Berlin, 1936–1939). |

# GLOSSARY

A glossary of technical terms was included in Checklist I, 217–218, supplemented by three changes as noted in Checklist III, 36. This glossary of terms is specific to silver-stained roundels.

*dutchman* — a flat lead strip applied across the front or back of a piece of glass for support of a break or weakened leads

*efflorescence* — a crust or blooming on the surface of the glass

*embedded frit* — isolated and unfused ingredients suspended in the glass

*Hausmark* — (German) a personal or family cipher or mark

*iridescence* — a rainbow-like diffraction of light across the surface of the glass

*reamy glass* — slightly raised wavy patterns across the surface of the glass

*roundel types*

    *replicas* — nearly exact duplicates

    *variants* — roundels with minor compositional or stylistic changes

    *versions* — copies with pronounced compositional or stylistic changes

*straw marks* — an impression of lines left on the surface of the glass when a warm sheet is placed on a bed of straw to cool

*surface accretions* — dirt, corrosion products, or other deposits on the surface of the glass

*vidimus* — in roundel studies, a copy of the design that served both as a full-scale cartoon and a contractual document, clearly establishing what the glass painter would produce and what the patron would receive

# PHOTOGRAPHIC CREDITS

Except as noted below, photographs were provided by the owners of the panels.

| | |
|---|---|
| California | Altadena, Axt Collection (T.H.)<br>Glendale, Forest Lawn (M.H.C.)<br>Hillsborough, Private Collection (T.H. except 323, 332, 326, 350, 366, 376, 394, 400, 402, 404, 418, 420, 422, 426, 430, 448, 450, 454, 455, 561, 571, 574, 678A, 678B, 685 to Constancio del Alamo); Addendum (T.H.) |
| Connecticut | Greenwich, George A. Douglass Collection (Leland A. Cook)<br>New Haven, Yale University, Berkeley College (T.H.) |
| Florida | Miami Beach, Claire Mendel Collection (T.H.)<br>Palm Beach, Bethesda-by-the-Sea Episcopal Church (T.H.)<br>Winter Park, The Charles Hosmer Morse Museum of American Art (T.H.) |
| Illinois | Chicago, Loyola University, The Martin D'Arcy Gallery of Art (T.H.) |
| Iowa | Des Moines, Salisbury House, Iowa State Educational Association, David Penney |
| Kentucky | Louisville, The J. B. Speed Art Museum (T.H.) |
| Maryland | Private Collection (T.H.)<br>Private Collection (T.H.) |
| Massachusetts | Cambridge, Harvard Lampoon (T.H.)<br>Charlestown, Private Collection (Leland A. Cook) |
| Michigan | Bloomfield Hills, Cranbrook Educational Community, Cranbrook House and Cranbrook Academy of Art Museum (T.H.)<br>Grosse Pointe Shores, Edsel & Eleanor Ford House (Leland A. Cook) |
| Minnesota | Winona, Watkins House |
| New York | East Hampton, Saint Luke's Episcopal Church (T.H.)<br>New York, Blumka Collection (T.H.)<br>New York, Private Collections (T.H.)<br>Westchester, Victoria and Eric Sternberg Collection (Marilyn M. Beaven)<br>Westchester, Private Collection (T.H.) |
| North Carolina | Durham, Duke University Museum of Art (T.H.)<br>Greensboro, Dr. Henry Hood Collection (T.H.)<br>Reidsville, Chinqua-Penn Plantation (T.H.) |
| Ohio | Cleveland, The Cleveland Museum of Art (T.H.) |
| Pennsylvania | Narperth, Mrs. Isabell Hardy Collection (T.H.)<br>Pittsburgh, The Carnegie Museum of Art (T.H.)<br>Pittsburgh, University of Pittsburgh, University Art Gallery (T.H.) |
| Rhode Island | Newport, Private Collection (Leland A. Cook except stairwell window c4 to T.H.) |
| South Carolina | Greenville, Bob Jones University (T.H.) |
| Tennessee | Memphis, Walter R. Brown/Richard K. Tanner Collection (T.H.)<br>Nashville, Vanderbilt University, Vanderbilt Art Collection (T.H.) |

# INDICES

# INDEX TO ROUNDELS

Margaret, St. 180
  with St. Hippolytus 56
Mark, St. 138
Martin of Tours, St.
  dividing his cloak and the beggar 82, 86, 133, 181
  with the beggar 184
Martyrs, two unidentified 64
Mary Cleopas, at the Crucifixion 169
Mary Magdalen, St. 85, 137
  with Christ 189
  at the Crucifixion 169
  in the wilderness 214
Mary, Mother of Christ see Virgin Mary, Christ
Matthew, St. 105
Maximilian I, portrait 72
Michael, St., Archangel
  slaying the dragon 123, 129, 196
Mercury, with Jupiter and Pollux 186
Monastery of Zevenburren 174
Monastic scene, clerics at table 53
Monk see Figures, clerical
Mordecai
  overhears the conspirators Bigthan and Teresh 77, 147
Moses 23
  and the brazen serpent 98
Nebuchadnezzar, as a wild man 51
November, Labor of the Month 210
October, Labor of the Month 104, 210
Ornament 196
  head of a lion 129
  leaded panel surrounds 21, 43, 58, 122, 175, 176, 218, 226
Paris, Judgment of 201
Passion of Christ see Christ
Paul, before Areopagus 24, 26
Pegasus, with Amor and Venus 51
Perseus, with Andromeda 215
Personifications
  Alchemist's elements
    Air 209
    Earth 173, 209
    Fire 173, 209
    Water 209
  Charity 175
  Harvest or Fall 46
  Senses
    Sight 86
  Seven Liberal Arts
    Arithmetic 172, 187
    Geometry 187
    Grammar 187
    Logic 172
    Rhetoric 187
Peter, St. 159, 181
  with St. Andrew 194
  hearing the cock crow 54
  as Pope with Canon Peter Verstrepen 162
Philip, St., with a Dominican monk 71
Pollux, with Jupiter and Mercury 186
Portraits
  General Gustavus Horn 10, 186
  Maximilian I 72
  Roman wives 42
  Ulrich von Württemberg 55
Procession of Putti 191
Prodigal son (Parable of Christ) 24, 25
  is banqueted 165–166

bids father farewell 164, 165–166, 198
in the brothel 50, 84, 96
driven from the brothel 47, 96
feasting 170
gambling 82, 165–166
given the best coat 165–166
receives his share 45, 165–166
returns 49
seeks work 47, 165–166
sets out 165–166, 192
as a swineherd 45, 47, 165–166
Putti see Angels
Pyramus, and Thisbe 185
Raphael, Archangel 53
Rebekah, Isaac asks for her hand 183
  and Isaac 16, 17
Renault, St. 94
Romans
  executing their treasonous sons 176, 226
  exhorting the crowds 176, 226
  portraits of wives 42
Sacrifice in the temple 155
Saint(s) (identifiable)
  Agnes
  Andrew
  Anne
  Anthony the Abbot
  Barbara
  Benedict
  Catherine of Alexandria
  Christopher
  Cornelius
  Elizabeth
  Eustache
  Francis
  George
  Herbert
  James Major
  John the Baptist
  John the Evangelist
  Judocus
  Lawrence
  Louis XI
  Margaret
  Mark
  Martin of Tours
  Mary Magdalen
  Matthew
  Peter
  Philip
  Renault
  Stephen
  Thomas Didymus
Saint(s) (unidentifiable)
  bishop 37, 40
  Dominican Abbess with donatrix 41
  female with phoenix 230
  monk with helmet 217, 222
  martyrs 64
  pilgrim 37, 215
Salvator Mundi 151
Samson
  and Delilah 153
  and the lion 173
Saul 24
  sacrificing 50

# INDEX OF PERSONAE
## Interim Owners, Dealers, and Artists

The second index is a listing of persons associated with the stained glass collections. Interim owners (provenance), many of whom were dealers, are designated in roman; artists (including designers, glass painters, or others whose drawings were adapted) are in small capitals.

# INDEX OF LOCATIONS

The third index is a location index. Original locations are in italics, and roundels from this location are noted immediately afterward. Artists working in the location are listed next in small capitals. Interim owners from the same city are noted on the following lines in roman. American place names and interim owners are also in roman.

# INDEX TO ADDENDUM

## INDEX OF SUBJECTS

## INDEX OF PERSONAE
Interim Owners, Dealers, and Artists

The second index is a listing of persons associated with the stained glass collections. Interim owners (provenance), many of whom were dealers, are designated in roman; artists (including designers, glass painters, or others whose drawings were adapted) are noted in small capitals.

## INDEX OF LOCATIONS

The third index is a location index. Original locations are in italics, and panels whose original location are known are noted immediately afterward. Interim owners from the same city are noted on the following lines in roman. American place names and interim owners are also in roman.

# STATUS OF CORPUS VITREARUM PUBLICATIONS

The Corpus Vitrearum Medii Aevi publishes under the auspices of the Comité international d'histoire de l'art and the Union académique internationale. Status of publications: 1 July 1990.

## AUSTRIA (8 volumes planned)

PUBLISHED

I. *Die mittelalterlichen Glasgemälde in Wien*, by Eva Frodl-Kraft, Vienna, 1962

II, 1. *Die mittelalterlichen Glasgemälde in Niederösterreich, I.: Albrechtsberg-Klosterneuberg*, by Eva Frodl-Kraft, Vienna, 1972

III, 1. *Die mittelalterlichen Glasgemälde in der Steiermark, I.: Graz und Strassengel*, by Ernst Bacher, Vienna, 1979

IN PREPARATION

IV. *Die mittelalterlichen Glasgemälde in Niederösterreich, 2.: Kremstetten-Zwettl*, by Eva Frodl-Kraft and Elisabeth Oberhaidacher

V. *Die mittelalterlichen Glasgemälde in der Steiermark, 2.: Admont-Vorau*, by Ernst Bacher

VI. *Die mittelalterlichen Glasgemälde in Kärnten*, by Ernst Bacher and Elisabeth Oberhaidacher

VII. *Die mittelalterlichen Glasgemälde in Salzburg, Tirol und Vorarlberg*, by Elisabeth Oberhaidacher

VIII. *Die mittelalterlichen Glasgemälde in Oberösterreich*, by Elisabeth Oberhaidacher

Published by the Bundesdenkmalamt and by the Österreichische Akademie der Wissenschaften; Hermann Böhlaus Nachf., Vienna/Cologne/Graz (Dr. Karl Lueger-Ring 12, A-1014 Vienna 1)

## BELGIUM (9 volumes planned)

PUBLISHED

I. *Les vitraux médiévaux conservés en Belgique, 1200–1500*, by Jean Helbig, Brussels, 1961

II. *Les vitraux de la première moitié du XVIe siècle conservés en Belgique. Anvers et Flandres*, by Jean Helbig, Brussels, 1968

III. *Les vitraux de la première moitié du XVIe siècle en Belgique. Brabant et Limbourg*, by Yvette Vanden Bemden, Ghent/Ledeberg, 1974

IV. *Les vitraux de la première moitié du XVIe siècle en Belgique. Luxemburg et Namur*, by Yvette Vanden Bemden, Ghent/Ledeberg, 1981

IN PREPARATION

V. *Les vitraux de la première moitié du XVIe siècle conservés en Belgique. Hainault. Fascicule I. Les vitraux de la collégiale Sainte Waudru de Mons*, by Yvette Vanden Bemden

Published by the Ministère de la Communauté Française, Brussels. Distributed by the Office International de Librairie, Brussels (30, Avenue Marnix, B 1050 Brussels)

## CZECHOSLOVAKIA (1 volume planned and published)

*Mittelalterliche Glasmalerei in der Tschechoslowakei*, by Frantisek Matous, Prague, 1975

Published by the Czechoslovak Academy of Sciences, Prague; Verlag Academia Prag (Distributed in Western countries by Hermann Böhlaus, Nachf., Vienna/Cologne/Graz; Dr. Karl Lueger-Ring 12, A-1014 Vienna 1)

## FRANCE (25 volumes planned)

PUBLISHED

I, 1. *Les vitraux de Notre Dame et de la Sainte-Chapelle de Paris*, by Marcel Aubert, Louis Grodecki, Jean Lafond and Jean Verrier, Paris, 1959

IV, 2. *Les vitraux de l'église Saint-Ouen de Rouen*, vol. 1, by Jean Lafond with the assistance of Françoise Perrot and Paul Popesco, Paris, 1970

IX. *Les vitraux de la cathédrale de Strasbourg*, by Victor Beyer, Christiane Wild-Block and Fridtjof Zschokke, Paris, 1986

"Etudes" series:

I. *Les vitraux de Saint-Denis.*, vol. 1, by Louis Grodecki, Paris, 1976

"Recensements des vitraux anciens de la France" series:

I. *Les vitraux de Paris, de la région parisienne, de la Picardie et du Nord-Pas-de-Calais*, Paris, 1978

II. *Les vitraux du Centre et des Pays de la Loire*, Paris, 1981

III. *Les vitraux de Borgogne, Franche-Comté, et Rhône-Alpes*, Paris, 1986

IN PREPARATION

VIII, 1. *Les vitraux de Saint-Nicholas-du-Port*, by Michel Hérold

XII, 1. *Les vitraux de la cathédrale de Lyon*, by Catherine Brisac

"Recensements des vitraux anciens de la France" series:

IV. *Les vitraux de Champagne, Lorraine, et Alsace*

Published by the Caisse Nationale des Monuments Historiques et de Sites and the Centre National de la Recherche Scientifique, Paris (295, rue St. Jacques, F-75005 Paris)

## GERMANY: Federal Republic of Germany (15 volumes planned)

PUBLISHED

I, 1. *Die Glasmalereien in Schwaben von 1200–1350*, by Hans Wentzel, Berlin, 1958 (out of print)

I, 2. *Die mittelalterlichen Glasmalereien in Schwaben von 1350–1530 (excluding Ulm)*, by Rüdiger Becksmann, Berlin, 1986

II, 1. *Die mittelalterlichen Glasmalereien in Baden und der Pfalz (excluding Freiburg-im-Breisgau)*, by Rüdiger Becksmann, Berlin, 1979

IV, 1. *Die mittelalterlichen Glasmalereien des Klöner Domes*, by Herbert Rode, Berlin, 1974

XIII, 1. *Die mittelalterlichen Glasmalereien im Regensburger Dom*, by Gabriela Fritzsche, 2 vols., Berlin, 1987

IN PRESS

Volume supplémentaire

I. *Entwurf und Ausführung. Werkstattpraxin in der Nürnberger Glasmalerei der Dürerzeit*, by H. Scholz

IN PREPARATION

I, 3. *Die mittelalterlichen Glasmalereien in Ulm*, by H. Scholz

II, 2. *Die mittelalterlichen Glasmalereien in Freiburg-im-Breisgau*, by Rüdiger Becksmann

VII, 2. *Die mittelalterlichen Glasmalereien in Niedersachsen, Teil 2: Heideklöster*, by Rüdiger Becksmann and Ulf-Dietrich Korn

XII. *Die mittelalterlichen Glasmalereien in Augsburg und Bayerisch-Schwaben*, by Rüdiger Becksmann

XIII, 2. *Die mittelalterlichen Glasmalereien im Regensburg (ohne Dom) und Oberfalz*, by Gabriela Fritzsche.

Published by the Akademie der Wissenschaften und der Literatur zu Mainz and der Deutscher Verein für Kunstwissenschaft, Berlin; Deutscher Verlag für Kunstwissenschaft, Berlin (Lindenstrasse 76, D-1000 Berlin 61)

**GERMANY: German Democratic Republic** (15 volumes planned)

PUBLISHED

I, 1. *Die mittelalterlichen Glasmalereien in den Ordenskirchen und im Angermuseum zu Erfurt*, by Erhard Drachenberg, Karl-Joachim Maercker and Christa Schmidt, Berlin, 1976 (out of print)

I, 2. *Die mittelalterlichen Glasmalereien im Erfurter Dom*, by Erhard Drachenberg; text, Berlin, 1980; plates, Berlin, 1973

V, 1. *Die mittelalterlichen Glasmalereien im Standaler Dom*, by Karl-Joachim Maercker, Berlin, 1989

IN PREPARATION

II. *Die mittelalterlichen Glasmalereien in Mühlhausen*, by Christa Richter

IV. *Die mittelalterlichen Glasmalereien in Halberstadt*, by Karl-Joachim Maercker and Christa Richter

V, 2. *Die mittelalterlichen Glasmalereien in Standal* (ohne Dom), by Karl-Joachim Maercker

VI, 1. *Die mittelalterlichen Glasmalereien in Salzwedel, Werben und Kloster Neuendorf*, by Marina Flügge

VI, 2. *Die mittelalterlichen Glasmalereien in Havelberg und Wilsnack*, by Angela Nickel

Published by the Institut für Denkmalpflege der DDR, Berlin; Academie-Verlag, Berlin (Distributed in Western countries by Hermann Böhlaus Nachf., Vienna/Cologne/Graz; Dr. Karl Lueger-Ring 12, A-1014 Vienna 1)

**GREAT BRITAIN** (number of volumes not yet determined)

PUBLISHED

I. *The County of Oxford. A Catalogue of Medieval Stained Glass*, by Peter Newton with the assistance of Jill Kerr, London, 1979

II. *The Windows of Christ Church Cathedral, Canterbury*, by Madeline Harrison Caviness, London, 1981

*The Medieval Painted Glass of York Minster, fascicule 1: The West Window*, by Thomas French and David O'Connor, London, 1988

Supplementary volume I. *The Window of Kings College Chapel: Cambridge*, by Hilary Wayment, London, 1972

Occasional Paper III. *The Medieval Painted Glass of Lincoln Cathedral*, by Nigel Morgan, London, 1983

IN PREPARATION

*The Medieval Painted Glass of York Minster*, by Thomas French and David O'Connor

*The City of Oxford. A Catalogue of Medieval Stained Glass*, by Jill Kerr and Peter Newton

*The City of Norwich. A Catalogue of Medieval Stained Glass*, by David King

*The County of Northhamptonshire. A Catalogue of Medieval Stained Glass*, by Richard Marks

*Kent. A Catalogue of Medieval Stained Glass*

*Stanford-upon-Avon. A Catalogue of Medieval Stained Glass*

*St. Peter Mancroft. A Catalogue of Medieval Stained Glass*

Occasional Volume. *Netherlandish Roundels in Great Britain*, by Dr. William Cole

Published by the British Academy, London; Oxford University Press, London (Distribution Services, Saxon Way West, GB-Corby/Northants NN18 9ES)

**ITALY** (5 volumes planned)

PUBLISHED

I. *Le vetrate dell'Umbria*, by Guiseppe Marchini, Rome, 1973
Published by the Consiglio Nazionale della Ricerche under the patronage of the Unione Accademia Nazionale; De Luca Editore, Rome (via S. Anna 11, I-00186, Rome)

II. *Lombardy I: Le vetrate del Duomo di Milano* (1400–1530), by Caterina Gilli-Perina, Florence, 1987

IN PREPARATION

*Le vetrate di Firenze*, by Luciano Bellosi
*Le vetrate della Toscana*, by Renée K. Burnam
*Le vetrate della Lombardia*

Published by the Amministrazione Provinciale di Milano (Le Monnier, via A. Meucci 2–50015 Grassina, Firenze)

**NETHERLANDS** (3 volumes planned)

IN PREPARATION

I. *De Goudse glazen: De ramen uit de voorreformatorische periode (1555–72)*, by Christiane Coeberg-Surie, H. van Hartenboers and Zsuzsana van Ruyven-Zeman

II. *De Goudse glazen: De Werktekeningen (cartons of "patronen") van de Goudse glazen*

III. *Les vitreaux de l'église St.-Jean de Gouda (choeur et la Chapelle Van der Vorm)*

**POLAND** (1 volume planned and in preparation)

*Die mittelalterlichen Glasmalereien in Polen*, by Lech Kalinowski with the assistance of Helene Malkiewicz

**PORTUGAL** (1 volume planned and published)

*O vitral em Portugal, Séculos XV-XVI*, by Carlos Vitorino da Silva Barros, Lisbon, 1983

Published under the patronage of the Commissariado para a XVII Exposiçao Europeia de Arte, Ciencia e Cultura do Conselho da Europa von der Banco Espirito Santo e Comercial de Lisboa (Museu Nacional de Arte Antiga, Rua Luciano Cordeiro, 49, 4 20–D^{to}, P-Lisbon 1100)

**SCANDINAVIA** (1 volume planned and published)

*Die mitteralterlichen Glasmalereien Skandinaviens*, by Aaron Andersson, Sigrid Christie, Carl A. Nordman and Aage Roussel, Stockholm, 1964

Published by Kungl. Vitterhets Historie och Antikvitets Akademien (Distributed by Almquist & Wiksell, Stockholm; P.O. Box 45150, S-104–30, Stockholm)

**SPAIN** (number of volumes not yet determined)

PUBLISHED

I. *Las vidrieras de la catedral de Sevilla*, by Victor Nieto Alcaide, Madrid, 1969

Published by the Laboratorio de Arte de la Universidad de Sevilla and the Instituto Diego Velázquez del Consejo Superior de Investigaciones Cientificas, Madrid (14, Duque de Medinaceli, E-Madrid 14)

II. *Las vidrieras de la catedral de Granada*, by Victor Nieto Alcaide with the assistance of Carlos Muñoz de Pablos, Granada, 1973

Published by the Universidad de Granada, Departamento de Historia del Arte, Secretariado de Publicaciones (Plaza de la Universidad, E-Granada)

VI. *Catalonia I: Els Vitralls Medievals de l'Eglésia de Santa Maria del Mar a Barcelona,* by Joan Ainaud I de Lasarte, Joan Vila-Grau, M. Assumpta Escudero I Ribot
VII. *Catalonia II: Els Vitralls de la Catedral de Girona,* by Joan Ainaud I de Lasarte, Joan Vila-Grau, M. Assumpta Escudero I Ribot, Antoni Vila I Delclòs, Jaume Marquès, Gabriel Roura, and Josep M. Marquès

Published by the Institut d'Estudis Catalans, Barcelona (C. del Carme 47, E-08001, Barcelona)

IN PREPARATION
III. *Las Vidrieras de Castilla Leon (Avilia, Segovia, Salamanca)*
IV. *Las Vidrieras de Castilla Leon (Catedral de Leon)*

**SWITZERLAND** (5 volumes planned)

PUBLISHED
I. *Die Glasmalereien der Schweiz vom 12. bis zum Beginn des 14. Jahrhunderts,* by Ellen J. Beer, Basel, 1956
III. *Die Glasmalereien der Schweiz aus dem 14. und 15. Jahrhundert, ohne Königsfelden und Berner Münsterchor,* by Ellen J. Beer, Basel, 1965

Published by the late Hans R. Hanloser; Birkhäuser Verlag, Basel (P.O. Box 34, CH-4010 Basel)

IN PREPARATION
IV. *Die mittelalterlichen Glasgemälde des Berner Münsters,* by Brigitte Kurmann-Schwarz

**UNITED STATES OF AMERICA** (9 volumes planned)

PUBLISHED
Checklist Series (in: *Studies in the History of Art*)
I. "Stained Glass before 1700 in American Collections: New England and New York," *Studies in the History of Art* 15, edited by Madeline H. Caviness, Washington, 1985
II. "Stained Glass before 1700 in American Collections: Mid-Atlantic and Southeastern Seaboard States," *Studies in the History of Art* 23, edited by Madeline H. Caviness, Washington, 1987
III. "Stained Glass before 1700 in American Collections: Midwestern and Western States," *Studies in the History of Art* 28, edited by Madeline H. Caviness and Michael W. Cothren, Washington, 1989
IV. "Stained Glass before 1700 in American Collections: Silver-Stained Roundels and Unipartite Panels," *Studies in the History of Art* 39, by Timothy B. Husband, edited by Madeline H. Caviness and Marilyn M. Beaven, Washington, 1991

Published for the National Committee of the Corpus Vitrearum USA by the National Gallery of Art, Washington. Distributed by the University Press of New England (17 1/2 Lebanon St., Hanover, NH 03733)

**Occasional Papers:**
I. *Studies in Medieval Stained Glass: Selected Papers from the XIth International Colloquium of the Corpus Vitrearum, New York, 1–6 June 1982,* edited by Madeline H. Caviness and Timothy Husband, New York, 1985

Published and distributed for the National Committee of the Corpus Vitrearum USA by the Metropolitan Museum of Art, New York (Special Service Office, Middle Village, NY 11381)

IN PREPARATION
I, 1. *European Stained Glass in the Metropolitan Museum of Art, New York* (Corpus Vitrearum, United States, Volume I), by Jane Hayward
2. *Stained Glass from before 1700 in New York State Collections (excluding New York City),* by Meredith Parsons Lillich
3. *Stained Glass from before 1700 in New York City Collections (excluding the Metropolitan Museum of Art),* by Linda Morey Papanicolaou, Mary Shepard, and Meredith Parsons Lillich
4. *Stained Glass from before 1700 in New England Collections,* by Madeline H. Caviness and Naomi Reed Kline
II. *Stained Glass from before 1700 in the Glencairn Museum,* by Michael W. Cothren
III, 1. *Stained Glass from before 1700 in the Detroit Institute of Arts,* by Virginia C. Raguin
2. *Stained Glass from before 1700 in Ohio Collections,* by Helen Jackson Zakin
3. *Stained Glass from before 1700 in Illinois and Indiana Collections,* by Elizabeth Carson Pastan
4. *Stained Glass from before 1700 in the Philadelphia Museum of Art,* by Renée George Burnam
5. *Stained Glass from before 1700 in Northern California Collections,* by Virginia C. Raguin et al.